THE LONDON RESTAURANT, 1840–1914

The London
Restaurant, 1840–1914

BRENDA ASSAEL

OXFORD
UNIVERSITY PRESS

OXFORD

UNIVERSITY PRESS

Great Clarendon Street, Oxford, OX2 6DP,
United Kingdom

Oxford University Press is a department of the University of Oxford.
It furthers the University's objective of excellence in research, scholarship,
and education by publishing worldwide. Oxford is a registered trade mark of
Oxford University Press in the UK and in certain other countries

Published in the United States of America by Oxford University Press
198 Madison Avenue, New York, NY 10016, United States of America

British Library Cataloguing in Publication Data

Data available

Library of Congress Control Number: 2018931631

ISBN 978–0–19–881760–4

Printed and bound by
CPI Group (UK) Ltd, Croydon, CR0 4YY

For Sammy and Martin

Acknowledgements

Like all scholars, my greatest debt is to the archivists and librarians responsible for the various collections, without access to which this project would have been impossible. In particular, I would like to thank the staff at the British Library, The National Archives, London Metropolitan Archives, Bishopsgate Institute Library, New York Public Library Rare Books Division, Burnett Archive on Working-Class Autobiography at Brunel University, Museum of London Library, City of Westminster Archives Centre, London Guildhall Library, Royal Borough of Kensington and Chelsea Library, Savoy Hotel Archive, and Women's Library, London (now housed in the London School of Economics). Ian Glen, the Academic Librarian at Swansea University, and his team, including Bernie Williams, had ingenious and imaginative ways of locating some materials that were otherwise hard to track down. The London Library very kindly offered me a Carlyle Membership in the two years leading up to the completion of this book.

The initial research for this book was funded by a Large Research Grant from the British Academy. The History Department at Swansea University granted me generous sabbatical leave. I am also grateful to the University of Cincinnati, where I was a Charles Phelps Taft Residential Fellow and, subsequently, McMicken Scholar in the College of Arts and Sciences. Many of the key themes in this book were first explored at seminars and conferences at the Institute of Historical Research and the Institute of English Studies, both in the University of London, the University of Warwick, the Leeds Centre for Victorian Studies in Trinity All Saints College, and the Leighton House Museum, London. Commentators and audiences at all these events, and at the North American Conference on British Studies, provided me with many insights for which I am grateful.

I found a very happy home at OUP, and in particular I want to thank the editorial and production team, including Cathryn Steele, Hilary Walford, and Ranjithkumar Shanmugam. I am also grateful to my anonymous readers for their empathetic, but intellectually rigorous, responses to my manuscript. My single most important debt at OUP is to my Commissioning Editor, Stephanie Ireland, whose enthusiasm and support seamlessly guided this project to the printed page.

I remain indebted to all those people who made highly valuable interventions in shaping the conceptualization and content of this book, and who have been a source of encouragement. This list would have to include: Stephen Brooke, Deborah Cohen, Ross Forman, Anne Humpherys, Seth Koven, Peter Mandler, John Spurr, and Alex Windscheffel. I have also benefited from the support of close friends in academic disciplines far removed from nineteenth-century British history, especially Rhiannon Ash, Diana Burton, Ayman El-Desouky, Grace Koh, and David Sarphie. My family, as ever, has always been a source of inspiration, and I must thank my parents, Alyce and Henry Assael, in particular. I wish that my mother-in-law, Barbara Francis (1933–2012), were here to celebrate the completion of this book.

The most important person who helped see me through this project is my husband (and fellow historian), Martin Francis. He has been there at the first spark of an idea and the last push to get the project home. There is a photograph that he took of me holding the publishing contract from OUP; he felt as proud as I did on that day, and he remains so. For this, and so much more, I dedicate this book to him and our son, Sammy, who manages to combine in equal measure a fiery intelligence and a *joie de vivre* that make us feel, every day, as though we have won the jackpot.

B.A.

London
January 2018

Contents

List of Illustrations

Introduction

Foregrounding the Restaurant

'Come with me now and see one of the most strangely human sights that the world can show. It is that of the biggest city there is, and the one containing most varieties of human life, being fed during an ordinary day.'[1] So wrote the little-known writer J. C. Woollan, in his contribution to *Living London* (1901–3), a multi-volume series of essays about the kaleidoscopic variety of metropolitan life at the turn of the twentieth century. *Living London* contained pieces concerned with topics as diverse as religious observance, politics, shopkeeping, street life, policing, popular leisure and sport, sanitation, transportation, philanthropy, schools, and even idiosyncratic subjects such as pets and ballooning. Woollan's contribution, entitled 'Table Land in London', used both the temporal (discussing meals at different times of the day) and the spatial (mapping public eating across the city) to display the scale and heterogeneity of eating out in the metropolis. He went on:

> Very likely it has never struck you that there is anything remarkable in this process. But when you come to know or reflect that there are some hundreds of people breakfasting in the city at four o'clock in the morning, that—so it has been calculated—there are nearly a million people lunching in restaurants within a few miles of the Strand every day, and that each evening some thousands of dinners are laid on West-End restaurant tables which, with wine, cost an average of a sovereign each, whilst, on the other hand, there are far more Londoners who live each day—and live not at all badly either—on a single shilling each—when you come to think of all this, and hundreds of other facts of a more detailed and more interesting character which could be adduced, you will begin to perceive that the Table Land of London must indeed be one of the biggest wonders of this glorious Metropolis.[2]

[1] J. C. Woollan, 'Table Land in London', in George R. Sims (ed.), *Living London* (3 vols; London: Cassell and Co., 1901–3), vol. i, sect. 2, p. 297.
[2] *Ibid.*

This book shares the premise of Woollan's somewhat breathless characterization of eating out in late Victorian and Edwardian London.[3] The quotidian nature of taking a meal in public during the working day or evening has, ironically, obscured the significance of the restaurant as a critical component in the creation of modern metropolitan culture. Between the 1840s (and especially from the 1870s) and the First World War, the London restaurant both emblematized, and contributed to, the myriad forces and formations that constitute what has been labelled (for want of an agreed alternative) 'modernity'.[4] The restaurant is a critical site for observing the expansion of commercial leisure, the introduction of technology, the democratization of the public sphere, greater mobility (of things and people), and the engagement of local cultures with the forces of globalization. London's restaurant sector expanded dramatically in the last third of the nineteenth century, deeply imbricated as it was in the dramatic rise in the population of the capital's urban core, and by a noticeable blurring of distinctions related to class, gender, and race. No less critically, the decades immediately after 1870 also saw the increased rapidity and volume of international trade. The restaurant became a beneficiary of this development, which made food cheaper, facilitated a rise in immigrant labour, and increased the availability of disposable income. Public eating in London in this period reflected the consciousness of a society that presented itself as democratic, self-governing, and entrepreneurial.[5]

The relationship of the restaurant to some of the less materially grounded aspects of modernity, notably the emergence of reflexive selfhood, is undoubtedly more problematic. Some contemporaries were highly self-conscious about 'dining out' as a novel form of the urban experience, even if it required them to disregard the fact that Londoners had been eating in coffee taverns and eating houses for generations. By contrast, returning to

---

[3] Generally, the use of the terms 'dining', 'public eating', and 'eating out' in this book should be understood to be equivalent and interchangeable. The term 'dining' does usually connote a more formal type of public eating, but the use of the term should not be assumed to apply only to more rarefied establishments, or to eating at a particular time of the day (i.e. evening). A similar protocol applies to the use of the term 'diner'.

[4] For studies of modernity in the context of this period, see Martin Daunton and Bernhard Rieger (eds), *Meanings of Modernity: Britain from the Late-Victorian Era to World War Two* (Oxford: Berg, 2001); Mica Nava and Alan O'Shea (eds), *Modern Times: Reflections on a Century of English Modernity* (London: Routledge, 1996).

[5] For how this self-understanding of British society played out in the political and intellectual establishment, see Peter Mandler, 'The Consciousness of Modernity? Liberalism and the English National Character, 1870–1940', in Daunton and Rieger (eds), *Meanings of Modernity*. For a more detailed explication (one that registers the conservative challenge to liberal ideas of national identity after the 1880s), see Peter Mandler, *The English National Character: The History of an Idea from Edmund Burke to Tony Blair* (New Haven and London: Yale University Press, 2006), 27–142.

Woollan's appraisal, many Londoners would have been unlikely to have regarded eating out as in any way 'remarkable'. Similarly, the fact that the restaurant experience encompassed both the anomie of the alienated diner and the pleasures of heterosociability suggests that it serves as a useful site to explore some of the fundamental contradictions associated with the modern condition. Whatever the specific associations, contemporaries certainly believed they were participating in a new dining culture at the close of the nineteenth century, one that was marked by the increasing complexity and heterogeneity of metropolitan society. Despite this, in the rich and expansive field of social and cultural history (both prior, and subsequent, to the so-called cultural turn) of late-nineteenth- and early twentieth-century London, the restaurant remains surprisingly overlooked.

The long-established study of urban leisure (and its relationship to official and moral regulation) has not extended to the restaurant, despite the physical proximity and wider symbiosis between West End dining rooms and theatres.[6] Of course, cultural historians have often been guilty of failing to acknowledge that the metropolis was also a place of work and production, and not merely of leisure and consumption.[7] Social histories of London's economy have shown negligible interest in the restaurant, either as a business enterprise or in its role in fuelling London's working population.[8] Historians concerned with gender have had little to say about the restaurant as a site for the performance of femininity and masculinity. A preoccupation with sexuality in metropolitan life and identity has had the unfortunate effect of undervaluing the pursuit of other needs and

---

[6] Note, for instance, the absence of the restaurant from Andrew Horrall, *Popular Culture in London, c.1890–1918: The Transformation of Entertainment* (Manchester: Manchester University Press, 2001). Early scholarship on nineteenth-century urban leisure includes Peter Bailey, *Leisure and Class in Victorian England: Rational Recreation and the Contest for Control, 1830–1885* (London: Routledge, 1978); Hugh Cunningham, *Leisure in the Industrial Revolution, c.1780–1880* (London: Croom Helm, 1980); J. M. Golby and A. W. Purdue, *The Civilisation of the Crowd: Popular Culture in England, 1750–1900* (London: Batsford, 1984); and more specifically on theatreland, Peter Bailey (ed.), *Music Hall: The Business of Pleasure* (Milton Keynes: Open University Press, 1986); Tracy C. Davis, *Actresses as Working Women: Their Social Identity in Victorian Culture* (London: Routledge, 1991).

[7] A notable exception would be Christopher Breward, *The Hidden Consumer: Masculinities, Fashion and City Life, 1860–1914* (Manchester: Manchester University Press, 1999).

[8] For example, Alison C. Kay, 'A Little Enterprise of her Own: Lodging-house Keeping and the Accommodation Business in Nineteenth-Century London', *London Journal*, 28/2 (2003), 41–53; Ranald C. Michie, *Guilty Money: The City of London in Victorian and Edwardian Culture, 1815–1914* (London: Pickering and Chatto, 2009). Exceptionally, Jerry White does mention the restaurant, but relies mostly on London guidebooks such as Baedeker's. Jerry White, *London in the Nineteenth Century* (London: Vintage, 2008), 286–7.

appetites, food chiefly among them.[9] Some recent interventions have shown a promising interest in the restaurant, notably single chapters dedicated to the subject, but the topic remains largely unexplored in the scholarship on modern metropolitan culture.[10]

If historical geographers have isolated the significance of particular urban sites for understanding the formation and performance of identities, they have focused on buildings, monuments, and gardens rather than the restaurant, despite the fact that it offers an obvious example of the intersections between the local and the global.[11] There has been a welcome recognition of London's significance as an imperial capital since the 1990s.[12] But the question of how this may have impacted on what particular types of food were being served (and the national, racial, and ethnic groups that consumed it) in London's eating houses has not been considered. The increasing deployment of the visual turn has brought rich rewards to those studying London in this period, but the restaurant is absent from the scholarship here also, possibly because the sheer ubiquity discussed by Woollan is all too evident in artistic, particularly photographic, representations of the city at this time.[13] The regular presence of the words 'dining room', 'restaurant', 'oyster rooms', 'chop house', 'tea room', 'grill room', 'café', 'eel and pie house', and 'fish bar' in the extraordinary bricolage of shopfront signs and advertising hoardings that characterized so many of London's streets has inexplicably been insufficient to attract scholarly interest (see Figure 0.1).[14]

---

[9] For example, Judith R. Walkowitz, *City of Dreadful Delight: Narratives of Sexual Danger in Late-Victorian London* (Chicago: University of Chicago Press, 1992); H. G. Cocks, *Nameless Offences: Homosexual Desire in the Nineteenth Century* (London: I. B. Tauris, 2003); Seth Koven, *Slumming: Sexual and Social Politics in Victorian London* (Princeton: Princeton University Press, 2004). In *Shopping for Pleasure: Women in the Making of London's West End* (Princeton: Princeton University Press, 2000), Erika Rappaport does acknowledge the restaurant, but only in the context of shoppers.

[10] See Rachel Rich, *Bourgeois Consumption: Food, Space and Identity in London and Paris, 1850–1914* (Manchester: Manchester University Press, 2011), and Judith R. Walkowitz, *Nights Out: Life in Cosmopolitan London* (New Haven: Yale University Press, 2012). The latter focuses on the Italian restaurant only, and mainly during the interwar years. The restaurant has also been granted recognition in a recent popular history, Jonathan Conlin, *Tales of Two Cities: Paris, London and the Birth of the Modern City* (London: Atlantic Books, 2013).

[11] See, for instance, the contributions in Felix Driver and David Gilbert (eds), *Imperial Cities: Landscape, Display and Identity* (Manchester: Manchester University Press, 1999).

[12] Most notably, Jonathan Schneer, *London 1900: The Imperial Metropolis* (New Haven and London: Yale University Press, 1999).

[13] Examples include Lynda Nead, *Victorian Babylon: People, Streets and Images in Nineteenth-Century London* (New Haven and London: Yale University Press, 2000); Nancy Rose Marshall, *City of Gold and Mud: Painting Victorian London* (New Haven and London: Yale University Press, 2012).

[14] For example, see some of the images reproduced in Philip Davies, *Panoramas of Lost London: Work, Wealth, Poverty and Change, 1870–1914* (Croxley Green: Transatlantic Press, 2011).

Figure 0.1. Harris Restaurant next to the Metropole Dining Rooms in Aldgate Street, 1909. (Reproduced with permission of the London Metropolitan Archives, City of London)

As food historian Jeffrey M. Pilcher has described it, there has been, in the last few decades, 'if not a culinary turn in scholarship, at the very least an academic food fad'.[15] The historical study of food has become a burgeoning field, with particular emphasis on the relationship between

---

[15] Jeffrey M. Pilcher, 'The Embodied Imagination in Recent Writings on Food History', *American Historical Review*, 121/3 (June 2016), 861.

food and the body, the role of food in creating socially based notions of taste, and the moral, political, and social discourses that surround the extremes around hunger and obesity. Much of this work has emerged as an aspect of the new cultural history, but food has also been granted particular significance by those committed to, if not world history, at least notions of historical change that embrace the transnational and the global. The majority of works in the historical study of food have concerned themselves with the early modern period and with non-British topics.[16] The food history of modern Britain has been largely relegated to popular histories or rather narrowly defined studies of individual culinary celebrities, cookbooks, and individual commodities.[17] In the much smaller academic scholarship concerned with food in nineteenth-century Britain, the restaurant is equally absent.[18]

While food historians have generally neglected the restaurant, there have been a number of studies that suggest how public eating can be used as a dynamic site on which to consider the wider formation of social and national identities. Mark Swislocki has used the food culture of Shanghai since the late Imperial period to show the complex relationship between regional, national, and global identities in Asia.[19] Various studies of food cultures of New York in the nineteenth and twentieth centuries have inevitably underlined the function of food as an expression of ethnic and

[16] For example, Marcy Norton, *Sacred Gifts, Profane Pleasures: A History of Tobacco and Chocolate in the Atlantic World* (Ithaca, NY, and London: Cornell University Press, 2010); Marcy Norton, 'Tasting Empire: Chocolate and the European Internalization of Meso-american Aesthetics', *American Historical Review*, 111/3 (June 2006), 660–91; Jordan Goodman, *Tobacco in History: The Cultures of Dependence* (London and New York: Routledge, 1993).

[17] Ruth Cowen, *Relish: The Extraordinary Life of Alexis Soyer, the Victorian Celebrity Chef* (London: Weidenfeld & Nicolson, 2006); Margaret Beetham, 'Good Taste and Sweet Ordering: Dining with Mrs Beeton', *Victorian Literature and Culture*, 36 (2008), 391–406; Kathryn Hughes, *The Short Life and Long Times of Mrs Beeton* (London: Fourth Estate, 2005); Lizzie Collingham, *Curry: A Biography* (London: Chatto and Windus, 2005). Collingham's recent wide-ranging, if episodic, *The Hungry Empire: How Britain's Quest for Food Shaped the Modern World* (London: Bodley Head, 2017), has no reference to the nineteenth-century restaurant.

[18] For example, Keir Waddington, ' "We Don't Want Any German Sausages Here!" Food, Fear, and the German Nation in Victorian and Edwardian Britain', and Nadja Durbach, 'Roast Beef, the New Poor Law, and the British Nation, 1834–1863', both in *Journal of British Studies* 52/4 (2013), 1017–1042, 963–89, respectively. The five chapters of John Burnett, *England Eats Out: A Social History of Eating out in England from 1830 to the Present* (Harlow: Pearson, 2004), dedicated to the period 1830–1914, offer a largely pedestrian narrative. While nominally concerned with the period since 1850, Panikos Panayi, *Spicing up Britain: The Multicultural History of British Food* (London: Reaktion, 2008), offers an essentially post-1945 narrative.

[19] Mark Swislocki, *Culinary Nostalgia: Regional Food Culture and the Urban Experience in Shanghai* (Stanford: Stanford University Press, 2009).

racial difference at the very same time that, taken together (and interacting with each other), these distinct food cultures contributed to the creation of a common urban (and, more widely, American) identity.[20] Perhaps the most acclaimed work that demonstrates the ability of public eating to contribute to larger narratives about politics, culture, and society is, of course, Rebecca Spang's arrestingly titled *The Invention of the Restaurant*. This work links the development of public gastronomic sensibility in revolutionary France to the emergence of modern life, in particular conceptions of public and private space, and the creation of new forms of social interaction in an urban setting.[21] While *The London Restaurant* shares Spang's desire to tell a bigger story, her conceptualization of 'the restaurant' as an abstraction is not one taken up here. Rather, the emphasis is on the restaurant as a site of material practice, and, as a consequence, while generalizations are regularly made, the reader will find reference to individual restaurants, some of them illustrious, some of them less well known, and others lacking names altogether. However, while the afore-mentioned works do not necessarily provide precise models for a study of the London restaurant, they help reinforce the necessity of an analysis of public eating that contributes to wider historiographical debates and issues.

This book is, therefore, not intended primarily as a contribution to food history. Rather, it should be seen as making a number of, related, inter-ventions in the historiography of modern Britain. First, the London restaurant raises important questions about issues of geography and scale in the writing of the history, not merely of London, but of Britain and its relationship to the wider world. At a most basic level, this study urges the necessity of looking at the creation of identities across all parts of (what later came to be termed) Greater London. While the focus of this book is largely on the metropolitan boroughs (with less attention paid to the outer suburbs), it still insists that we need to go beyond the primary focus on the West End that has characterized the most influential cultural histories of late Victorian and Edwardian London. It pays particular attention to the City of London, the emergence of which as a centre of both wealth creation and employment was perhaps the most important development

---

[20] Cindy R. Lobel, *Urban Appetites: Food and Culture in Nineteenth-Century New York* (Chicago: University of Chicago Press, 2014); Hasia R. Diner, *Hungering for America: Italian, Irish, and Jewish Foodways in the Age of Migration* (Cambridge, MA: Harvard University Press, 2001); Donna Gabaccia, *We are what we Eat: Ethnic Food and the Making of Americans* (Cambridge, MA: Harvard University Press, 1998; repr. 2000).

[21] Rebecca L. Spang, *The Invention of the Restaurant: Paris and Modern Gastronomic Culture* (Cambridge, MA: Harvard University Press, 2000); cf. Brian Cowan, *The Social Life of Coffee: The Emergence of the British Coffeehouse* (New Haven and London: Yale University Press, 2005).

in the capital's fortunes. However, it also recovers sites of public eating in the overlooked nooks and crannies of the urban infrastructure—for instance, around the docks and in the vicinity of railway stations.

Most significantly of all, the restaurant culture of this more broadly conceived London has to be placed within a transnational and globalized context. Those who ate out in London, the meals they consumed, and the staff who served them were all part of a genuinely international matrix. The association between cosmopolitanism and certain categories of consumption has long been recognized, but the restaurant reveals how this relationship played out, not merely in the realms of the elite and the fashionable, but in the more everyday experiences of public eating among a range of social actors. Unsurprisingly, Britain's formal empire had an important role to play in this culture of what I have termed 'gastro-cosmopolitanism', but the restaurant also revealed the ongoing connections between Britain and parts of the globe that lay outside it, notably continental Europe, China, the Americas (North and South), and the Middle East. This study of the restaurant therefore aligns itself with scholarship that has urged the need to go not merely beyond the nation, but also beyond empire. A turn from imperial history to world history has often privileged historical actors (or material goods and commodities) that move across national, imperial, and regional demarcations. By contrast, the London restaurant provides an ostensibly fixed point on which one can see the playing-out of these forces.[22] As a consequence, it raises important questions about the nature of scale in history, revealing how larger global questions of culture and identity can be dramatized in the smallest of spaces, whether the cramped dining room or even the plate from which the diner ate.

Second, paying attention to the restaurant requires us to recover categories of social actors whose 'unstoried' experiences have been either overlooked, or entirely erased, from the existing practices of social history.[23] Waiting staff, chefs, kitchen hands, managers, and restaurant proprietors: none of these important occupational groups has succeeded in finding a champion among economic, social, cultural, or labour historians. This is in part an inevitable consequence of the often transient nature

---

[22] For a slightly different approach to the interrelationship between the local and personal, on the one hand, and the global, on the other, see Erika Rappaport, *A Thirst for Empire: How Tea Shaped the Modern World* (Princeton: Princeton University Press, 2017).

[23] This notion of recovering 'unstoried' experiences has been most usefully demonstrated in studies of how domestic servants shaped elite colonial women's gendered relationships to home and history. For example, Ann Laura Stoler and Karen Strassler, 'Castings for the Colonial: Memory Work in "New Order" Java', *Comparative Studies in Society and History*, 42/1 (2000), 4–48.

of restaurant work, but it would be wrong to believe that those employed in the trade lacked the ability to seek forms of organization and recognition, in the form of either trade-union or professional groups. Having said that, the idiosyncrasies of the restaurant confound straightforward categorization of the workers involved, underlining the need for a more nuanced approach to issues of occupation and class identity in the late-nineteenth-century metropolis. Women played an important role in the restaurant, increasingly as diners, but also as workers, and indeed proprietors. This presence of women in these different public roles adds further support, if it is needed, to the case against simplistic models of separate spheres in pre-1914 Britain. However, this book also tries to offer a more reflective and dynamic conception of domesticity, recognizing that eating out could often blend forms of public sociability with the more traditional association of food with the realms of the domestic and intimate.

Third, consideration of those who worked in the restaurant trade, as opposed to its consumers, requires us to acknowledge the central role of the service sector in the creation of metropolitan modernity. The focus on consumption in much of the existing literature dedicated to modern London is in part a reflection of the preferences, and possibly comfort zones, of cultural historians.[24] Economic and social historians have emphasized London's economic significance as a manufacturing centre, despite the absence of large-scale industrial production.[25] However, both categories of historical analysis have largely neglected service industries, despite the fact that this sector of the economy transcended the production–consumption binary and thereby facilitated, not merely new forms of employment, but also new forms of social practice.[26] Paying attention to the restaurant also reminds us of the importance of small-scale

---

[24] For an exception, which considers both consumption and production, see Lara Kriegel, *Grand Designs: Labor, Empire, and the Museum in Victorian Culture* (Durham, NC: Duke University Press, 2007).

[25] On London's economic significance as a manufacturing and industrial centre, see White, *London in the Nineteenth Century*, 172–81; Michael Ball and David Sunderland, *An Economic History of London, 1800–1914* (London: Routledge, 2001), esp. pp. 293–319; James A. Schmiechen, *Sweated Industries and Sweated Labor: The London Clothing Trades, 1860–1914* (London: Croom Helm, 1984); Andrew Godley, 'Immigrant Entrepreneurs and the Emergence of London's East End as an Industrial District', *London Journal*, 21/1 (1996), 38–45; on the earlier period, see David R. Green, *From Artisans to Paupers: Economic Change and Poverty in London, 1790–1870* (Aldershot: Scolar Press, 1995); L. D. Schwarz, *London in the Age of Industrialisation: Entrepreneurs, Labour Force and Living Conditions, 1700–1850* (Cambridge: Cambridge University Press, 1992).

[26] Ball and Sunderland, *An Economic History of London*, includes a very short chapter on 'Domestic, Clerical and Professional Services', but the content is limited to domestic service, laundry services, and clerks, in addition to lawyers and accountants. The restaurant trade is entirely absent.

enterprises. While there were examples of consolidation and standardization, most venues for public eating remained small scale and independent. Nevertheless, they articulated a robust private-enterprise culture that should be accorded its full significance (even in an era of national and local government expansion) in the shaping of metropolitan life.

Fourth, while eating out could be associated with cultural anxiety (in issues ranging from food contamination to hostility to foreign waiters), most of the time it represented one of the more congenial aspects of urban culture. The overwhelming experience of those who ate out in London might best be characterized as either unremarkable or enjoyable. People either ate out to fuel their appetites during interludes in the working day, or did so as an opportunity to enjoy the food on their plate or the (increasingly heterosocial) company of family, friends, or colleagues. This observation might risk appearing sanguine (not to say glib), but it is important to provide some form of mitigation to a cultural history that often emphasizes the more discomfiting or fraught (and, critically, exceptional and spectacular) aspects of the modern experience.[27]

The chronological parameters of this study are the middle decades of the nineteenth century, on the one hand, and the outbreak of the First World War, on the other. The selection of 1914 as a termination date is appropriate, given that the Great War caused a serious disruption in London's restaurant sector. Among the various dislocations created by the war (notably difficulties of food provision), the international labour market that was so important to London's public eating was ruptured by the expulsion of German waiting staff and the return of many Italians to their homeland after Italy had joined the war in 1915. The start date of this study is more arbitrary, and is largely determined by the nature and availability of source material. While public eating in London clearly predated the Victorian era, it left (with the exception of one or two famous establishments frequented by men of letters) very little in the way of historical record. References to the London restaurant become more frequent between the 1840s and 1870s, and thereafter they attain a regularity in the historical record commensurate with their significance in the economy and culture of the late Victorian and Edwardian metropolis.

The fact that the restaurant was both quotidian and yet also potentially quite ephemeral poses particular challenges in the location of sources

[27] The classic text in this regard is Walkowitz, *City of Dreadful Delight*. For a highly effective reminder of how modernity could be reconciled to a culture of reassurance, through an emphasis on the everyday and the unremarkable, see Alison Light, *Forever England: Femininity, Literature and Conservatism between the Wars* (London and New York: Routledge, 1991).

required for its scholarly study. Publicity materials provide a material trace of the encounter between consumer and eating house. Some restaurants actually provided lavish brochures, especially to coincide with the opening of a new establishment. For example, when it reopened in 1894, the Holborn Restaurant published a thirty-five-page brochure with illustrations of (among others) its dazzling King's Hall (complete with an orchestra), up-to-date kitchen, and intimate and comfortable smoking lounge.[28] If such materials tend to privilege the more spectacular or successful concerns, archives such as the Bishopsgate Library also contain the handbills for modest establishments. Of course, such survivals are relatively rare, and it should also not be forgotten that the vast majority of eating houses advertised through sandwich boards or blackboards, whose content can be recovered only from their tantalizing but intermittent presence in street photography. A similar problem of rates of survival exists in regard to menus, an obvious resource for the history of the restaurant. The Evanion Collection in the British Library includes a sizeable collection of London restaurant menus, although not on the scale that exists for New York held in the New York Public Library's Buttolph Collection of Menus. There is a handful of memoirs by, or sketches of, restaurant proprietors, managers, and chefs, but not on a large scale, and, again, these fail to give a sense of the range of restaurant businesses in London at the time.

Given that records produced by individual restaurant businesses themselves have rarely survived (with the notable exception of Lyons), the historian is much more likely to be rewarded by looking at sources from the wider culture in which other eating took place. References to public eating crop up in novels, short stories, even popular song. Newspapers, journals, and magazines regularly discussed restaurants (both individual establishments and broader trends in dining), and, by the Edwardian period, we start to see something approaching the modern restaurant reviewer. Official records, including Metropolitan Police reports and Parliamentary Papers (notably Royal Commission and Select Committee reports), also contain references to restaurants. Most notably, the records of the City of London's Commissioner of Sewers and the LCC's Medical Officer of Health in the Public Health Department allow us to scrutinize the restaurant's relationship to public health and the environment, while the publications of pressure groups (notably trade unions) and philanthropic organizations (such as temperance and vegetarian societies) tell us much about the restaurant's significance in narratives of social

---

[28] Frederick Leal, *Holborn Restaurant Illustrated* (London: Holborn Restaurant, 1894), D 93.2 London Collection Pamphlets, Box 323/38, Bishopsgate.

advancement and improvement. Post Office directories can give some sense of the scale and location of public eating. References to restaurants can also be retrieved from works authored by those associated with theatrical and literary London. If such sources seem inevitably eclectic, a more comprehensive source base of the restaurant is the trade press, which encompassed both description and commentary. Publications such as the *Caterer* and the *Restaurant* regularly registered a range of perspectives on public eating. While the voice of restaurant proprietors and managers was sometimes prioritized, the experiences and concerns of waiting and kitchen staff were regularly discussed, and due consideration was given to the experience of diners. The trade press was, not surprisingly, eager to boost the interests of the restaurant sector, and to defend it against its critics. However, it was no less willing to confront the deficiencies and idiosyncrasies of the restaurant, an approach that invests these trade publications with a much broader historical value than might have been assumed. Indeed, the trade press, through its ability to highlight the critical interrelationship between cultural practice and commerce, is particularly suited to the broader agenda of this book.

Chapter 1 offers a typology and geographical survey of the Victorian and Edwardian restaurant. After providing a quantitative overview, it then introduces a variety of categories (for example, chophouses, working-class eating houses, small-scale owner-managed dining rooms, and women's, vegetarian, and temperance restaurants) while at the same time emphasizing that the polyglot nature of eating often renders such categorization problematic. The restaurant is shown here to be more than just a fashionable West End establishment; it also encompassed modest refreshment rooms spread across the metropolis, in particular the City of London.

Chapter 2 examines the restaurant as a business. It offers an explanation for the dramatically contrasting fortunes of London's restaurants, a sector of the economy characterized by both success and expansion, and failure and bankruptcy. Consideration is given to how restaurants were financed, how they secured staff and supplies, the incorporation of new technology, and the often ingenious ways that they sought out customers. Restaurant proprietors and managers (and even cooks and chefs) explored a variety of schemes to establish their status as professionals, but these rarely compromised the vigorous pursuit of financial reward, in a sector of the economy in which profit margins were often relatively small. In an era characterized by a moving frontier between state and economy, the restaurant revealed the ongoing commitment in Victorian and Edwardian culture to the power of free enterprise and the maintenance of a robust commercial domain.

Chapter 3 focuses on one important player in the restaurant's workforce, the waiter, regularly represented in popular culture as marginal, disenchanted, and melancholy. While real-life waiters were often keen to share a variety of grievances about their working conditions, it would be inaccurate to present them universally as degraded victims of exploitation. Some waiters were able to capitalize on the open and dynamic nature of the restaurant service economy, which created opportunities for mobility and reward. Even tipping, which remained an ongoing bone of contention, for both waiters and those they served, could prove to be an important source of supplementary income. For all the idiosyncrasies of the waiter's position, he represented the broader significance of the service sector in the shaping of London in this period. The extensive public attention given to foreign-born waiters and (newly emergent) waitresses underlines the heterogeneity that characterized, not merely the restaurant, but the wider metropolitan culture in which it was located.

Chapter 4 links the restaurant to issues of public health. Restaurants faced the problem that, even if they attained superior standards of hygiene within their kitchens and dining rooms, they were still prone to episodes of contamination and adulteration emanating from suppliers, wholesalers, and markets. Concerns that the restaurant might be a site of pollution and disease inevitably accorded it a significant place in the discourses of official regulation. The culture and conduct of restaurant inspection, while definitely inscribed with the practices of liberal governance, were also required to accommodate themselves to the prerogatives of commercial forces. Moreover, attention to inspectors should not obscure the fact that the restaurant sector itself was eager to reassure customers that it made every effort to ensure the highest standards of hygiene. Temperance and vegetarian establishments will also be discussed here, as sites on which healthy eating was yoked to the pursuit of moral purity and rationalism.

Chapter 5 presents the restaurant as a valuable site for mapping patterns of transnational global and cultural exchange. London's diners were exposed to a variety of new, often hybrid, culinary cultures, which call into question simplistic binaries between Britain and the world beyond. The presence in London's restaurants of French menus, Indian dishes, Italian cooks, Swiss proprietors, German waiters, and Chinese and American diners illustrates the complexity of the relationship between populations and places. London's 'gastro-cosmopolitanism', my shorthand for this multilayered culture, reveals not merely the extent to which Britain's imperial metropolis was exposed to transnational forces, but that these influences were genuinely global and not confined to Britain's formal empire.

Chapter 6 offers a sketch of those who ate out in London. It emphasizes the diversity of diners, defined in terms of both social class and, critically, gender. Here diners are mapped onto broader patterns of social change in the metropolis, notably suburbanization, the expansion of the service sector, and changing leisure patterns. Attention to the increased presence of women eating out allows us to locate the restaurant in wider discussions about the interconnections between the domestic and public spheres, and the emergence of new forms of heterosociability. Inserting the restaurant diner into our understanding of Victorian and Edwardian metropolitan culture obliges us to qualify, and even repudiate, some of the dominant scholarly interpretations of how identities were fashioned and performed at this time.

In the chapters that follow the reader will encounter a range of characters located in a variety of, often arresting, situations. A restaurant owner is seriously discomfited when he tries to establish who, among the forty women seated in a waiting room at Liverpool Street station, are the four he had requested to meet him there in order to be interviewed for a waitressing position at his establishment. The owner of a modest eating house in Paddington resorts to the courts, when the police order the horse-drawn 'carmen' (who make up her core clientele) to desist from parking outside her premises. An Italian waiter at the Cavour restaurant in Leicester Square chases a co-worker to Victoria station, after the latter, for whom he had provided free board and lodging, had run off with his host's life savings. A group of waiters become self-appointed informants, passing on to the Public Health Department lurid details of poor hygiene in the kitchens of a number of prestigious West End restaurants. Conversely, two friends succumb to food poisoning after dining on the Strand, but then return to eat at the same restaurant the following evening. A retired army officer turned restaurant reviewer dines with an American actress in the Haymarket. A Japanese painter resident in London is perplexed when he is taken out by a group of English actors to what purports to be a 'Samurai dinner' at a restaurant. However, many of the people who feature in this book are more anonymous, their presence registered only fleetingly in the margins and the shadows. For example, a Greek pastry cook is mentioned only in passing in the description of a coffee tavern recommended by a patron to the readers of a temperance journal.

A similar variety characterizes the settings in which we encounter these people. Fashionable West End restaurants were lavishly decorated with marble staircases, palm trees, ornate balconies, enormous mirrors, and spectacular chandeliers, with diners eating to the accompaniment of an orchestra. The refreshment rooms run by Spiers and Pond, and later Lyons, prioritized a self-consciously modern functionalism in the layout of their interiors. The majority of diners ate out in modest eating houses of which little visual or descriptive record survives. Moreover, the requirements of either poverty or economy meant that many others ate adjacent to the shop windows, street carts, and mobile kitchens from which they purchased their food. To return to the testimony of J. C. Woollan, with which this chapter began, the heterogeneous nature of London's public eating was also a consequence of people taking meals at different times of the day. Any study of the restaurant needs to encompass, not just the leisured and affluent evening diners in theatreland, but also dock workers grabbing breakfast in coffee houses, City clerks desperately perambulating the Square Mile in search of a meal during their lunch break, and employees in the theatre in search of a late-night supper after curtain call. Appreciating this social, spatial, and temporal spectrum underlines the myriad intersections between the restaurant and the wider metropolitan culture to which it was intrinsically linked. Most critically of all, the restaurant is a testimony to the heterogeneity of Victorian and Edwardian London, a place and a time that can fully be understood only when we pay proper attention to the complex interrelationships that existed between culture and commerce, and the global and the local.

1

Finding the Restaurant

Musing on the subject of dining out in London, actor–playwright Charles Selby, writing under the wonderful pseudonym of Tabitha Tickletooth, professed that the times when 'merchants and tradesmen lived at their places of business and dined with their families at one o'clock on a plain joint', when 'clerks and shopmen bought half a pound of mutton-chop or beef-steak at a butcher's hard by, and cooked it for themselves on a gigantic common gridiron for a penny', and 'when "Templers" and other "limbs of the law" were contented with a basin of mock turtle, a cut of the joint and a pint' were long gone and now only 'curious matters of history'. Instead, he continued, 'clerks and shopmen' and other workers 'take their dinners...at some...renowned "Dining Room", where for fifteen pence they can have a sufficing plateful of fine, well cooked meat, bread, and vegetables, with a slice of pudding or pie, a pint of porter, a "skim" at the "Times", and a "thank you, sir", from the bland waiter' for their custom.[1] Selby was writing in 1860, but the dramatic change in public eating habits that he recorded was to become even more apparent in the remaining decades of the century. Observers in the 1880s and 1890s testified not merely to the change in the nature of metropolitan catering, but also to the concomitant increase in venues. The wife of journalist E. T. Cook, W. T. Stead's successor as editor of the *Pall Mall Gazette*, remarked in 1887 that 'revolutions have been worked' with respect to the growth of dining places in the previous twenty years, while another observer later commented that 'we have fifty times as many good restaurants in the London of 1895 as we had eight-and-thirty-years ago...'.[2]

Such anecdotal impressions about growth are borne out by statistics. Counting the number of public eating establishments listed in Kelly's

[1] Tabitha Tickletooth [Charles Selby], *The Dinner Question, or how to Dine Well and Economically* (London: Routledge, 1860), 139. Selby's real name was George Henry Wilson.

[2] Mrs E. T. Cook [Emily Constance Baird Cook], *Highways and Byways in London* (London: Macmillan, 1887; repr. 1902), 321; 'The Origin of Restaurants', *Hotel*, 18 September 1895, p. 21.

Table 1. Numbers of dining rooms, refreshment rooms, and restaurants per decade, 1840–1910

Establishments	1840	1850	1860	1870	1880	1890	1900	1910
Dining rooms	106	302	358	403	440	587	882	1,009
Dining/coffee rooms*	—	35	89	73	69	178	224	177
Refreshment rooms	n.a.	n.a.	n.a.	94	235	344	461	769
Restaurants	n.a.	n.a.	n.a.	n.a.	12	38	92	n.a.
TOTAL	106	337	447	570	756	1,147	1,659	1,955

* This denotes a subcategory within the larger category of 'coffee rooms' referred to in Kelly's as 'also dining rooms' and indicated by an asterisk in the directory.

Note: Between 1840 and 1860, only dining rooms appeared in Kelly's. From 1870 onwards, Kelly's listed dining rooms and refreshment rooms under two separate categories. Between 1880 and 1900, Kelly's also listed restaurants under the category of Hotels, &c., while continuing to list dining rooms and refreshment rooms. N.a. = not applicable.

Sources: *Post Office London Directory* (London: W. Kelly and Co., 1840–1910): 'Dining Rooms', *Post Office London Directory for 1840*, 409; 'Coffee Rooms', *Post Office London Directory for 1850*, 1227–8, 1207–11; 'Dining Rooms', 'Coffee Rooms', *Post Office London Directory for 1860*, 1586–7, 1558–63; 'Dining Rooms', 'Coffee Rooms', 'Refreshment Rooms', *Post Office London Directory for 1870*, 1528–30, 1502–6, 1725–6; *Post Office London Directory for 1880*, 1546–7, 1514–19, 1783–4; *Post Office London Directory for 1890*, 1682–4, 1644–9, 1966–7; *Post Office London Directory for 1900*, 1997–2000, 1952–7, 2336–8; *Post Office London Directory for 1910*, 1527–30, 1492–5, 1811–13.

London trade directories at the beginning of each decade between 1840 and 1910 can give a fairly reliable index of this change (see Table 1). Initially, Kelly's listed only the category of 'dining rooms', but in 1850, the category of 'coffee rooms' began to include a subcategory 'and also dining rooms'. In 1870, 'refreshment rooms' were granted a category of their own. From that point, Kelly's allocation of an establishment as either 'dining room', 'dining/coffee room', or 'refreshment room' often appears arbitrary, with similar institutions appearing in one of these three categories, or indeed in none. To complicate matters further, in the two decades after 1880, the annotation 'r' (for restaurant) was appended to a number of institutions listed in the established category of 'hotels, inns, taverns, and principal coffee houses', although several legendary London dining venues, notably the Cock and the Cheshire Cheese, appeared in this sprawling category without the specific 'r' designation. Given the difficulty of substantiating, in every case, whether patrons ate, as opposed to drank or slept, in hotels, taverns, inns, and coffee houses, the analysis of figures derived from Kelly's that follows will be confined to the following four categories: (1) 'dining rooms'; (2) establishments designated as 'also dining rooms' within the category of coffee rooms; (3) 'refreshment rooms'; and (4) those institutions that received the 'r' designation in the category of 'hotels, inns, taverns, and principal coffee houses'. By 1910, the 'r' designation was dropped and institutions that might have expected to appear under it were folded into the category of 'refreshment room'.[3]

Irrespective of this categorical mish-mash, it is hard not to conclude from the raw figures that there was a dramatic growth in the number of public eating establishments in the second half of the century. The combined total of the four categories isolated here rose from 106 in 1840 to 570 in 1870, and 1,147 in 1890. By 1910, the total had reached 1,955, which represented close to a fourfold increase since 1870.

The linguistic slippage between 'dining room', 'refreshment room', and 'restaurant' is intriguing in Kelly's trade directories, a publication produced by that highly regulatory body, the Post Office, which had clear instrumental reasons for ordering and categorizing the metropolis. If it was obliged to accommodate imprecision about how to label these establishments, then we can assume the general public was likely to be similarly inexact, especially considering the names of some establishments such as the Silver Grill Café and Restaurant, Pearce's Dining and Refreshment Rooms, St James's Restaurant and Tavern, Southwark Coffee Palace and Dining Room, the British Tea Table Co., and the Grand Hotel, Buffet and Grill Room. Thus, if Kelly's appears unsure about the terminology underpinning public eating, then it is because establishments themselves co-opted multiple labels. For the purposes of this discussion, a highly elastic definition of 'restaurant' must be taken to reflect the slippage evident in the historical record where these categories were blended or used to incorporate an establishment's multiple labelling. Such fastidious attachment to Kelly's sometimes haphazard labelling has its risks— notably the likelihood of underestimating the number of dining establishments in London. To take just one example, Lockhart's Cocoa Rooms, palpably a significant presence in London's restaurant scene, was for much of this period listed under the category of 'coffee rooms', but without the asterisk denoting 'also dining rooms'.[4] However, a survey of Kelly's trade directories offers the most effective way of providing a global picture of the numerical and geographical scale of public eating.

[3] This change appears in 1902. See 'Refreshment Rooms, Restaurants, Cafes, &c.', *Post Office London Directory for 1902* (London: W. Kelly and Co., 1902), 2164.

[4] By 1910, Lockhart's Cocoa Rooms migrated to the category of 'Refreshment Rooms'. See *Post Office London Directory for 1910* (London: W. Kelly and Co., 1910), 1493. But for 1880 (when there were 7 establishments), 1890 (when there were 54), and 1900 (when there were 63), Lockhart's was listed only as a coffee room. See *Post Office London Directory for 1880* (London: W. Kelly and Co., 1880), 1558; *Post Office London Directory for 1890* (London: W. Kelly and Co., 1890), 1647; *Post Office London Directory for 1900* (London: W. Kelly and Co., 1900), 1955.

Table 2. Numbers of dining rooms, coffee rooms designated as 'also dining rooms', refreshment rooms, and restaurants in London sorted by postal code, 1840–1910

Postal code*	1840	1850	1860	1870	1880	1890	1900	1910
E	4	25	31	80	101	149	160	238
EC	46	119	123	180	239	387	499	538
SE	9	28	22	48	81	104	151	190
S**	0	7	29	0	0	0	0	0
SW	6	24	30	41	61	94	144	154
W	19	55	82	89	115	191	327	379
WC	22	37	51	59	86	126	144	146
N	0	14	23	33	31	46	95	124
NW	0	17	27	40	42	36	91	120
NE**	0	11	29	0	0	14	48	66
TOTAL	106	337	447	570	756	1,147	1,659	1,955

* Before 1857, Kelly's did not list postal codes after the street addresses. For the sake of consistency in my decennial sample, I have inserted the postal codes for 1840 and 1850 establishments by matching street addresses against the postal-code boundaries of 1857.

** The NE district was abolished in 1867, but the Post Office acknowledged that streets once belonging to NE could be integrated into the Eastern districts, or the letters NE and E could be used interchangeably. The S district was abolished in 1868.

Note: In this table, each eating house is counted separately even if owned by the same individual or company.

Sources: 'Dining Rooms', *Post Office London Directory for 1840*, 409; 'Coffee Rooms', *Post Office London Directory for 1850*, 1227–8, 1207–11; 'Dining Rooms', 'Coffee Rooms', *Post Office London Directory for 1860*, 1586–7, 1558–63; 'Dining Rooms', 'Coffee Rooms', 'Refreshment Rooms', *Post Office London Directory for 1870*, 1528–30, 1502–6, 1725–6; *Post Office London Directory for 1880*, 1546–7, 1514–19, 1783–4; *Post Office London Directory for 1890*, 1682–4, 1644–9, 1966–7; *Post Office London Directory for 1900*, 1997–2000, 1952–7, 2336–8; *Post Office London Directory for 1910*, 1527–30, 1492–5, 1811–13.

If we use Kelly's to establish, not just numbers, but locations, what is immediately apparent is that public eating establishments were scattered across the entire metropolis. Noting and collating the postal codes of all the individual establishments listed under the categories of 'dining rooms', those coffee houses designated as 'also dining rooms', 'refreshment rooms', and 'restaurants' every ten years between 1840 and 1910 provides a rough and ready measure of the geographical distribution of public eating, as Table 2 demonstrates. Represented in percentages (see Table 3), these figures demonstrate where in the metropolis public eating was concentrated.

A global view of the regional distribution shows that most eating houses lay adjacent to centres of commercial activity, and in each decade EC (comprising the City of London) had the lion's share in the form of dining rooms or, after 1850, both dining rooms and coffee rooms designated as 'also dining rooms', or, after 1870, refreshment rooms, coffee rooms designated as 'also dining rooms', and dining rooms, or, between 1880

Table 3. Percentage of dining rooms, coffee rooms designated as 'also dining rooms', refreshment rooms, and restaurants in London sorted by postal code, 1840–1910 (%)

Postal code	1840	1850	1860	1870	1880	1890	1900	1910
E	3.77	7.40	6.94	14.04	13.36	13.00	9.60	12.20
EC	43.40	35.30	27.50	31.58	31.60	33.70	30.07	27.50
SE	8.50	8.30	4.90	8.42	10.70	9.07	9.10	9.70
S	0.00	2.08	6.49	0.00	0.00	0.00	0.00	0.00
SW	5.66	7.12	6.71	7.19	8.07	8.20	8.68	7.90
W	17.90	16.30	18.34	15.60	15.20	16.65	19.70	19.40
WC	20.75	10.97	11.40	10.35	11.38	11.00	8.68	7.50
N	0.00	4.15	5.15	5.79	4.10	4.01	5.70	6.30
NW	0.00	5.04	6.04	7.02	5.55	3.13	5.49	6.10
NE	0.00	3.26	6.49	0.00	0.00	1.22	2.89	3.40

Sources: 'Dining Rooms', *Post Office London Directory for 1840*, 409; 'Coffee Rooms', *Post Office London Directory for 1850*, 1227–8, 1207–11; 'Dining Rooms', 'Coffee Rooms', *Post Office London Directory for 1860*, 1586–7, 1558–63; 'Dining Rooms', 'Coffee Rooms', 'Refreshment Rooms', *Post Office London Directory for 1870*, 1528–30, 1502–6, 1725–6; *Post Office London Directory for 1880*, 1546–7, 1514–19, 1783–4; *Post Office London Directory for 1890*, 1682–4, 1644–9, 1966–7; *Post Office London Directory for 1900*, 1997–2000, 1952–7, 2336–8; *Post Office London Directory for 1910*, 1527–30, 1492–5, 1811–13.

and 1900, restaurants, refreshment rooms, coffee rooms designated as 'also dining rooms', and dining rooms. To be sure, in 1840, EC was home to roughly 43 per cent of all eating establishments, a figure that dipped to about 35 per cent in 1850, and fell again slightly in the next few decades, but the area still dominated in relation to other districts in London. The relative decline in the middle decades of the century related to the relative increase in areas such as west (W) and west-central London (WC), where theatreland—clearly important but far from dominant in this trans-metropolitan story—was located, east London (E), and, to a lesser extent, residential and commercial areas in the south (SE and SW) and north (NW, N, and NE).

The statistics in Table 3 suggest that public eating accords with the shifts in metropolitan population growth over this period. When mapping London's eating houses in this period, it is notable that they often existed cheek by jowl with other businesses, trade associations, social institutions, and the transportation infrastructure. For example, Spiers and Pond's, a cheap and cheerful behemoth in the world of popular dining, had multiple locations at railway stations throughout the metropolis from the 1870s onwards along the London, Chatham and Dover lines, St John's Wood railway, the Metropolitan District and Metropolitan Western Extension lines, Midland railway, and the Great Eastern and Great Western lines.

Joseph Lyons and Co., which became an even bigger chain with its thirty-seven locations spread throughout the metropolis at the end of the century, followed a similar pattern. Yet, the persistent clustering of restaurants in EC relates to the rise and consolidation of the City as a key centre of economic activity in late-nineteenth-century London. The concentration of catering in this area is evidenced by the continued growth of small-scale proprietors who hoped to make their fortune (or at least a profit) by locating their establishments in this very congested economic hive, as a Mrs Sarah Lucy Seabright apparently hoped to do in 1890 with her modest refreshment room in London Street, a mean little road that was near not only Fenchurch railway station but also the East and West India Dock company warehouses and Leadenhall market, both of which probably supplied food for her kitchen.[5] While there is no other trace of her establishment apart from a listing in Kelly's, Mrs Seabright's customers might have included clerks from City offices or the nearby Custom House, merchants from local commercial salesrooms, dock workers, or visitors to the Tower of London. If location was anything to go by, Mrs Seabright cleverly positioned herself in a commercial web of opportunity, and the fact that she remained on this site ten years later, according to Kelly's, suggests something about her good business sense.[6] She did well to hold her own in this area especially given that, of the thirty-seven J. Lyons and Co. refreshment rooms, eighteen were located in EC and at least one—at 31 Fenchurch St—was in Mrs Seabright's immediate vicinity, though perhaps their customer base differed.[7]

Combing through Kelly's listing of these establishments also offers a fleeting glimpse into the world of public eating in other parts of the metropolis, where, while less concentrated, they were woven, literally street by street, into the fabric of daily life. For instance, in 1900, in west London, on Praed Street, a Mrs Emma Newman set up her refreshment room probably in order to capitalize on the foot traffic to and from Paddington Station, but perhaps also from the nearby residences. While further south-west in Vanston Place, in the leafy, middle-class section of Fulham near the Walham Green and Parsons Green railway stations, was Mrs Harriett Wynn's dining room, a place within the easy reach of a local church, several chapels and schools, a butchers' asylum, a post office, and a brewery, thus perhaps an integral part of the neighbourhood for local

---

[5] Listing for Mrs Sarah Lucy Seabright, *Kelly's Post Office Trades' and Professional Directory for 1890* (London: Kelly's Directories, Ltd, 1890), iii. 1967.
[6] Listing for Mrs Sarah Lucy Seabright, *Kelly's Post Office Trades' and Professional Directory for 1900* (London: Kelly's Directories, Ltd, 1900), iii. 2337.
[7] Listing for J. Lyons and Co., *ibid.* iii. 2337.

residents. Meanwhile in north London, one Mrs Maria Elliott had her dining room in Newington Green Road between Canonbury and Mildmay Park stations, near a conference hall, timber yard, hospital, lecture hall, and bricklayers' asylum, possibly attracting residents, local workers, and visitors to this area, which, according to Charles Booth, was comfortably middle class.[8] Apart from their proximity to centres of commercial trade, social organizations, and railway lines, these restaurant-keepers had another (rather obvious) thing in common, which is that they were all married (or widowed) women, suggesting something about the respectability and acceptability about this type of business ownership for women. Their presence in the trade is also a reminder of the reality that females played an important role in the productive and service sectors of the metropolis, which made them markedly different from the female consumers who have been the focus of existing historiography on the Victorian city.[9]

What Kelly's directories show is that public eating establishments were ubiquitous across the metropolis and were clearly folded into the commercial and economic structure of London as a whole. What they cannot reveal is any sense about individual establishments, and the differences or commonalities between them. What follows is a brief typology of public eating in nineteenth-century London. By isolating a number of types, it is important to appreciate that many establishments could be remarkably eclectic and incorporate elements from more than one type. Moreover, they could change their character over time in order to keep up with the changing trends and markets.

In this growing and complex eating culture, the traditional chophouse was to become proportionately less significant. While its precise origins are obscure, the term 'chophouse' first appeared at the end of the seventeenth century. The term was often used quite loosely, but it can certainly be distinguished from both public houses, which were primarily for drinking,

---

[8] Listings for Mrs Emma Newman, Mrs Harriett Wynn, Mrs Maria Elliot, *ibid.* 1999, 2000, 1998.

[9] For a discussion of women as consumers, see Erika D. Rappaport, *Shopping for Pleasure: Women in the Making of London's West End* (Princeton: Princeton University Press, 2000); Thomas Richards, *The Commodity Culture of Victorian England: Advertising and Spectacle, 1851–1914* (Stanford: Stanford University Press, 1990); Lynne Walker, 'Vistas of Pleasure: Women Consumers of Urban Space in the West End of London, 1850–1900', in Clarissa Campbell Orr (ed.), *Women in the Victorian Art World* (Manchester: Manchester University Press, 1995); Lori Loeb, *Consuming Angels: Advertising and Victorian Women* (Oxford: Oxford University Press, 1994). On the (limited) literature on female businesswomen, see Alison C. Kay, 'A Little Enterprise of her Own: Lodging-House Keeping and the Accommodation Business in Nineteenth-Century London', *London Journal*, 28/2 (2003), 41–53; Jennifer Aston and Paolo Di Martino, 'Risk, Success, and Failure: Female Entrepreneurship in Late Victorian and Edwardian England', *Economic History Review*, 70/3 (2017), 837–58.

and the rooms made available in taverns for private dining by social clubs. The interiors of chophouses were characterized by boxes, curtained partitions, and benches. The meals served emphasized culinary simplicity and relatively speedy delivery of food at the table. London chophouses were sufficiently important in eighteenth-century culture to feature in both popular verse and Boswell's *London Journal*.[10] They were still a key part of London's public eating culture well into the middle decades of the nineteenth century. Precisely when they began to decline in significance is not entirely clear. Writing at the turn of the century, the theatre critic Clement Scott insisted that, as late as 1860, 'there were very few restaurants of any importance in London ... the old tavern and chop house life had not been obliterated'.[11] If Scott was correct, then the decline of the chophouse was decidedly precipitate, since, by the 1880s, there was already a growing consensus that it was no longer flourishing.

This is not to deny that essayists, illustrators, and photographers were attracted to the historical, sentimental, and even whimsical aspects of these venerable establishments. A gushing portrait of the Cheshire Cheese in Wine Office Court off Fleet Street that appeared in 1889 in the *English Illustrated Magazine* celebrated its 'heavily timbered windows, the low planked ceiling, the huge projecting fire-place with a great copper boiler always on the simmer, the high, stiff-backed settles which box off the guests, the solitary picture of a great departed waiter'.[12] In this atmosphere of 'decorous simplicity', from which had been banished 'all the new-fangled ideas of the fashionable restaurants now in vogue, with their garishness and their glitter', one could find dishes—point steaks, gargantuan chops, floury potatoes, rump steak, and oyster pudding, all washed down with tankards of 'creaming stout'—that embodied a reassuring 'England of solid comfort, and solid plenty'.[13] Two years later, a profile of Baker's Chop House in Cornhill in the City swooned over the decor— sanded floors, high partitions dividing the seats, the preference for benches over chairs—that recalled 'the times of our grandsires'.[14] As at the

---

[10] For example, 'The London al-n's taste, or Pretty Sally of the chop-house. The address of a gentleman whose inclinations induced him to taste her commodities' (London, 1750). Clifton's chophouse in Butcher Row near Lincoln's Inn was a particular favourite of Boswell's. See Frederick A. Pottle (ed.), *Boswell's London Journal, 1762–1763* (New Haven: Yale University Press, 1950; repr. 2004), 236–7, 240–1, 254–7, 262, 268, 270–2, 282, 324.

[11] Clement Scott, *How they Dined us in 1860 and how they Dine us now* (London, n.d. [c.1900]), 4.

[12] W. Outram Tristram, 'A Storied Tavern', with illustrations by Herbert Railton, *English Illustrated Magazine*, 75 (December 1889), 220.

[13] *Ibid.*

[14] Clipping, 'Baker's Chop House', *City Press*, 1891, Norman Collection, London Guildhall Library.

Cheshire Cheese, the diner at Baker's need not have feared encountering modish continental fare, and 'if an unwary visitor merely suggests any dainty at all out of the way he is soon recalled to his senses by the waiter— himself a relic of the past'.[15]

However, such eulogies barely concealed an underlying anxiety about the future prospects of chophouses and their ability to hold their own against their more modern competitors. These essays were often exercises in nostalgia, rather than a convincing case for contemporary relevance. The portrait of the Cheshire Cheese, in particular, dedicated more space to anecdotes about the establishment's literary associations—it was said to have been frequented by Herrick, Johnson, Garrick, Goldsmith, and Chatterton, and later Dickens, Tennyson, and Thackeray—than it did to its culinary accomplishments.[16] Significantly, the article was accompanied by illustrations (by Herbert Railton) that referenced the chophouse's architectural and historical charms, rather than the cuisine served, a trend reiterated in photographic and postcard reproductions (see Figure 1.1).[17] Moreover, articles on both the Cheshire Cheese and Baker's acknowledged that, while these particular institutions had survived, many other prominent chophouses had not. The Cheshire Cheese was declared to have been fortunate to have been spared the 'deplorable fate which overtook its great rival and prototype', the Cock, a sixteenth-century house, also on Fleet Street, which was demolished in 1887.[18]

Indeed, the passing of the chophouse became almost a journalistic cliché at the end of the century. The otherwise notoriously acerbic Clement Scott recalled with fondness his experience of dining in the middle decades of the nineteenth century with fellow journalists and literary men at various London chophouses such as Dolly's in the City, Izant's in Holborn, the Cock, the Cheshire Cheese, and the Rainbow, all in Fleet Street, Stone's in Panton Street, and the Albion near Drury Lane.[19] He noted their 'attraction for bohemian journalists and literary men', but also testified to the fact that they were 'cosy with boxes polished or plain, they prided themselves on their hospitable ways, their roaring fires, and [their visitors] never disdained a good old fashioned bowl of whiskey or plain punch'.[20] Scott also recalled the archaic forms of food preparation associated with chophouse dining: 'it was the fashion to choose your own chop or steak out of the glass cupboard at the door,

---

[15] *Ibid.*   [16] Tristram, 'A Storied Tavern', 222–3.
[17] See, e.g., postcards held in C23.1, Noble Collection, London Guildhall Library (now in the London Metropolitan Archives [hereafter LMA]).
[18] Tristram, 'A Storied Tavern', 225–6. The Cock then moved across the street to 22 Fleet Street from 201 Fleet Street.
[19] Scott, *How they Dined us in 1860*, 7.   [20] *Ibid.*

THE CHOP ROOM.

Figure 1.1. *The Chop Room* in the Cheshire Cheese, by Herbert Railton, in W. Outram Tristram, 'A Storied Tavern', *English Illustrated Magazine* (December 1889). (Reproduced with permission of the Bishopsgate Institute)

hand it to the cook at the fire and see it prepared on a simple gridiron, not in those days on a golden or silver grill'. Here the venerability of the chophouse is underlined by placing it in a continuum with earlier, less formalized practices of public eating, notably the expedient by which butchers sold meat that was then cooked on a gridiron for a small fee.[21] Scott insisted that these were 'survivals of chop houses of another century'. While the precise historical provenance of some of these institutions was questionable, there is no doubt that many of them had been commercial establishments since the eighteenth century, if not earlier still. When, in

[21] *Ibid.*

1882, Dolly's Chop House was pulled down so that the offices of an adjoining business could be expanded, the press noted the passing of an institution with 'an illustrious history' that had allegedly survived the Great Fire of 1666 and catered to Addison, Steele, Pope, Swift, and Congreve.[22]

A similar notion that the chophouse had had its day was shared by writers in the trade press. Citing the specific example of the Rainbow chophouse in Fleet Street, a writer for the *Tourist and Traveller, and Hotel Review* noted the transformation of what had once been a solidly English establishment, in terms of both fare and personnel: 'Here the homely, appetizing bill of fare is now called the "menu", and the English waiter has been replaced by the ubiquitous German . . . '.[23] In a more positive vein, a writer in the *British Journal of Catering* commented that 'the old chop houses are not nearly so common in London [now in 1889] as they were twenty years ago'. Instead, clean and cheap eating houses, many of which favoured 'the French style of cooking', were so numerous 'that it is almost impossible to walk fifty yards along a thoroughfare in the City without passing two or three . . . ' of them.[24] Others rejected the notion that traditional British institutions were losing out largely to continental restaurants. A year earlier, the *Caterer*, taking issue with the journalist George R. Sims, who had claimed that the British were being 'snuffed out' as 'refreshment-caterers', drew attention to the emergence of 'well-fitted and comfortable dining halls, where solid and sensible British fare is obtainable at moderate prices'.[25] Nevertheless, they acknowledged (albeit far from sadly) that these developments had been at the cost of 'the stuffy chop house and malodorous cookshop', both of which had been 'widely replaced'.[26] Writers may have disagreed over the merits of the venerable chophouse, but there was a consensus that it was in decline.

Clearly, these articles in the trade press attribute the eclipse of the chophouse to changing tastes and trends in dining, with one challenge coming from the continental restaurant with its diverse menu, another emerging from the growth of establishments offering traditional British fare, but in a more attractive and comfortable setting. Moreover, both these types of newer establishments appeared to be more welcoming to

---

[22] Clipping: 'Dolly's Chop House', Restaurant Files, box C–F, London Press Cuttings [hereafter, London Cuttings], Bishopsgate Institute Library, London [hereafter, Bishopsgate].

[23] 'Dining Experiences in London', *Tourist and Traveller, and Hotel Review*, 1 January 1885, p. 11.

[24] 'Cheap Dinners', *British Journal of Catering*, 1 February 1889, p. 33.

[25] 'Foreign v. English Caterers', *Caterer*, 15 June 1888, p. 218. This article was a response to comments made by George R. Sims under the pseudonym 'Dragonet', which appeared in his column, 'Mustard and Cress', in the *Referee*, a Sunday sports and entertainment paper.

[26] *Ibid.*

female diners, a point of attraction that, for many commentators, reinforced their association of these new venues with a modernity that was absent in the more primitive and robustly masculine chophouse.[27] Clearly, the chophouse was having difficulty accommodating itself to changing configurations of masculinity, characterized by an emphasis on self-discipline in personal deportment, the pleasures of heterosociability in the public sphere, and the lionization of hearth and home.[28] In this regard, the inadequacies of the chophouse had already been anticipated in a letter written by H.P., 'a gentleman', in 1851 to the famous French chef, Alexis Soyer, in which the former, having railed against the inedible food, surly staff, poor ventilation, ugly decoration, and lack of hygiene to be found in the chophouse, concluded by stating that 'there are none at all suitable to men accustomed to have everything good, clean, and comfortable at home'.[29]

H.P. was specifically concerned with the lack of attractive dining options for 'gentlemen in the habit of dining in the City . . . at present often driven to dine at home from the want of comfortable accommodation'.[30] By contrast, four decades later, the *City Press* declared 'the City man will soon have little or no reason to complain of the facilities afforded him for getting his midday meal'.[31] It insisted that, in every thoroughfare in the Square Mile, there 'is now being opened a restaurant of the new order', but singled out a recently opened branch of Slaters as representative of the attractions of the new popular eating houses that had expanded in the closing decades of the century.[32] Cleanliness, good ventilation, tasteful decoration, bright lighting, and good food were all emphasized in press puffs for these places in an attempt to characterize their embrace of modernity. Convenience and efficiency were also important motifs in the discourses surrounding the new restaurant. *Windsor Magazine* reported that Slaters, serving an average of five hundred lunches daily, had each seat 'filled six times between 1 and 3 pm, showing that City men do not linger long over their meals'.[33] This rapid turnover of diners can possibly be attributed to the fact that there was no opportunity to linger over a drink after their plate had been cleared—which put even more clear blue water between it and the venerable chophouse, for Slaters

[27] See Scott, *How they Dined us in 1860*, 12.

[28] John Tosh, 'Masculinities in an Industrializing Society: Britain, 1800–1914', *Journal of British Studies*, 44/2 (April 2005), 330–42.

[29] Alexis Soyer, *Memoirs of Alexis Soyer, with Unpublished Receipts and Odds and Ends of Gastronomy*, ed. F. Volant and J. R. Warren (London: Kent & Co., 1859), 229.

[30] *Ibid.* 233, 232.

[31] 'A New Restaurant', *City Press*, 5 December 1894, Restaurant Files, box Q–S, London Cuttings, Bishopsgate.

[32] The branch in question was in Aldersgate Street.

[33] W. J. Wintle, 'Round the London Restaurants', *Windsor Magazine* (1896), 450.

Figure 1.2. 'Where I Dined Today', Slaters Popular Restaurant, 27 Leadenhall Street, EC, London. (Reproduced with permission of the London Metropolitan Archives, City of London)

was run along strictly temperance lines. However, this distinctive characteristic should not detract from its broader typicality. Slaters was identified with the new dynamic commercial forces that were reshaping public eating across London. In particular, Slaters was seen as a pioneer of the benefits of integration between provision, preparation, and consumption, combining 'the businesses of butchers, bakers and greengrocers, [and] thus dispensing altogether with the middleman'.[34] Slaters also reflected another key element in the new commercial culture of public eating—namely, the emergence of the chain. By 1900, Kelly's listed eleven branches of Slaters refreshment rooms (located predominantly in the City, but also in West London and the West End) (see Figure 1.2).[35]

One of the most ambitious chain restaurant projects in this era was the one belonging to John Pearce, whose name was associated with a new breed in the catering world that fused the confectioner's, sandwich, coffee, tea, and light refreshment room. In an interview given at the end of the century, Pearce claimed to have started his business from a simple coffee

---

[34] 'A New Restaurant', *City Press*, 5 December 1894, Restaurant Files, box Q–S, London Cuttings, Bishopsgate. The *Caterer* also referred to there being 'half a dozen butcher shops and about double the number devoted to the sale of game and poultry, fruit and greengrocery' (15 October 1898, p. 483).
[35] Listing for Slaters, *Kelly's Post Office Trades' and Professional Directory for 1900*, 2000.

stall on the corner of East Road and City Road, where, between 1866 and 1879, he tried to attract working-class custom, even calling his stand 'the Gutter Hotel'.[36] Having saved a little money, he opened a shop in Aldersgate in 1879, and then moved it three years later to Farringdon Street, running it alone until 1886, when 'a few wealthy gentlemen who were interested in my experiment formed a company' and expanded the business whose capital worth was £20,000.[37] From its central depot at Farringdon Street in the City of London, it distributed food to the company's thirteen 'dining and refreshment rooms' located across the metropolis in 1890, a figure that rose to eighteen just seven years later.[38] In a tribute to Mr Pearce, the *Caterer* noted that 'an average of 40,000 meals are served daily' at his refreshment rooms with 'the average expenditure of each customer...a little over seven farthings' (or less than two pennies).[39] The paper was quick to add that 'it must be remembered that frequenters of "Pearce & Plenty" establishments are mostly poor, possessed of large appetites but small means to satisfy them'.[40] Pearce himself said that most of his patrons were workmen and, of these, many were Irish Catholics who demanded a light lunchtime meal of haddocks and eggs on Fridays, not for religious reasons but because of a lack of cash. Indeed, 'they often come back in the evening after paytime and indulge in a good square meal'. This might include beef-steak pudding made from 'half a pound of thoroughly good beef and a well-made crust' and a cheap cup of tea, though the 'demand for cocoa has also largely increased of late years'.[41] Although it was run along temperance lines, spirits in the place were nonetheless high, as one reporter for the *New Penny Magazine* commented on the 'shouting, swallowing throng of newsboys, printers' "devils", bricklayers' labourers, carters, and sweeps', who, in a lunchtime scrum, pushed their way to the counter to get their food, since there were no waiters to take orders.[42] In his memoirs of the *fin de siècle* East End, the notorious underworld figure Arthur Harding recalled how his father worked odd jobs at a hat shop next door to Pearce and Plenty's, where 'cup a tea a halfpenny, slice of bread and marge a halfpenny, and one could buy a three course lunch for 4*d*'. Whether he ate there himself he failed to

[36] Wintle, 'Round the London Restaurants', 447.

[37] *Ibid*; 'Representative Temperance Caterers: No. 1 Mr. John Pearce, London', *Temperance Caterer*, 30 July 1887, p. 137.

[38] Listing for Pearce and Plenty, *Kelly's Post Office Trades' and Professional Directory for 1890*, 1683; 'A People's Caterer', *Caterer*, 15 January 1897, p. 38. A year earlier, in 1896, Pearce claimed to have twenty-two.

[39] 'A People's Caterer', *Caterer*, 15 January 1897, p. 38.   [40] *Ibid*.

[41] Wintle, 'Round the London Restaurants', 447, 448.

[42] 'How London Feeds', *New Penny Magazine*, 7 (1900), 597.

disclose—his father earned 2 shillings or 24 pence for eighteen hours work, so it is unlikely—but the mere fact of its existence, with the Royal Standard next door, where 'some of the great melodramas of the age were dramatized for the people of the East End', spoke volumes about the small pleasures derived from small means.[43]

If the Pearce and Plenty restaurants were potentially accessible to working-class patrons, Pearce also created a chain of eateries in 1892 that were more likely to attract 'young City clerks and others who, while requiring something superior to the arrangements of "Pearce and Plenty", found themselves unable to pay high prices'.[44] His British Tea Table refreshment rooms, 'daintily fitted up and furnished', provided 'excellent fare . . . served by neat waitresses at remarkably low prices'.[45] According to Pearce, his tea tables supplied 15,000 meals daily, ranging from eggs on toast, ham and salad to soups, chops, and steaks.[46] For 1 shilling (or 12 pence), 'the young lady typewriter or city clerk' was able to 'lunch quite sumptuously', and the surroundings were 'quite refined with respectable company seated around at the many marble-slab tables', as noted by the *New Penny Magazine* reporter.[47] There was also a smoking lounge for those wishing 'to indulge in the fragrant weed after dining', as was increasingly customary in many such establishments. The *Caterer* identified the British Tea Table restaurants as filling the void between the A.B.C. (or Aerated Bread Company), which was more 'tea and buns', and the more elaborate version of the 'popular restaurant'—for instance, Slaters.[48] While, in 1897, the year the company went limited, the British Tea Table had twenty-five locations, three years later, it had thirty-seven branches across the metropolis—twenty-six were in the City—with a depot at Farringdon, 'where we keep forty bakers hard at work'.[49]

If he wanted to model his tea table on a successful establishment, Pearce needed to look no farther than Lockhart's, a temperance chain that attracted to its Fetter Lane location in 1880, for instance, 'many persons on their way

[43] Raphael Samuel (ed.), *East End Underworld: Chapters in the Life of Arthur Harding* (London: Routledge and Kegan Paul, 1981), 10. This book is based on a series of oral interviews with Harding conducted by Samuel in the 1970s when Harding was in his late eighties and early nineties.

[44] Wintle, 'Round the London Restaurants', 448.

[45] 'A People's Caterer', *Caterer*, 15 January 1897, p. 38.

[46] Wintle, 'Round the London Restaurants', 448.

[47] 'How London Feeds', *New Penny Magazine*, 7 (1900), 594.

[48] 'A People's Caterer', *Caterer*, 15 January 1897, p. 38.

[49] Advertisement, *British Tea Table (1897) British Restaurants London Guide* (London: British Tea Table Co., Ltd, 1908), Food and Drink Box A5, Ephemera Collection, Museum of London; Listing for British Tea Table Ltd, *Kelly's Post Office Trades' and Professional Directory for 1900*, 2336–7; Wintle, 'Round the London Restaurants', 448.

to and from London bridge' or those arriving by steamboat at the nearby docks, 'most of them preferring the basement where marble slabs and stools enable them to feel quite at home'.[50] It was open from 5 a.m. to midnight. The artist Yoshio Markino recalled how, after working for 12½ pence a day as a model, he went to a branch near Westminster Bridge, where he ate a plate of steak and fried onions, 'which was a great dinner for me then', for sixpence.[51] In addition to its dining room, Lockhart's offered 'a smoking room' and 'ladies' room', in which several daily papers could be found 'for those who wish to learn the latest news'. Also capitalizing on a popular desire for a homelike atmosphere, especially among men, was the Spread Eagle Bread Company. Founded in 1884, it had seven City restaurants in as many years later 'that appear to be much appreciated by the gentlemen in the banking houses adjoining'. Like Slaters' and Pearce's, the Spread Eagles were run along temperance lines, and served tea and coffee, with cold lunches to an estimated 5,000 diners daily by 1890.[52] What made them distinct was their explicit offer of a 'saloon or divan where, after lunch, the man of commerce may enjoy a quiet whiff before he again returns to the busy office, or still busier mart'.[53] At Broad-street House, the restaurant took over the entire basement, where a partition divided the luncheon room from the smoking divan, with the doors between them remaining open and 'in the former the atmosphere is always clear and free from even the faintest hint of tobacco'.[54] Comparing the Spread Eagle establishments to other such places, one writer for the *City Press* noted that the former were well furnished and well ventilated, 'two all-important matters [that] have received little attention, managers having apparently entertained the idea that, as long as facilities were afforded for a quiet smoke, young fellows would not object to the saloon being scantily and cheaply furnished, badly lighted, and imperfectly ventilated'.[55] If these new Spread Eagle houses had a clublike atmosphere (albeit one without snifters), then they also reflected a persistent (if not also defensive) movement to exclude a growing population of female clerks, who took their hard-earned pence to alternative establishments, such as Lockhart's.

Another restaurant behemoth in this period was the myriad dining establishments owned and managed by Felix Spiers and Christopher Pond,

[50] 'A Want Supplied', *City Press*, 11 August 1880, Restaurant Files, box G–L, London Cuttings, Bishopsgate.

[51] Yoshio Markino, *A Japanese Artist in London* (London: Chatto and Windus, 1910), 42.

[52] 'The Spread Eagles', *City Press*, 7 June 1890, Restaurant Files, box Q–S, London Cuttings, Bishopsgate.

[53] 'A Luxury for City Men', *City Press*, 18 November 1891, Restaurant Files, box Q–S, London Cuttings, Bishopsgate.

[54] *Ibid.*   [55] *Ibid.*

two English-born entrepreneurs who met in the early 1850s in Australia, where they laid the foundations for a catering enterprise they would later export to Britain.[56] Spiers and Pond, as mentioned earlier, had refreshment rooms near centres of activity, especially in metropolitan railway stations, thereby confirming the complex interrelationship between dining and transportation. In the period before Joseph Lyons's meteoric rise, Felix Spiers and Christopher Pond operated railway refreshment rooms on the Metropolitan Railway and the London, Chatham, and Dover Railway lines. By 1866, they had established the Silver Grill restaurant 'possessed of artistic beauty' inside the arch at Ludgate Station, a space originally designated as an inspector's office.[57] So wide was the company's reach that by 1888, the *Hotel News* dubbed Spiers and Pond Limited '"the Smiths" of the refreshment department on our railways', with 'buffets and luncheon rooms and restaurants from Dundee and Glasgow in the North to Dover and Plymouth in the South, and Ilfracombe and Liverpool in the west'. In that year, the paper noted that the firm had 211 railway buffet and refreshment rooms, the smallest of which catered a variety of cold meats, veal-and-ham pies, pork pies, sausage rolls, hard-boiled eggs, sandwiches, cakes and buns, biscuits, bread and butter, tea and coffee, and spirits, beers, and wines. At their railway restaurants, they offered 'the most ample bill of fare, which many who are not travellers take advantage of systematically'.[58] For those wishing to sacrifice neither refreshment nor speed, a luncheon basket—containing a cold luncheon for 3 shillings or a well-cooked hot chop with potatoes and all accessories for 3/6—could be secured by giving notice at one of many stopping stations to a guard, who then will 'have it forwarded by telegraph without any charge' to the next station, where the basket would be handed into the carriage and 'consumed at the passenger's leisure'.[59] On long journeys with few stopping points, a 2 shilling breakfast or dinner was sometimes served. In the 1870s, Spiers and Pond both expanded and diversified their restaurant empire by entering the domain of the theatre–restaurant, purchasing (and extravagantly refashioning, with their acclaimed 'liberality and good taste') the Criterion and the Gaiety (see Figure 1.3).[60]

[56] 'The Genesis of Spiers and Pond', *Caterer*, 15 April 1898, p. 188.
[57] 'Messrs Spiers and Pond's Silver Grill', 6 January 1866, Restaurant Files, box Q–S, London Cuttings, Bishopsgate.
[58] 'Railway Travellers and their Refreshments', *Hotel News*, 16 June 1888, p. 11.
[59] *Ibid.*; 'Correspondence', *Caterer*, 16 March 1891, p. 88.
[60] 'The Restaurateur: The Gaiety Restaurant', *Caterer*, 7 December 1878, p. 133; 'The Restaurateur: The Criterion and Theatre', *Caterer*, 4 March 1879, pp. 30–1. Spiers and Pond were also major players in the metropolitan and provincial hotel business, owning at various points the Holborn Viaduct Hotel, Bailey's in South Kensington, and palatial hotels in various seaside resorts. See John Burnett, *England Eats out: A Social History of Eating out in England from 1830 to the Present* (Harlow: Pearson, 2004), 98.

Figure 1.3. Detail from menu showing Criterion in the top right, Spiers and Pond Ltd, January 1890. (Reproduced with permission of the Rare Books Division, The New York Public Library, Astor, Lenox and Tilden Foundations)

Spiers and Pond's restaurant initiatives aimed to balance diversification and ubiquity with innovation, most notably in the adaptation of the *System Duval* in the Palsgrave, a restaurant the company (Pond died in 1881) opened in the Strand in 1886.[61] The Duval system involved the diner, on entering the restaurant, being presented with a printed ticket 'on which the price of each article is marked by the waitress as it is ordered'. When the diner has completed the meal, the ticket 'is summed up and checked at the desk, and the diner pays the cashier as he goes out'.[62] This streamlined system compensated for the Palsgrave's modest prices (by ensuring a swift turnover of diners and precluding customers from leaving without paying, a not uncommon problem), but it also satisfied the stipulations of rational efficiency. The waitresses themselves, of which there were about thirty, each wore a plain silver broach bearing her number, 'which she is required to mark on the tickets of all her customers'.[63] This systematic method of dining ensured 'the welcome absence of all bustle, scramble, and harassing delay'.[64] Reviews of the Palsgrave in the trade press commended its efficiency and economy, not least its ambition to serve up to 1,500 meals a day on the Duval plan, at prices that were appealing to those who, 'whilst appreciating cheapness, desire that their food should be presented in as appetizing form as possible'.[65] Soups cost between 4 and 8 pence, fish dishes ranged between 8 and 10 pence, while meat entrées cost anywhere from 9 pence to 2 shillings and vegetables cost between 2 and 4 pence. For those desiring only vegetables, diners could repair to the firm's adjoining vegetarian restaurant.[66]

The presence of the Duval system in the Palsgrave restaurant satisfied the stipulations of progress and uniformity, and it was appropriate that Spiers and Pond had first deployed this expedient when acting as caterers for the Inventions Exhibition at South Kensington the year before.[67] The motif of rationalization was also evident in Spiers and Pond's attempt to create 'a unique and comprehensive system', which allowed them to act as

[61] 'Death of Mr Christopher Pond', *City Press*, 3 August 1881, London Cuttings, Restaurant Files, box Q–S, Bishopsgate. After Pond's death, the company continued to call itself Spiers and Pond.

[62] 'Dining a la Duval: A Visit to the Duval Restaurant', *Tourist and Traveller, and Hotel Review* (May 1886), 126.

[63] 'Duval Dinners in London', *Caterer*, 15 April 1886, p. 98. This culinary and commercial influence was a reciprocal process. Spiers and Pond later opened an English restaurant on the Boulevard des Capucines in Paris. See *Caterer*, 15 November 1893, p. 478.

[64] 'Dining a la Duval: A Visit to the Duval Restaurant', *Tourist and Traveller, and Hotel Review* (May 1886), 125.

[65] 'Notes of the Month', *Refreshment World and Hotel Supplies Journal*, 1 May 1886, p. 3.

[66] 'Correspondence', *Caterer*, 15 December 1886, p. 374.

[67] *Anti-Adulteration Review and Food Journal* (March 1885), 919.

their own providers and eliminate the profits of the middleman.[68] At their central depot in Ludgate-hill station, the company had wine cellars, a grocery, and a provision store, as well as bakery, meat, poultry, and fish markets, where managers of the company's individual branches bought what they needed to stock their kitchens, 'thereby saving time, trouble, and temptation inseparable from the ordinary marketing'.[69] These markets not only served the needs of Spiers and Pond's restaurants, but also traded with the public 'in the ordinary way'.[70] For those in parts of the metropolis and suburbs too far from the depot, the company operated a daily delivery service. In a comment that was made after a visit to their Duval restaurant, but that could have applied to the entire concern, one contemporary was moved to write that 'the enterprise of Spiers and Pond Ltd slumbers not, nor sleeps'.[71]

Spiers and Pond provided the template for the most famous catering empire in this period, that of Joseph Lyons. As with Spiers and Pond's enterprise, Lyons' catering ventures began in the domain of exhibitions, notably the Newcastle Exhibition (1887), the Glasgow Exhibition (1888), the Paris Exhibition (1889), and those at Olympia in London that included Barnum and Bailey's 'Greatest Show on Earth' (1889–90), Imre Kiralfy's 'Venice in London' (1891–2), and 'Constantinople' (1893–4). Lyons' first teashop opened in Piccadilly in 1894, and the number grew to thirty-seven by the end of the century, as we have seen. By 1910, there were approximately 150 branches throughout the metropolis, marking a rise of over 300 per cent.[72] So impressive was this growth that one contemporary put the number of Londoners fed daily by Lyons at half a million.[73] The Lyons teashop (and its successor, the Lyons Corner House, which first appeared in 1909) obviously became a prominent part of the commercial and the popular imaginary of the metropolis.[74] Lyons' successful formula was built around popular prices, comfortable and bright surroundings, and the much-remarked-upon charms of the company's waitresses, selected on

---

[68] 'The Restaurant Business', *Caterer*, 15 December 1890, pp. 460–1.
[69] *Ibid.* 460.   [70] *Ibid.* 461.
[71] 'Dining a la Duval: A Visit to the Duval Restaurant', *Tourist and Traveller, and Hotel Review* (May 1886), 126.
[72] As counted by the author in *Kelly's Post Office Trades' and Professional Directory for 1900*, 2337; *Kelly's Post Office Trades' and Professional Directory for 1910* (London: Kelly's Directories, Ltd, 1910), 1812.
[73] 'Feeding Half-A-Million Daily', *Organiser* (December 1910), 459, 462. The number of branches is confirmed in this article.
[74] For example, see 'Peggy of "Lyons": A Romance of the Famous Tea-Shops', *Weekend*, 31 March–15 September 1910; and Alfred Hitchcock's *Blackmail* (1929), in which Frank Webber, a Scotland Yard detective, takes his girlfriend, Alice White, to a Lyons Corner House.

the basis of being young, single, and slim, and who, by the standards of the day, were rewarded with eye-catching uniforms.[75] Some teashops, especially those in the City, had a clublike atmosphere, but many branches offered the possibility of heterosocial dining and were popular with both single working women and married couples. However, it is important to appreciate that the Lyons teashop was not unique, but was merely preeminent among a competitive field that included not merely the established chains such as the A.B.C., Slaters, Lockhart's, Pearce and Plenty, and Spiers and Pond, but also new arrivals like the Duval Restaurant Company. Lyons' success was predicated not merely on ubiquity, but also on securing its presence in particularly lucrative locations—for example, its Throgmorton Street branch opened in 1900, which allowed it to compete in the intense market for lunchtime diners working in the Stock Exchange. (The A.B.C. already had a branch there.)[76] The upmarket pretensions and expensive furnishings of the Throgmorton Street branch demonstrated that Lyons' expansion of the relatively mundane teashop was increasingly accompanied by investment in prestige projects. For example, the Trocadero, a theatre and restaurant in Piccadilly Circus, had opened in 1896. More significantly, J. Lyons and Co. was characterized by an extension of Spiers and Pond's integration of provision and catering through the construction of Cadby Hall, Lyons' 10-acre headquarters and supply centre, which incorporated bakeries, cold-storage rooms, butchers' shops, stables, workshops, and administrative offices. J. Lyons and Co. also clearly benefited from its involvement in the import, production, and retailing of tea, cocoa, and coffee, which were sold not only from its teashops but also from its wagons, which visited individual households.[77]

While J. Lyons and Co. and Spiers and Pond appeared to combine innovation with a presence throughout the metropolis, another category of restaurants that became important from the 1880s onwards was much more specifically situated within the West End. These illustrious restaurants included the Hotel Continental, Verrey's, Nicols' Café Royal (all in Regent Street), Adelaide Gallery, the Tivoli (in the Strand), Café Monico (Shaftesbury Avenue), St James's Hall (in Piccadilly), and, admitted one commentator in 1885, 'this list could be readily extended but the

[75] Peter Bird, *The First Food Empire: A History of J. Lyons & Co.* (Chichester: Phillimore & Co., Ltd, 2000), 43.

[76] *Cenitic*[?], 12 March 1898, and *Madam*, 19 March 1898, ACC 3527/423, Lyons Archive, LMA.

[77] A shareholders' report refers to the house-to-house supply of bread, but tea was also sold. Report to the Directors and Balance Sheet for year ending 31 March 1895, ACC 3527/2, Lyons Archive, LMA.

houses mentioned will suffice as examples'.[78] Four years later, the Savoy Hotel Company was founded and included the Savoy, Claridge's, the Berkeley (which were world-class hotels with high-end restaurants), and Simpson's in-the-Strand. By the outbreak of the First World War, this body of restaurants had been supplemented by the Ritz, the Carlton, Maxim's, and the Waldorf.[79] Clearly their emergence was symptomatic of a broader expansion of the West End as a pleasure zone for men and women who increasingly defined themselves through leisure, consumption, and spectacle. Customers were attracted by their renowned cooking and new methods of serving, expensive wine cellars, lavish furnishings, electric lights, mirrors, musical accompaniment, and name recognition, all of which made dining out possibly more attractive than dining at home. The fact that patrons could take their meals at different times of day in a variety of settings under one palatial roof—in the grill room, luncheon room, coffee room, buffet, ladies' salon, winter garden, gallery, and restaurant proper—made these places even more appealing. With their banquet rooms, many offered catering for wedding and other private functions. For those staying in the hotels, restaurant dining was an extension of their home away from home. The presence of these restaurants in the West End suggested a symbiotic relationship to other forms of conspicuous consumption and leisure in the neighbourhood, notably the theatres. Indeed, some theatre programmes recommended restaurants in their vicinity that audiences might repair to, either before or after the play, while some theatres, such as the Savoy, had restaurants attached to them. Illustrator and *Punch* cartoonist Edward Linley Sambourne described a visit to the Savoy Theatre in 1893 to see a Gilbert and Sullivan opera with his wife. After failing to find a carriage on the Embankment, he joined a group of ladies for supper at the Savoy Restaurant, a gathering he found tiresome, but which his wife enjoyed.[80] The clientele of these fashionable houses mostly belonged to an internationalized plutocracy (which had already by this point extended beyond the traditional territorial elite) with a possible smattering of upper-middle-class professionals, politicians, the literati, and figures from the world of celebrity culture.[81] This new culture

---

[78] 'London', *Supplement to the Tourist and Traveller, and Hotel Review* (April 1885), 3.

[79] Bon Viveur, *Where to Dine in London* (London: Geoffrey Bles, 1937), 15–17.

[80] Diary entry from 7 December 1893, Edward Linley Sambourne Diaries, Royal Borough of Kensington and Chelsea Libraries, Local Studies Division.

[81] Prestigious restaurants were also the venue for banquets in honour of prominent individuals and the annual dinners of various guilds, societies, and military regiments. These dinners had their own specific conventions, and are therefore not treated in this book. A useful selection of menus produced for these occasions is in the Buttolph Collection of Menus, New York Public Library.

had a guide and a booster in the form of Lieutenant-Colonel Nathaniel Newnham-Davis, a retired army officer, and arguably the first restaurant reviewer, who introduced readers of the *Pall Mall Gazette* in 1897–8 to a number of notable restaurants. At one level these fashionable restaurants were exclusive, but their referencing in contemporary writing also kept them in the popular imaginary, thus allowing interested observers to enter vicariously the portals of the dining room without reaching for their purse.

The possible apotheosis of this type of dining experience could be found in a description of Verrey's in Regent Street, 'the rendezvous of the more aristocratic foreign visitors to London', where Newnham-Davis reportedly took a Mrs Myra Washington, an American living abroad who 'knows most people who are worth knowing in Europe, has been to most places worth seeing, and is in every way cosmopolitan', before they ventured to a ballet at The Empire afterwards.[82] In the dining room, with its silver arches to the roof, Newnham-Davis noted how 'the room's suave dark-green panels' formed an excellent background to Mrs Washington's 'cream-coloured miracle of a dress', all of which was 'caught and reflected a hundred times by the mirrors'. For her part, Mrs Washington took the measure of the room, observing 'the company dining at the many little square tables, lighted by wax red-shaded candles': 'the ruddy-haired prima donna', 'the celebrated musician who was dining with his wife', 'the well-known journalist whose love for dogs forms a bond between him and the Messrs Krehl [the management]', and 'her banker in Paris, who was entertaining a party of a dozen'. The food that was served tickled their taste buds and dazzled their eyes, particularly the Venetian salad, 'a little tower of many-coloured vegetables' that looked 'like poker chips'.[83] The price of the meal for two—£2 4s. 2d.—was certainly in line with other prestige dining establishments—the Savoy, for example, cost Newnham-Davis £2 17s.[84] However, it clearly required deeper pockets than dining at Lyons, where a three-course meal for two could be secured for one-tenth of the price.[85]

Both the chain restaurant and the fashionable West End restaurant required considerable capital investment. However, the great majority of dining establishments in London in this period remained on a much more modest scale. Such establishments were largely ephemeral and have left a less extensive trace in the archive. In many cases, the only evidence for

[82] Charles Eyre Pascoe, *London of Today: An Illustrated Handbook for the Season* (London: Sampson Low & Co., 1885), 48; Nathaniel Newnham-Davis, *Dinners and Diners: Where and how to Dine in London* (London: Grant Richards, 1899), 54. The *Pall Mall Gazette* reviews were republished in this book.
[83] Newnham-Davis, *Dinners and Diners*, 56.   [84] *Ibid.* 57, 88.
[85] Lyons Teashop Tariff, 1901, ACC 3527/395, Lyons Archive, LMA.

their existence is the listing of a proprietor's name in Kelly's (the afore-mentioned Mmes Seabright, Newman, Wynn, or Elliott, for instance). Small establishments usually did not produce printed menus, relying instead on the blackboard, street boys with sandwich boards, window displays, or on the customer being informed by the waiter on arrival. They remained largely outside the purview of restaurant reviewers and the trade press more generally. We are therefore dependent on fleeting references from the accounts of visitors to London or other social observers. For example, Nathaniel Hawthorne ate at the Albert Dining Rooms in the 1850s and wrote of being served a mutton chop, bread, potatoes, and beans 'each of which was proffered to me separately'. While it appeared not to be a 'disreputable place, but an honest place of resort for people whose circumstances were just adapted to that measure of comfort', he nonetheless described it as 'the very meanest and dirtiest eating place I ever chanced upon'. Taken together—the 'filthy table cloth, covered with other people's crumbs; iron forks; a leaden salt-cellar, the commonest of earthen plates' and the 'dark little stall' in which he ate—it rendered him 'much wearied' by the end of the meal.[86]

If the owner of the Albert Dining Rooms might have had mixed feelings about the attention that Hawthorne accorded to them, he might at least have consoled himself with the thought that such modest institutions (like his) were usually overlooked, even by those interested in food and the curiosities of metropolitan life.[87] Some of these more modest dining establishments had foreign-born proprietors, and undoubtedly played a significant role in accommodating the needs of overseas visitors and diasporic populations in the metropolis. Joseph Salter of the London City Missionary Society wrote of a 'Mahammedan' who kept an eating house in north London that was patronized by a Sikh military officer 'whose fidelity to the British during the Indian Mutiny was duly rewarded' and his nephew. While Salter said nothing of what was eaten there, he did comment that, 'being a Sikh, [the officer] could only eat a certain class of food', rendering houses like these essential for foreign visitors with specific dietary requirements.[88] The Sikh officer, who had had difficulty finding accommodation owing to his 'not knowing any English', resided, during

[86] Diary entry for 7 September 1855, Nathaniel Hawthorne, *The English Notebooks, 1853–1856*, ed. Thomas Woodson and Bill Ellis (Columbus: Ohio State University Press, 1997), 308.

[87] One rare opportunity to pierce the wall of silence that surrounded the small-scale owner-managed dining room—the legal case surrounding Mrs Baker, the Paddington eating-house keeper who catered to 'carmen'—will be discussed in Chapter 2.

[88] Joseph Salter, *East in the West; or, Work Among the Asiatics and Africans in London* (London: S. W. Partridge & Co., n.d. [1896]), 139–40.

his stay in London, in a room above this eating house. Other proprietors of modest dining rooms accommodated overseas patrons in other ways, such as by receiving letters for them, as did one little French house set among the 'foreign settlement in Soho'. At such places, as one commentator noted in 1879, meals did not need to be ordered in order for regulars to feel welcome: 'They chat to the proprietor or his wife, and sit down and smoke, not quite as if the house belonged to them, but most certainly as if they belonged to the house.'[89] With the delivery of a letter and news from home, conversations between patron and proprietor might move back and forth between the old world and the new one, demonstrating that these types of eating houses played an important role in aiding foreign visitors and recently arrived immigrants in the process of negotiating their place in the urban fabric. What little evidence we have for such establishments comes from self-styled bohemians who often sought out these eateries for their supposedly unadorned foreign authenticity. The writer and traveller Morley Roberts described 'a little French house', 'known only by Bohemians or French workers', in which the menu was written on a slate hanging from a string on a nail in the dingy papered wall underneath a broken clock.[90] Roberts commended the intimacy and hospitality that he encountered after he entered 'its dingy unremarkable portals to be treated like a friend, being neither overwhelmed with servility . . . nor scowled at ferociously . . .'.[91] Its 'half-domestic kindness' was encapsulated in the presence of the proprietor's young son, who 'toddles round confidently to such of the customers as he looks upon as friends'.[92] Roberts refused to disclose the name and location of this particular establishment lest its charm be erased by 'the uproar of a new crowd'.[93]

Indeed, if the diner was not already in the know, these small foreign-owned dining rooms were sometimes hard to find, as one observer attested in his recommendation that diners hoping 'to see how comparatively poor foreigners enjoy their evening meals' might be advised to visit an Italian restaurant in Hatton Garden, the location of which was rather unhelpfully specified as merely 'down Eyre-street hill, on the left'. Upon entering this particular place, 'frequented by the pensive organ grinder and better class of Italian worker', the visitor finds 'two large tables clothed for business proper while a third is minus the snowy covering'. For this (presumably English) writer, there was economy in 'the monumental plate of macaroni dressed with a rich tomato-tasting sauce' and (in a nod to culinary hybridity) 'the stewed veal covered with a rich sauce and accompanied

---

[89] 'Soho and its Restaurants', *Caterer*, 1 November 1879, p. 151.
[90] Morley Roberts, 'Waiters and Restaurants', *Murray's Magazine*, 7 (1890), 539.
[91] Ibid. 540.   [92] Ibid. 540, 539.   [93] Ibid. 540.

by two or three delicately roasted potatoes', for fourpence each. However, for the regular clientele of this establishment, company and cultural practices were just as important, the visitor citing the presence of 'sundry Italians who frivol with claret and lemonade limited and conversation unlimited over a game of cards', all under the attentive eyes of 'a portly hostess known familiarly as Maria, her slim and pretty niece', and 'a cheap oleograph' of King Victor Emmanuel and his consort.[94] Unfortunately, such extended descriptions of the ambience and the cuisine found in such dining rooms are rare, which is a pity, since it is undoubtedly in these smaller, owner-managed establishments that the majority of Londoners, whether overseas visitors, immigrants, or the more established population, ate.

It is also important to recognize that many Londoners ate in establishments that provided food that was largely intended to be consumed outside. An anonymous memoir of working-class London life in the 1880s recalled a cookshop in Hackney which sold 'hot peas-pudding, a baked mixture of bread and meat and onions called "faggots", blood puddings, all sorts of sausages, and other things no doubt'.[95] Some cookshops and shops selling fried fish, eels, confectionery, or sausages provided a table or two for customers who wished to consume the food they had purchased on the premises. James McKenzie, a showman, recalled, during his working-class boyhood in 1870s London, one fried fish shop in Clerkenwell that sold a plate of fish and tatters 'for tuppence or threepence' to customers who might eat at the shop's single table.[96] Eyeing the patron's unfinished food through the shop's front window, McKenzie and his friends then 'used to hide out of site [*sic*] of the owner and as soon as a customer emerged took it in turns to dive in quickly and scoop everything left on the plate', an improvised plebian smorgasbord that might include bones, chips, and bread.[97] They then 'shared out the haul' in the back passage of the Clerkenwell Tavern, relishing these crumbs and celebrating their panache for scavenging. The eel shop was another staple in the neighbourhood, according to McKenzie, where lady servers, standing behind a counter, wore 'cleanwhite [*sic*] aprons' and served stewed eels

---

[94] 'Foreign London at Dinner: The Resorts of Our Permanent Visitors', 1897, Norman Collection, London Guildhall Library.

[95] *Narrow Waters: The First Volume of the Life and Thoughts of a Common Man* (London: W. Hodge & Co., 1935), 54.

[96] James H. McKenzie, 'Strange Truth: The Autobiography of a Circus Showman, Stage and Exhibition Man', TS 473, Working Class Autobiography, Special Collections, Brunel University Library, p. 22. For the broader place of fish and chips in British (especially working-class) culture, see John Walton, *Fish and Chips, and the British Working Class, 1870–1940* (Leicester: Leicester University Press, 1992); Panikos Panayi, *Fish and Chips: A History* (London: Reaktion, 2014).

[97] McKenzie, 'Strange Truth', 22.

from steaming containers.[98] Price varied according to size, but most portions could be purchased for a penny or a halfpenny. These places also provided a source of unintended diversion. McKenzie recalled the stall outside the eel shop with its steel tray about 3 feet square containing a 'live writhing mass of live eels . . . slither[ing] about until the customer required them'. After a selection was made and the price agreed, the stall keeper cut off their heads and, while they still wriggled, wrapped them up into a parcel. McKenzie noted that 'in theory all the heads and offal should have gone into a bucket under the stall but often they were lying around the pavement and many a row has been caused by folk slipping on them', a sight he witnessed through the eel shop's window while he enjoyed his 'pennoth' basin of eel 'juice'. For McKenzie, the drama of working-class life continued in other quarters as well, notably a confectionery shop owned by Old Mother Pudney, 'a short very fat woman with a face that was always streaming with sweat' and a temper to match.[99] 'Periodically she would be drunk and then the fur flew. In her northern accent she would start swearing and cursing her husband', 'a dwarf of a man with one leg very much shorter than the other and [who] always had to use a stick to get around'. These arguments, he recalled, led to a 'throwing stage', by which point those customers who had not already beaten a hasty retreat were chased out of the shop, allowing Old Mother Pudney the opportunity to assail her husband with an assortment of kitchen implements. During these domestic altercations, 'us kids would flock th[ere] and have a grandstand view from the other side of the street'. While McKenzie's recollections lean towards the Rabelaisian picaresque, his stories demonstrate the significance of humble fried fish, eel, and bake shops in the vivid fabric of a robust working-class metropolitan life.

There was also the opportunity to secure a meal on occasion in the private hotel, the quotidian public house, and coffee house. In private hotels, meals were typically taken at the *table d'hôte* (literally, host's table), where a multi-course *prix-fixe* menu was served at set times, a custom that contrasted with the *à la carte* system. Reporting on one such meal that was 'French in form and order' at an establishment in Soho in 1879, the *Caterer* made the point that 'it would be better if this form and order was less adhered to, and the menu made more limited; but the customers probably prefer the arrangement as it stands'.[100] Indeed, by the end of the century, the *table d'hôte* still prevailed at many hotels, attracting not merely residents but a wider public.[101] We have already encountered

[98] *Ibid.* 27.   [99] *Ibid.* 30.
[100] 'Soho and its Restaurants', *Caterer*, 1 November 1879, p. 152.
[101] 'Taking Meals away from Home', *Hotel*, 27 June 1895, p. 7.

some venerable taverns that were an important (albeit declining) part of the London dining scene. However, it was undoubtedly also possible to secure food in the commonplace public house. Indeed, the Temperance Refreshment House Movement was at times troubled by the possibility that the added enticement of food would expose working men to the evils of the licensed drink trade.[102] However, while there was undoubtedly opportunity to secure food in the public house, the range of other modestly priced eating options considered in this chapter demonstrates that any notion that the public house was the primary site of working-class eating out is inaccurate, if not disingenuous.

In addition to the public house, another venue for public eating that was not exclusively concerned with the provision of food was the coffee house, which had a long-standing and ongoing presence in the metropolis. Coffee houses in the City such as the Jerusalem Coffee House beside the Royal Exchange or Garraway's in Exchange Alley were traditionally meeting grounds for commercial men pursuing business over coffee, but they were also places where food could be obtained. In comparison with these venerable places, most of London's coffee houses belonged to a less distinguished variety that was far more numerous. There were an estimated 1,700 of these coffee houses spread across the metropolis by 1884.[103] While many undoubtedly prioritized hot beverages, some also served food at modest prices largely for the benefit of working-class patrons. For instance, George Gissing, in the form of his alter ego Henry Ryecroft, an impoverished writer, recalled eating a midday meal of meat and vegetables for sixpence at a coffee house on Oxford Street.[104] These coffee houses also offered an opportunity for lighter lunches (a sandwich or a meat pie, for example) rather than something heavier.[105] Coffee houses were also a place of resort for the working classes on Sunday, a day on which larger English-owned establishments were usually closed.[106] They were also resorts at night for 'thousands of persons who have not the comforts of domesticity at home' attracted by a good fire, bright light, and a supply of newspapers and magazines, as well as a cheap meal.[107] Some extended their services further

---

[102] For more detailed discussion of the relationship between the temperance movement and London's restaurants, see Chapter 4.

[103] 'Coffee and Coffee Houses', *Anti-Adulteration Review* (October 1884), 820.

[104] George Gissing, *The Private Papers of Henry Ryecroft* (London: Archibald Constable & Co., 1903), 37.

[105] 'Taking Meals away from Home', *Hotel*, 27 July 1895, p. 7.

[106] 'Sunday Refreshments', *Hotel*, 21 August 1895, p. 13; 'The Looker On', *Hotel*, 6 November 1895, p. 19.

[107] George Dodd, *The Food of London: A Sketch* (London: Longman, 1856), 514. This point is also made in the article from the *Globe*, reprinted in 'Cafés and Coffee-Houses', *Caterer*, 15 July 1887, p. 253, and *Temperance Caterer*, 30 July 1887, p. 135.

by offering beds for the night or places to bathe and use the lavatory, as did the Britannia on Brompton Road.[108]

Despite being an important part of the urban fabric, the coffee house was poorly regarded in much contemporary commentary. Some bemoaned their failure to match the standards and charm of the continental café.[109] Coffee houses might have expected to find a supportive voice in the temperance movement, but even here they were often taken to task for their dirtiness, lazy staff, and unsavoury refreshments.[110] That said, the temperance movement did play an important role in an attempt to reinvigorate the coffee house in the 1880s and 1890s with the so-called coffee palace movement, whose purpose was 'to provide counter attractions to the public house, and thus to mark the commencement of a new era in the history of social recreation and enjoyment'.[111] The attempt to establish model coffee houses across the metropolis was sufficiently attractive to encourage the participation of major players in the catering trade, such as Slaters, Pearce and Plenty, Lockhart, and the Spread Eagle Bread Company, not to mention the endorsement of evangelical philanthropists and politicians such as Samuel Morley and the Earl of Shaftesbury.[112] However, by the end of the century, the emergence of the model coffee house had failed to stem the decline of coffee houses in general. As early as 1882, the *Caterer* concluded that, whereas the model coffee house movement had achieved some success in the provinces, in London it had been 'by no means uniformly successful' and had 'scarcely progressed beyond the experimental stage'.[113] Some of the more venerable coffee houses, such as the Jamaica Coffee House, drew on their antiquity and refashioned themselves as wine houses or restaurants.[114] Others copied the growth areas of the market, producing something akin to Lyons with well-lit and salubrious interiors.[115] However, it would be unwise to assume that the coffee

[108] Handbill, Britannia Coffee Palace, *c*.1880s, Evanion Collection 6799, British Library.

[109] Article from the *Globe* reprinted in 'Cafés and Coffee-Houses', *Caterer*, 15 July 1887, p. 253, and *Temperance Caterer*, 30 July 1887, p. 135.

[110] 'The On Looker', *Coffee Tavern Gazette and Journal of Food Thrift* [an organ of the Coffee Tavern Protection Society], 23 November 1886, p. 247.

[111] 'Coffee Palaces', *Anti-Adulteration Review* (September 1884), 795.

[112] 'People's Café Company', *City Press*, 17 April 1875, Restaurant Files, box M–P, London Cuttings, Bishopsgate; 'Opening of Another "People's Café"', *City Press*, 15 May 1875, Restaurant Files, box M–P, London Cuttings, Bishopsgate. The Earl of Shaftesbury was president of the company, while Samuel Morley was a staunch supporter.

[113] 'Catering Prospects', *Caterer*, 16 January 1882, p. 1.

[114] 'The Jamaica Coffee-House', *City Press*, 18 May 1889, 22 May 1889, Restaurant Files, box G–L, London Cuttings, Bishopsgate.

[115] For instance, 'A New City Tea and Coffee Room', *City Press*, 30 January 1889, Restaurant Files, box G–L, London Cuttings, Bishopsgate.

house had become entirely enfolded within broader and more contemporary catering rubrics—notably that of the refreshment or dining room. Kelly's still chose in 1910 to identify coffee rooms as a discrete business category, providing a list of establishments that ran to nearly 1,200 premises (as we have seen, 177 of these were labelled 'also dining rooms'), reflecting the refashioning of older understandings of the cultures of public eating even in a rapidly changing metropolitan environment.[116]

London's diverse restaurant culture also incorporated the needs of highly specific categories of diners, notably those seeking a late-night meal, women in search of all-female dining facilities, and vegetarians. Despite the oft-repeated criticism among thespians and audiences alike that there were few places one could eat after curtain call, theatrical types had resort to a number of well-established institutions, notably Evans' in Covent Garden, known for its 'chop suppers'.[117] In *Twice Round the Clock* (1858), George Augustus Sala wrote of an expedition there at one o'clock in the morning, after returning from a play and consuming some oysters from a street stall in the Haymarket, in order to satisfy his craving for meat. There, amid the 'pyramids of dishes', he was dazzled by 'the steaming succession of red-hot chops, with their brown, frizzling caudal appendages sobbing hot tears of passionate fat', 'serene kidneys . . . weltering proudly in their noble gravy', and 'corpulent sausages'. 'These sturdy rations' were moistened with 'pints of stout . . . pints of sparkling pale ale, or creaming Scotch, or brownest Burton . . .'.[118] If the diner was inclined to linger, Evans' also offered the possibility of entertainment in the form of song. Clearly, Evans' was a haunt for writers and other contemporary celebrities, as Hawthorne testified when he visited it in the early hours of 13 April 1856 in the company of the Alpinist Albert Smith, after attending the latter's lecture on his ascent of Mont Blanc held at the Egyptian Hall in Piccadilly. Hawthorne described Evans' as a very good place in which to see London life, remarking that he was introduced to various other notables, including Mr Edwin Lawrence, the author of a *Life of Fielding*, and to the music critic of *The Times,* as well as the superintendent of the rooms, a Mr Green, 'who expressed himself in the highest degree honoured by my presence'.[119] Late-night dining clearly attracted the city's demi-monde, in both its rarified and its vulgar incarnations.

---

[116] 'Coffee Rooms', *Kelly's Post Office Trades' and Professional Directory for 1910*, 1492–5.

[117] Tickletooth, *The Dinner Question*, 146.

[118] George Augustus Sala, *Twice Round the Clock, or the Hours of the Day and Night in London* (1858); with an introduction by Phillip Collins (Leicester: Leicester University Press; New York: Humanities Press, 1971), 340.

[119] Diary entry for 13 April 1856, Hawthorne, *The English Notebooks*, 489.

Approximately thirty years after Hawthorne's visit to Evans', a description of 'a London restaurant by midnight' detailed the assortment of rowdy mashers, 'would-be swells', '"Arries" in evening dress', 'décolleté damsels', ageing roués, and others 'making a night of it' who frequented an unnamed supper room.[120] The supper room's 'well-cushioned corners', table lamps that acted as screens, the gorgeously provocative dress of the female diners, 'displaying greater and yet greater an expanse of bare flesh' as the evening progressed, and the riotous horseplay of diners awaiting their meals, all suggested the possibility of sexual titillation, if not sexual exchange. Two 'elegantly dressed girls', having ordered their supper, were observed 'wait [ing] for some mug to come along and pay for it'.[121]

Conversely, there were many in late-nineteenth-century London who sought out dining experiences from which the opposite sex was absent. If the all-male world of the gentleman's club is well known, it should not be forgotten that some women, too, sought out homosocial environments in which to take their meals. Some of this demand, particularly among feminists, upper-class socialites, and suburban shoppers, was satisfied by the emergence of a female clubland, which, while it was never as extravagant or influential as its male counterpart, had a definite presence in the urban landscape of the West End.[122] However, there were also women, usually of more modest means, seeking a meal who were less concerned with political activism, sociability, or fashionability, and whose working lives placed them at a distance from the squares and avenues of Mayfair and Langham Place, where most women's clubs were clustered. This need was particularly acute in the City, where there was a notable increase of female clerks in the 1890s and yet few places they could go for lunch without, in the words of a correspondent in the *Caterer*, 'having to walk through a crowd of gentlemen, who look up at [them] as though [they] were some curiosity'.[123] For this writer, there was a good business opportunity for someone willing to cater for these women who 'require a comfortable (not necessarily luxurious) dining room to themselves, and a nicely cooked plain dinner for a shilling'. But others doubted the viability of such an enterprise, another commentator insisting 'in the City rents are, of course, enormously high, and unless the number of customers is very large, the profit on a shilling dinner for ladies only might not be sufficient to justify the experiment'.[124] For this reason, some industrious caterers set apart an entire floor of their establishments for

[120] 'A London Restaurant by Midnight', *British Journal of Catering*, 1 March 1888, p. 189.
[121] *Ibid.*   [122] Rappaport, *Shopping*, 85–107.
[123] 'Caterer's Notebook', *Caterer*, 15 December 1892, p. 492.   [124] *Ibid.*

women's only dining. Having done this, however, one caterer near the Mansion House found that 'a great many ladies prefer to dine with men...'. He added that a similar attempt was made with the 'ladies' carriage on the railway... [but there again] many ladies don't want it'.[125] If female clerks in the City appeared ambivalent about the attractions of single-sex dining, concern about insufficient dining options for these women remained a common subject of discussion in the *Caterer* throughout the 1890s.[126]

Sexual segregation at mealtimes was obviously a preoccupation of reformers and philanthropists keen to monitor and police the lives of young, working-class women in the metropolis. In the vicinity of Aldersgate Street were to be found three separate institutions, all run by 'a philanthropic lady', in which female factory workers could obtain a good lunch that included 'a nice helping of roast beef, mutton, or stewed steak, vegetables, pudding and some non-intoxicating drink' for as little as sixpence.[127] There was precedence for such experiments evidenced ten years earlier when a Mrs Fisher created 'The Welcome' near St Paul's, which aimed to attract approximately 20,000 young workers employed in various nearby handicraft industries. With its two dining rooms, it could seat 200 or 300 workers. But eating on the premises was not requisite, as meals 'could be fetched away if desired, and eaten in the workrooms and warehouses in which the young women were employed'. They were also permitted to bring their own food to the dining room and could then supplement it, if they desired, with articles sold on the premises—for instance, 'a cup of coffee may be had for a halfpenny, pudding for a penny, ham twopence or fourpence per plate'. 'The Welcome' also offered accommodation and, without leaving the building, access to the Young Men's Christian Association lecture hall where meetings were held daily at half past one.[128]

Intersections between moral improvement (and self-improvement) and the requirements of finding a meal also feature in another niche restaurant market in this period—namely, the vegetarian restaurant. As with the temperance restaurant or the restaurant for women-only diners, the vegetarian restaurant served a didactic function that was linked to a campaign for moral improvement, notably advocated by Fabian socialist H. S. Salt in the 1880s and 1890s and whose book, *A Plea for Vegetarianism* (1886), served as a clarion call for the movement. It was sold at some vegetarian

---

[125] *Ibid.*
[126] Most notably, 'How to Cater for Girls', *Caterer*, 15 February 1897, p. 73.
[127] 'Caterer's Notebook', *Caterer*, 15 December 1892, p. 492.
[128] 'The Welcome', *City Press*, 4 January 1882, Restaurant Files, box T–Z, London Cuttings, Bishopsgate.

restaurants, such as the Central, near Farringdon Street, frequented by Mohandas K. Gandhi, who, after reading the book, 'adopted vegetarianism from principle' and became associated with the well-established London Vegetarian Society.[129] (Memorial Hall, where it met, was located near the Central.) Another group, the Food Reform Society, was responsible for creating several vegetarian restaurants, including 'the first food reform restaurant in London', the Alpha, located at 23 Oxford Street, which one observer noted in 1880, two years after it had been founded, fed an average of four hundred diners daily. Among them were numbers of Crosse and Blackwell's clerical staff, reflecting that the vegetarian restaurant was not merely a resort for bohemians, intellectuals, and radical political activists.[130] Among the eight 'savouries' on an 1889 menu for the Alpha, three items featured lentils as a main ingredient, which the diner might have enjoyed after the initial course of lentil soup.[131] Contemporary observers certainly testified to the value of the vegetarian restaurant to low-paid young clerks and office workers acquiring quick and cheap meals. W. J. Wintle, writing for the *Windsor Magazine* in 1896, drawing on conversations held with restaurant managers, asserted that the popularity of vegetarian meals 'is not due to any very widespread acceptance of vegetarian principles, but simply to a preference for light and economical luncheons, the heavier meal being taken in the evening'.[132] The National Food Reform Association sought out followers possessed of even less significant means, offering 'cheap dinners for the poor at a cost of less than 3d per head' from its headquarters in the City.[133]

While the rise of vegetarian eating establishments was clearly part of a broader culture promoting the benefits for health and morality, there were also commercial forces at work, and these places were attractive to a large swathe of the population who found them throughout the metropolis. The *British Journal of Catering* was so convinced of its viability and longevity that it declared in 1889 that 'the age of vegetarianism is upon us judging by the ever increasing number of restaurants devoted exclusively to that school of feeding', adding that there were at least thirty of '"these health resorts" . . . in London today'.[134] That profit—as opposed to moral improvement—was a key factor in the proliferation of vegetarian

---

[129] 'Mr Gandhi's Narrative', *Vegetarian*, 20 June 1891, p. 336.

[130] 'The Extended Use of Vegetable Diet', *Chambers's Journal* (November 1880), 720; James Gregory, *Of Victorians and Vegetarians: The Vegetarian Movement in Nineteenth-Century Britain* (London: I. B. Tauris, 2007), 136.

[131] 'The Alpha', menu, 1889, Evanion Collection 6835, British Library.

[132] Wintle, 'Round the London Restaurants', 449–50.

[133] 'Chops and Changes', *Caterer*, 16 February 1885, p. 41.

[134] 'Editorial', *British Journal of Catering*, 1 December 1889, p. 9.

restaurants is evident from the fact that many were not vegetarian-owned, while other entrepreneurs chose to exploit the commercial potential of vegetarianism by offering vegetarian meals as sidelines in restaurants that also served meat (thereby inducing the ire of pristine vegetarian activists).[135] The fad for vegetarian dining peaked in the early 1890s, but failed to sustain momentum through the turn of the century. Both the prominent vegetarian reformer C. W. Forward and a correspondent in the *Caterer* testified to the fact that by the end of the 1890s the number of vegetarian restaurants in London was less than a quarter of what it had been at the beginning of the decade.[136]

The changing fortunes of the vegetarian restaurant encapsulated two dominant strains within the culture of public eating in the metropolis: the perennial pursuit of affordable eating options and the more uneven flows of culinary trends. By contrast, one aspect of public eating, while it satisfied the requirements of affordability, paid little, or no, attention to changing fads and fancies. The humble street cart, stall, or even handheld tray, all of them staples of preindustrial cities, remained an ongoing feature of London's food culture up until the First World War. At one level, the trade in cooked street food was obviously ephemeral, and any survey of it remains imprecise. In 1856, the journeyman writer George Dodd conceded that a numerical estimate of the number of people who worked in this trade was almost impossible to establish, but he noted that there was 'a rough guess some years ago, that there are ... 30,000 stall-keepers and costermongers, employed in selling food in London'.[137] Dodd failed to distinguish between those hawking prepared food and those engaged in selling raw fruit, vegetables, meat, and fish. By contrast, Henry Mayhew, writing a few years later, isolated street vendors selling prepared food, estimating that there were 6,347, although this figure changed according to the season.[138] Among the things they sold were hot pies, pickled whelks, hot eels, sheep trotters, kidney puddings, pea soup, hot green peas, ham sandwiches, baked potatoes, chestnuts, muffins, cakes, ice cream, and tarts. Drinkables included tea, coffee, cocoa, ginger beer, lemonade, 'Persian sherbet', and 'highly-coloured beverages which have no specific name'. 'In each of these provisions, the street poor find a midday or mid-night meal.'[139]

---

[135] Gregory, *Of Victorians and Vegetarians*, 136.
[136] 'National Vegetarian Congress: Friday's Sitting', *Vegetarian*, 23 September 1899, p. 454; 'A Vegetarian Banquet', *Caterer*, 15 January 1900, p. 15.
[137] Dodd, *The Food of London*, 502.
[138] Henry Mayhew, *London Labour and the London Poor* (4 vols; 1861–2; repr. New York, London, and Toronto: Dover, 1968), i. 208.
[139] *Ibid.* 159.

Depending on what they sold, the sellers roamed with their carts or trays or had fixed stalls in markets, major thoroughfares, and parks across the metropolis. For instance, the great majority of fried fish sellers were itinerant, and their sale was greatest from making rounds from one public house to another in populous neighbourhoods (they generally fried their fish beforehand in their garrets or low lodging houses). They also sold at races and fairs where there was a gathering of hungry revellers.[140] By contrast, pea soup, whelk, and hot-eel purveyors were generally stationary with stalls in the street: 'the savoury odour from them attracts more hungry-looking gazers and loungers than does a cook-shop window'.[141] According to Mayhew, the greatest concentration of these could be found in Old Street, but there were others in Windmill Street off Tottenham Court Road, the New Cut (opposite the Victoria Theatre), and the junction of Old and New Kent Roads (near the Bricklayers Arms), among other populous precincts belonging to the working poor.[142] However, Mayhew was alert to the growing challenge to street hawkers from less peripatetic purveyors, noting that 'the penny pie-shops, the street men say, have done their trade a great deal of harm', a development they attributed to the ability of the shops to sell larger pies for the same price.[143] By 1901, journalist and popular dramatist George R. Sims insisted that these street hawkers were less prevalent than they had been in the past, especially in the West End and the City: 'The trade in light refreshments which is left in the hands of the kerbstone purveyor is not so great as it used to be, except perhaps in the east and south of London and certain Saturday-night thoroughfares.' 'The oyster stalls', he continued, were now 'few and far between', the whelk stall had 'shown a modest retirement in the west', and 'the old lady with a basket [of] trotters... belongs to a rapidly disappearing body of street caterers'.[144] However, if the trotter woman's 'peculiar cry' was 'getting as rare as the muffin man's bell', Sims acknowledged that 'coster barrows and stalls' were still doing a lively trade in the East End, particularly on Saturday nights when poor Londoners tended to shop. The continued presence of refreshments sold from carts and stalls at the end of the century is also evident from working-class autobiographies. Arthur Harding's reminiscences of the East End included eel stalls that attracted 'crowds of ordinary people who could always be found along Shoreditch High Street up to midnight', when (as in Mayhew's day) they could obtain their plebian supper.[145] Percy Wall, who

---

[140] *Ibid.* 166.   [141] *Ibid.* 160.   [142] *Ibid.* 160–1.   [143] *Ibid.* 196.

[144] George R. Sims, 'London's Light Refreshments', in George R. Sims (ed.), *Living London* (3 vols; London: Cassell and Co., 1901–3), vol. iii, sect. 1, p. 52.

[145] Samuel (ed.), *East End Underworld*, 8–9.

grew up in Fulham at the turn of the century, recalled street vendors selling hot potatoes or chestnuts, as well as the 'muffin man, as he made his way through the streets, tray on head'.[146]

The sometimes elegiac motif that entered into Mayhew's and Sim's discussion of street vendors suggests that they attracted attention less for their contribution to the urban economy than for their value as subjects in a romantic, even exotic, rendering of metropolitan life. Sims compared street vendors with 'Arabs' who silently stole away 'into the shadowland of the outcasts', 'a human fringe to the pavements of London'.[147] These sentimentalized associations made the street cart a popular subject for illustrators. Among the various archetypes of London's street folk to be found in the first volume of Mayhew's *London Labour and the London Poor* are engravings, based on Richard Beard's daguerreotypes, of 'the Baked Potato Man', 'the London Coffee Stall', and 'the Coster Boy and Girl Tossing the Pieman'. Later on, street vendors attracted the attention of photographers, especially those concerned with providing a visual catalogue of the varieties of activities undertaken by the working poor. For example, one R. L. Sirus took photographs in the mid-1880s of street life that included ice-cream sellers, and a man carrying a bell in order to draw attention to the muffins and crumpets he was selling from a tray carried on his head.[148] One of the hawkers captured by Sirus was pictured with a pie can bearing the notice 'W. Thompson, Champion Pie Maker' (see Figure 1.4). In another of Sirus's photographs, an old man selling ginger cakes from a tray hanging from his neck looks plaintively straight into the camera (perhaps in an attempt to sell his wares to Sirus himself).[149] The potential poignancy of such evidence, however, should not blind us to the fact that these hawkers, their profit margins insubstantial even in the best of times, were both engaged in a struggle for daily survival and played an ongoing role in the public eating culture of the metropolis.

In conclusion, at the risk of offering an anodyne appraisal, London's public eating culture exhibited a distinctive blend of continuity and change. While contemporaries gave extended attention to clearly observable trends, such as the eclipse of the chophouse and the rise of both the West End elite restaurant and the chain restaurant, these narratives are

[146] Percy Wall, 'Hour at Eve', TS 186, 4, Working Class Autobiography, Special Collections, Brunel University Library.

[147] George R. Sims, 'Kerbstone London', in Sims (ed.), *Living London*, vol. i, sect. 2, p. 384.

[148] See photograph of a man selling muffins and crumpets, 12 September 1884, COPY 1/369/236, The National Archives.

[149] See photograph of a man with ginger cakes, 12 September 1884, COPY 1/369/226, The National Archives.

Figure 1.4. W. Thompson, Champion Pie Maker, by R. L. Sirus, 1884. (Reproduced with permission of The National Archives, ref. COPY1/369/259)

best understood as part of a broader, more complex, story. It was a story that encompassed a much wider range of establishments, including the oft-neglected owner-managed dining room, which not merely was responsible for feeding a large part of London's rising population, but contained an important subcategory of foreign-owned modest restaurants that played a significant role in the growing diversification of London's culinary culture. It is particularly important to appreciate that the dramatic growth of London's restaurants was matched by an impressive geographical dispersal. The focus on the West End as a predominant zone of consumption in the late-nineteenth-century metropolis works less effectively when it comes to a consideration of public eating. Those who required meals in London in this period were not just the privileged members of the upper class and bohemian set. We also need to recognize the existence of establishments that served the needs of City clerks, warehousemen, merchants, financiers, office girls, and even the working poor. This diversity of demand also contributed to a distinct heterogeneity in supply. Some restaurants deliberately sought a niche market, but elsewhere entrepreneurial dynamism rendered fixed categories less pertinent. For example, Lockhart's, while it can be considered a restaurant chain (in the same mode as Spiers and Pond), can also be categorized as a temperance restaurant. The modest fried fish shop could be refashioned in more elaborate and rarified form, as in the case of Lynn's, a prestigious fish restaurant that opened in Fleet Street in 1888.[150]

Restaurant growth was often associated with innovation—for example, the introduction of the rational Duval system by Spiers and Pond or the emergence of the model coffee house in the 1880s. However, such new departures coexisted with older styles of public eating—for example, the traditional coffee house or the humble street cart. The growth of London's restaurant sector was also a consequence of its intersection with important external social forces and movements: the emergence of an extended plutocratic elite, the development of the West End as a zone of consumption and entertainment, the dramatic expansion of London's financial sector, suburbanization, and the emergence of the commuter requiring a meal away from home and (once home) in his neighbourhood, the activism of vegetarians, feminists, and various advocates of moral improvement, notably temperance. However, this cultural and social context should not distract from the fact that, whether it be the wretched pieman or the catering empire builder Joseph Lyons, public eating was a commercial venture, and it is to the restaurant as a business that we now turn our attention.

---

[150] 'New Building in Fleet Street', *City Press*, 19 December 1888, Restaurant Files, box G–L, London Cuttings, Bishopsgate.

2

Running the Restaurant

In 1911, the *Restaurant* carried the death notices of two prominent London restaurateurs: Giacomo Monico, owner of the eponymous restaurant on Shaftesbury Avenue that drew the fashionable and the famous, left an estate valued at £75,573 to his wife and three children, into whose hands the family business fell.[1] The second notice reported the death of Felix William Spiers, one of the founders of the Spiers and Pond chain, which had in this period thirty-one refreshment rooms across London, many of them located in or near railway termini.[2] Mr Spiers left his £151,327 estate entirely to his wife, who was thereby able to continue to reside on the tree-lined Avenue d'Iéna in Paris, known for its beaux-arts residences.[3] The *Restaurant* also disclosed to its readers, presumably for reasons of comparison, the value of the estates of a number of other restaurant proprietors who had died in recent years. The estate of Oscar Philippe of the Cavour restaurant was valued at £98,873, a sum that was left entirely to his bookkeeper and manageress, one Mrs George Dale.[4] That of Steffano Gatti (one of the Gatti Brothers, whose refreshment rooms bore the family name) amounted to £220,415. The value of Gatti's estate might seem exceptional, but it was comparable to the fortunes of Spiers's business partner, Christopher Pond (£221,776), and those of Edwin Levy of J. Lyons and Co. (£261,518).[5] The value of these estates compares favourably with the fortunes of leading provincial businessmen (Joseph Chamberlain left approximately £126,000), even if they did not quite reach the stratospheric heights of those possessed by City millionaires, such as Edmund Leopold de Rothschild (with an estimated £1.48 million at death).[6] These were obviously exceptional cases, and

[1] *Restaurant* (February 1911), 47.
[2] *Ibid.*; 'Refreshment Rooms', *Post Office London Directory for 1910* (London: W. Kelly and Co., 1910), 1813.
[3] 'Mr F. W. Spiers' Will', *Restaurant* (July 1911), 244.
[4] *Restaurant* (February 1911), 47.
[5] 'Mr F. W. Spiers' Will', *Restaurant* (July 1911), 244; *Restaurant* (February 1911), 47.
[6] William D. Rubinstein, 'The Wealth Structure of Britain in 1809–39, 1860–1, and 1906', in David R. Green, Alastair Owens, Josephine Maltby, and Janette Rutterford (eds),

establishing how much money could be made in the restaurant business is neither straightforward nor conclusive. We are usually dependent on random pieces of information—for example, the compensation paid in 1896 to one Mr Tenchio, whose refreshment house in Bayswater was compulsorily acquired by the Central London Railway Company, which intended to build a station on the site. Tenchio made a claim for £2,200 (of which he ultimately obtained only half), but during the hearing it was made clear that his establishment made an annual profit of £500, amounting to an all-round profit of 67 per cent.[7] Even if denied the expansive fulsome good fortune of Gatti or Levy, and even if located away from the rarified world of fashionable West End dining, it was clearly possible to make a decent amount of money in the restaurant business.

In stark contrast is the story of Jules Charles Gaillard, a little-known restaurant keeper in Pall Mall, who filed for bankruptcy in 1889, insisting that his debts were too great to manage and that he was losing money, according to his calculations, at a rate of £2 daily.[8] The testimony he provided before the bankruptcy court at the High Court revealed that he owed £35 to J. B. Delbane, a wine importer, £14 6s. to P. Van Danme, a cigar importer, £22 10s. to Jules Gandais for 'goods sold and delivered', and £3 4s. to the Scott Brothers for 'foreign produce', all these suppliers based in Soho and Fitzroy Square.[9] But there were many others who had called on him to collect what money he owed them. Perhaps what plagued Gaillard the most—and probably propelled his appearance before the law courts—was the massive £800 debt he owed to a building society for the building costs to his restaurant and home nearby. All told, he owed £938 17s. 1d. according to the bankruptcy court records filed against him by his creditors.[10] From this point on, Gaillard disappears from the historical record. We do not know if he later went on to reopen his restaurant, open a restaurant somewhere else, or moved into a different line of business. His story underlines the fact that the great majority of restaurant owners ran small establishments that often had a precarious, almost ephemeral, presence in the economic landscape of London. Mapping the fortunes of the

Men, Women, and Money: Perspectives on Gender, Wealth, and Investment, 1850–1930 (Oxford: Oxford University Press, 2011), 50.

[7] 'The Italian Restaurant Business', *Pall Mall Gazette*, 3 June 1896, p. 8.

[8] B 9/387, Public Examiner's Notes record no. 604, 1889, 11 July 1889, The National Archives [hereafter, TNA].

[9] B 9/387, Bankruptcy court record, High Court of Justice, J. C. Gaillard of 1, 2, 3 Prince's Court, 24 May 1889, TNA.

[10] B 9/387, Bankruptcy court record, High Court of Justice, Public Examination of Debtor, J. C. Gaillard, 13 September 1889, TNA.

vast majority of individual restaurants is therefore challenging, if not impossible.

Nevertheless, even if we are obliged to draw on sources that are far from comprehensive, it is possible to gain some sense of the way the restaurant functioned as a business enterprise in this period. This chapter offers an explanation for why some restaurants, like the Monico, flourished, while others, like Gaillard's, failed. It examines how restaurants were financed, how they secured staff and supplies, and how they incorporated techno-logical innovation, and it reveals the often ingenious ways that they sought out customers. The continued presence of the small-scale dining room with its owner–manager and modest blackboard suggested that intensive capitalization and self-conscious modishness were not essential to the success of an individual restaurant. However, it is equally true that consideration of the restaurant as a business reveals some of the ways in which it intersects with important aspects of late-nineteenth and early-twentieth-century modernity—notably, the emergence of a distinct man-agerial class, dramatically expanded economies of scale, and recourse to increasingly sophisticated forms of advertising. Restaurants that were faced with the necessity of excluding undesirable diners dramatized another aspect of modern urban life—namely, the increased democratization of, and greater mobility within, the public sphere. This chapter demonstrates the extraordinary range of challenges faced by those sustaining a restaurant business, in particular the need to remain competitive in a sector of the economy in which profit margins were often relatively small.[11] It will be seen that the restaurant trade was characterized by a healthy entrepreneurial spirit.[12] The restaurant, considered as a business, certainly offers powerful testimony to the continued salience of private enterprise in an era in which

[11] A similar precariousness characterized some other occupations, notably small retail merchants. See Michael J. Winstanley, *The Shopkeeper's World, 1830–1914* (Manchester: Manchester University Press, 1983). The continued dominance of the small shop in the retail sector before 1914, in spite of the rise of the multiple, is confirmed by Michael Ball and David Sunderland, *An Economic History of London, 1800–1914* (London: Routledge, 2001), ch. 6. Small-scale restaurants are a notable absentee even from John Benson, *The Penny Capitalists: A Study of Nineteenth-Century Working-Class Entrepreneurs* (New Brunswick: Rutgers University Press, 1983).

[12] Important works in the debate over whether there was a failure of entrepreneurship in late Victorian Britain (which has largely been settled in favour of those refuting this notion) would be: Martin J. Wiener, *English Culture and the Decline of the Industrial Spirit, 1850–1980* (Cambridge: Cambridge University Press, 1981; 2nd edn, 2004); Donald N. McCloskey, 'Did Victorian Britain Fail?', *Economic History Review*, 23/3 (December 1970), 446–59; W. D. Rubinstein, *Capitalism, Culture and Decline in Britain, 1750–1990* (London: Routledge, 1994); Martin J. Daunton, '"Gentlemanly Capitalism" and British Industry, 1820–1914', *Past and Present*, 122 (February 1989), 119–58; and Peter Mandler, 'Against "Englishness": English Culture and the Limits to Rural Nostalgia, 1850–1940', *Transactions of the Royal Historical Society*, 7 (1997), 155–75.

many commentators (across the political spectrum) were raising doubts about the effectiveness of an unregulated free market.[13]

Given the numbers and range of restaurant establishments in late-Victorian London, it is obviously impossible to generalize about how they were financed. However, in the 1890s, when the expansion of the restaurant sector was most evident, we are able to detect something of the manner in which restaurant businesses were set up by perusing the advertisement section of the trade paper the *Caterer*. The *Caterer* acted as a site of brokerage, both publicizing business opportunities to potential investors, and allowing entrepreneurs to seek out investors in a column devoted to this enterprise called 'Business for Disposal'. Some listings were terse, offering little by way of description. A not untypical example is an advertisement from 1896 seeking the 'quick sale' of a premises described as 'Coffee and Dining Rooms', the location of which was unhelpfully identified as 'central position, close to station'. At least the advertiser felt obliged to specify the rent on the property, set at £80, and the price of the business, in this case, £75.[14] Being close to a railway station seemed to be a particular selling point in this period.[15] Location was particularly priori-tized by advertisers, especially for properties in which there was no existing restaurant business, but which might be suitable for conversion, or in which an existing restaurant had failed. In 1896, an advertisement announced for sale two large shops in Soho suitable for an eating house that stood next door to 'Messrs Novell's new works, employing over 500 hands', who all needed feeding at mealtimes.[16] Other advertisements, especially for growing concerns, not only stressed location, but also recorded existing levels of profitability. A listing for a fully licensed restaurant and hotel 'at a most important City thoroughfare' also drew attention to annual profits of between £3,000 and £6,500 and 'the chance to increase liquor trade'. Not surprisingly, given these attractive profit margins, the price tag for the business was set at £4,000.[17]

However, even this sum was small fry compared to that demanded by fashionable West End restaurants like Krasnapolsky's in Oxford Street, which, the *Caterer* reported in 1892, sold to Messrs Hamp and Co. for £70,000. It was thereupon transformed into Frascati's, where 'musical dinners are a new a feature', making the place a favourite among diners,

---

[13] Frank Trentmann, *Free Trade Nation: Commerce, Consumption, and Civil Society in Modern Britain* (Oxford: Oxford University Press, 2008).

[14] 'Business for Disposal', *Caterer*, 15 May 1896, p. xlvi.

[15] For example, the 'growing concern facing the railway station, South London', *Caterer*, 15 December 1898, supplement.

[16] 'Business for Disposal', *Caterer*, 15 October 1896, p. li.

[17] 'Business for Disposal', *Caterer*, 15 October 1898, p. liii.

such as restaurant critic Nathaniel Newnham-Davis, seeking theatricality in the dining experience.[18] Prestigious West End and chain restaurants inevitably sought to offset high start-up costs by an ongoing commitment to paying dividends to shareholders. In 1897, the *Caterer* estimated that shareholders could expect returns of around 4.5–5 per cent in any investment made in top restaurants or hotels.[19] In fact, estimates for individual establishments, notably the Savoy Hotel and the chain restaurant Spiers and Pond, suggest that annual dividends in the late 1880s and 1890s could reach as high as 10 per cent, while those for the Lyons empire were probably even higher.[20] Many larger restaurants were floated on the stock exchange during this period. The *Caterer* claimed the first restaurant to become a limited company was the St James's Hall in 1887, and it was subsequently joined by Kettner's, the Holborn, and Frascati restaurants, all forming limited companies.[21] By contrast, most restaurants operated under very different financial environments. Given that modest restaurants attracted buyers and investors who did not possess the capital that was required for the purchase of prestigious West End restaurants, vendors often felt obliged to offer the possibility of payments by instalments. Others offered specific, or additional, inducements—for example, furnishings and fittings and existing liquor licences.[22]

Attaining a liquor licence was certainly a necessity for larger restaurant ventures, but how far it was necessary, or desirable, for smaller establishments is open to question. In the lead-up to the 1888 Local Government Act, concerted pressure by the temperance movement raised the possibility of restaurants and hotels having their application for a licence (or renewal of an existing licence) determined not by a legal tribunal, but by an elected body composed of ratepayers. Editorials in the *British Journal of Catering* were inevitably indignant about this 'revolutionary proposal', which threatened commercial enterprise with the irrational impulses of 'popular agitation'.[23] However, they also attempted to reassure their readers

---

[18] 'Chops and Changes', *Caterer*, 15 November 1892, p. 458.

[19] 'Hotels and Restaurants', *Caterer*, 15 December 1897, p. 692.

[20] 'Messrs Spiers and Pond', *Caterer*, 15 July 1887, p. 235; 'Hotel News', *Caterer*, 15 October 1892, p. 395; 'Hotel News', *Caterer*, 16 April 1895, p. 143; 'Odds and Ends', *Caterer*, 16 January 1899, p. 32.

[21] 'Odds and Ends', *Caterer*, 15 March 1887, p. 96; 'Chops and Changes', *Caterer*, 16 August 1897, p. 424; 'Chops and Changes', *Caterer*, 15 December 1897, p. 683; 'Odds and Ends', *Caterer*, 15 March 1898, p. 140. For the development of limited companies more generally, see Timothy L. Alborn, *Conceiving Companies: Joint-Stock Politics in Victorian England* (London: Routledge, 1998).

[22] For instance, 'Business for Disposal', *Caterer*, 15 June 1899, p. xlvii, 15 December 1899, p. xlv; 'Hotels and the "Hire System"', *Hotel Review and Catering & Food Trades' Gazette*, (November 1886), 131.

[23] 'Editorial', *British Journal of Catering*, 1 March 1888, p. 171, and 1 April 1888, p. 206.

that such 'reckless legislation' was likely to be stillborn, since the necessity of providing compensation for revoked licences both risked placing undue financial burden on the newly elected county councils and was opposed in principle by the temperance movement.[24] Nevertheless, in the very same year, reports in the trade press on individual establishments suggest that it was becoming more difficult to obtain a liquor licence. In May 1888, the *British Journal of Catering*, having reported that a certain Mrs Rutterman had failed to secure a licence for the restaurant she had acquired at Westminster-chambers, offered some consolation to her by stating that 'the confirmation of a licence is now quite a rarity, and it looks as though licences will be very much rarer still by and by'.[25] Twenty years later, an article in the *Restaurant* asserted that 'the question is an open one as to whether the license is worth all the extra cost and supervision'.[26] It insisted that there was no evidence that possessing what had once been considered a 'valuable monopoly' led to increased trade and custom. Even those restaurants that did have licences, it unequivocally stated, might no longer find it necessary to maintain a large stock in the cellars. The article failed to detail the changing tastes or character that had led to this shift, merely offering the cryptic statement that, especially in the City, 'men's ideas have altered in the matter of liquid refreshments'.[27] Presumably, what the author had in mind was the consequence of increased heterosociability, and the expansion of the white-collar workforce, in City dining rooms.

The decision whether to seek a liquor licence was obviously most pertinent in the case of smaller establishments, where both the securing of capital and expenditure operated under serious financial constraints. There is evidence that some smaller restaurants sought to circumvent licensing regulation by simply obtaining alcohol from neighbouring taverns or contacts in the wine trade. However, recourse to this expedient was limited by the problem of not being able to list the prices of the drinks, either in the restaurant window or on the menu (the law specifically forbidding the display of a list of excisable articles on unlicensed premises).[28] Such frustrations were obviously not a feature of larger establishments, whose horizons were inevitably financially and geographically more expansive. Indeed, while investment in London restaurants took

[24] 'Editorial', *British Journal of Catering*, 1 March 1888, p. 171.
[25] 'Hotel and Restaurant News', *British Journal of Catering*, 1 May 1888, p. 248. This characterization was supported in the Parliamentary Papers, *Royal Commission on Liquor Licensing Laws* (1899), 11. The report stated that, for the previous fifteen or twenty years, justices in England had abstained from granting new licences.
[26] 'Business Management: How to Start a Restaurant', *Restaurant* (August 1909), 7.
[27] *Ibid.*   [28] 'Legal Magisterial Notes', *Caterer*, 15 February 1892, p. 76.

place in a local marketplace, at times it was also connected to the much larger movements of global capital that characterized the age. In 1897, the *Caterer* carried a clumsily phrased, but intriguing, advertisement placed by a self-declared caterer who, 'having thorough experience in the [latest] American restaurant business', required a 'Capitalist to assist in establishing up-to-date Restaurant in London'. The advertiser in this case failed to identify him or herself except by the rather gnomic '1897', and asked for anyone offering 'entirely novel ideas' to contact him or her at the offices of the *Caterer*.[29] By contrast, some businesses sought investment from a more contained constituency. Vegetarian and women-only restaurants sought subscribers through cooperative groups and their publications.[30]

Having secured finance, the restaurant owner now needed personnel for his or her establishment. An obvious way of recruiting staff was through advertisements in newspapers or the trade press, placed by both employers and those seeking employment. Advertising did not necessarily secure the desired results. In one case, a restaurateur not only wasted time and effort, but also endured a considerable measure of embarrassment. Looking for waitresses, he received over 200 responses to his advertisement. Having isolated four of the most suitable applicants, he then, probably unwisely, arranged to meet them, 'for want of a better place', in the first-class waiting room of the Great Eastern Railway at Liverpool Street Station.[31] On arrival, the man in question, to his considerable dismay, discovered not four, but forty, women seated in the room. He was forced to approach the women in turn to ask each of them if she had been one of the ones who had responded to his advertisement. One woman responded that she was indeed waiting to meet a prospective employer, but one who had advertised, not for a waitress, but for a wet nurse. Another indignantly replied that she was waiting for her husband. The restaurateur, having failed to negotiate a new heterosocial culture, in which women were increasingly solicitous of their rights to move through public space free of male harassment, returned home crestfallen, 'no better off than when he started'.[32]

---

[29] 'Engagements Wanted', *Caterer*, 15 January 1897, p. xlv.

[30] As early as the 1870s, the Vegetarian Society tried to attract wealthy subscribers. See Francis William Newman, 'Vegetarianism', *Fraser's Magazine*, NS 11/62 (February 1875), p. 156; for a more grass-roots appeal, see 'Opening of a People's Café in Gracechurch Street', 13 November 1878, Restaurant Files, box M–P, London Cuttings, Bishopsgate. On women-only restaurants, see, for instance, 'Proposed Women's Cooperative Restaurant Society' (c.1916), correspondence file, 2 LSW/FL 368/1, Women's Library, London. Some niche investment schemes were even more narrowly focused; see reference to the Women's Vegetarian Union in 'Temperance Hotel and Restaurant Notes', *Caterer*, 15 March 1897, p. 143.

[31] 'The Hotel Club Scheme', *Caterer*, 15 October 1891, p. 385.　　[32] *Ibid.*

Restaurateurs were also able to seek staff through various employment agencies specifically devised for the catering trade. For example, in 1879, it was possible to secure employees through the British and Foreign Hotel Servants' Agency, by paying either a yearly annual subscription or an individual fee for each servant engaged.[33] A prospectus for this agency promised that proprietors 'who wish to avoid the delay and trouble of making enquiries into servants' characters may safely leave the selection to us'.[34] Similar services were offered in the decades that followed by (to take just two examples) the International Hotel Employés' Society and the City of London Licensed Victuallers and Restaurant Keepers' Trade Protection Society.[35] However, recourse to employment agencies was no guarantee of a successful match between employer and employee either. A coffee-room proprietor from Hastings was informed by a London agency that it had found somebody suitable to serve in his establishment. He then travelled to London to meet his prospective employee in person, only to find him unwilling to take on the job.[36] At least potential employers who participated in registry schemes were liable to registry fees only if they secured a servant at the end of the process. By contrast, many workers found themselves out of pocket after paying a fee to what was effectively a sham agency.[37]

The anecdotes about the embarrassed restaurateur accosting women at Liverpool Street station and the frustrated coffee-room proprietor from Hastings were both relayed in an article that appeared in the *Caterer* in 1891, authored by D. M. Sherwill of the Guildhall Tavern in the City. Sherwill, eager to save employers wasting precious time and effort in the search for staff, but also alert to a potential business opportunity, proposed the creation of a national register of every staff member currently employed in hotels, restaurants, and other catering establishments. Entries in this register would be supplied by proprietors, including 'full particulars as to their names, their history, age, references, causes of their change in different establishments, and every detail requisite to form a true report as

[33] 'Trade Employers Registration Offices', *Licensed Victuallers' Guardian*, 28 October 1879, repr. in *Hotel and Tavern Advertiser*, 8 November 1879, p. 1.

[34] 'The British and Foreign Hotel Servants' Agency', *Hotel and Tavern Advertiser*, 8 November 1879, p. 1.

[35] 'The International Hotel Employés' Society', *Caterer*, 15 March 1886, p. 80; 'Caterer's Notebook', *Caterer*, 15 February 1894, p. 60.

[36] 'The Hotel Club Scheme', *Caterer*, 15 October 1891, p. 385.

[37] 'Trade Employers Registration Office', *Licensed Victuallers' Guardian*, 28 October 1879, repr. in *Hotel and Tavern Advertiser*, 8 November 1879. References to sham registry offices in the trade press suggest this was a particular problem in the late 1870s, but there is no reason to assume that they were not still a feature of the labour market in the following decades.

to the character of the servant'.[38] This ambitious, or, perhaps more accurately, largely unrealizable, initiative was to be operated through a social club for proprietors and managers, paid for by subscription. Sherwill's grand scheme was not to be restricted to an employment list. He hoped to secure premises in London for a club, which would comprise not merely the conventional reading, smoking, and refreshment rooms and members' accommodation, but also arbitration rooms and 'suitable rooms for interviewing and engaging servants'.[39] He further suggested the club would create its own food and supply stores with a view to undercutting the Grocers' Association, and also supply legal advice to subscribers.[40] While Sherwill's prospectus, for what he termed the Hotel and Caterers' Union, did not explicitly exclude female proprietors, the list of forty-one prominent members of the hotel and catering community who had agreed to support the scheme did not include a single woman.[41]

Sherwill's main priority was obviously to protect the interests of proprietors. His employment register, what he termed a 'servants' roll', was intended not merely to procure more reliable staff, and to provide their employers with 'a more absolute guarantee of character'. He also saw it as a mechanism to detect and expose 'thieves and swindlers', who, he argued, had been a long-standing problem in the trade.[42] However, Sherwill deployed the language of moral uplift in order to argue that prospective employees would also be beneficiaries of his scheme. His 'servants' roll' would save young women from the perils of the employment registry office, where, having been liberated of their half-crown fee, they would encounter young men who would invite them for a drink. Once they had spent the afternoon together, 'later on, the poor girls are lost'.[43] By contrast, Sherwill's club promised interview rooms that were sexually segregated, which he hoped would free young women from the temptations offered by their male peers, even if it did not necessarily guarantee them protection from the overzealous inducements of their (presumably male) potential employers.

Sherwill's club scheme never came to fruition.[44] Significantly, the International Hotel, Club and Restaurant Protection and Benevolent Association, formed in 1903, while it shared several features with Sherwill's proposal (notably the provision of free legal advice to members and the aspiration for securing club premises in London), did not

[38] 'The Hotel Club Scheme', *Caterer*, 15 October 1891, p. 385.
[39] 'The Hotel and Caterers' Union', *Caterer*, 15 July 1891, p. 276.
[40] 'The Hotel Club Scheme', *Caterer*, 15 October 1891, p. 385.
[41] 'The Hotel and Caterers' Union', *Caterer*, 15 October 1891, p. 384.   [42] *Ibid.*
[43] 'The Hotel Club Scheme', *Caterer*, 15 October 1891, p. 385.
[44] 'The Hotel and Caterers' Union', *Caterer*, 16 May 1892, p. 181.

implement a 'servants' roll', although, even less feasibly, it did promise to create a 'black list' of troublesome customers.[45] While both unique and unimplemented, Sherwill's scheme reveals the anxieties and frustrations that faced all proprietors looking for workers. In contrast to Sherwill's emphasis on streamlining and rationalizing (and indeed collective solutions), most proprietors secured staff in ways that were more mundane or idiosyncratic. We need to remember that, in addition to waiting staff (who receive specific attention in another chapter), restaurants also employed kitchen staff and front-of-house employees. Some establishments needed kitchen maids, scullery men, porters, carvers, cashiers, doorkeepers, clerks, and bookkeepers. But, as the restaurant sector expanded and became much more part of the fabric of the London economy and culture, the two types of employee who were most illustrative of the restaurant's relationship to wider society were to be the chef and the manager.

The most rarified professional cooks in mid-nineteenth-century London were less likely to be found in restaurants than they were to be acting as *chefs de cuisine* in the households of leading aristocrats, or as resident chefs at clubs. Many of these were émigrés from France, a consequence of that nation's turbulent politics in the opening decades of the century. After serving as *maître d'hôtel* to Madame Letitia Bonaparte (his departure a consequence of matters 'arithmetical'), Louis Eustache Ude crossed the Channel and established himself in England, and for twenty years cooked for Lord Sefton.[46] Fellow émigré Antonin de Carême, known as the 'king of the kitchen', was put in charge of various royal kitchens across Europe, including the Prince Regent's. Former second cook to French statesman Jules, Duke de Polignac, Alexis Soyer, in addition to working in the households of notables such as the Duke of Sutherland and the Marquess of Waterford, proved to be an innovatory chief cook at the Reform Club between 1837 and 1850.[47] A year later, coinciding with the Great Exhibition, he attracted a wider public at the 'Universal Symposium' in Gore House, where, amid myriad spectacular displays, dinners and refreshments were served (Karl Marx was on the guest list of its first press lunch, representing *Neue Rheinische Zeitung*).[48]

---

[45] '"The International Caterers": Its Past, Present and Future', *Restaurant* (April 1910), 202.

[46] 'Famous *Chefs de Cuisine*: Louis Eustache Ude', *British Journal of Catering*, 1 March 1889, p. 25.

[47] For a description of Soyer's improvements, see 'Kitchens of the Reform Club House, Pall Mall', *Sharpe's London Magazine*, 24 October 1846, pp. 402–5.

[48] Ruth Brandon, *The People's Chef Alexis Soyer, A Life in Seven Courses* (Chichester: Wiley & Sons, 2004), 208.

While more likely to be found at a state banquet or a patrician London townhouse, some of these renowned chefs were engaged in the restaurant sector as it established itself and expanded in the later decades of the century. For example, Monsieur Suzanne, the *chef de cuisine* to the Duke of Bedford, took it upon himself to offer a commentary in the pages of the *Caterer* about the merits of various London restaurants. He credited Londoners with a growing appreciation of the continental restaurant, and declared that it was 'an indisputable fact that London now rivals Paris for the beauty, convenience, and comfort of its restaurants', the only drawback being the continued failings of the British waiter.[49] Other chefs made less direct interventions in the London restaurant scene, but undoubtedly had an indirect impact through the proselytizing of the latest developments in haute cuisine, which then found their way onto the menus of fashionable dining establishments. For example, Charles Elmé Francatelli, one-time *chef de cuisine* to the Earl of Chelmsford and *maître d'hôtel* and chief cook to Queen Victoria, drew on his daunting résumé to offer advice to British chefs in a series of publications that appeared between the 1840s and 1860s (to say nothing of the new editions that appeared later).[50] In a class by himself was Auguste Escoffier, the legendary 'king of chefs and chef of kings', initially employed as a chef at the Savoy in 1890, but who went on to even greater fame as a prominent figure in international hotel development, culinary writing, and the promotion of French cuisine. His attention to the specific and idiosyncratic needs of monarchs, dukes, plutocrats, and actresses had obvious continuities with the *chefs de cuisine* from earlier in the century.[51] However, the fact that his culinary creations were highly visible, served in the public spaces of the hotel dining room (and reported in the new illustrated press), made him a key player in the creation of a more modernized version of conspicuous consumption and the newly emergent celebrity culture with which it was associated.[52]

---

[49] M. Suzanne, *Chef de Cuisine* to the Duke of Bedford, 'Typical English Kitchens', *Caterer*, 15 April 1887, p. 117.

[50] See, e.g., Charles Elmé Francatelli, *The Modern Cook* (London: Richard Bentley, 1846); *A Plain Cookery Book for the Working Classes* (London: Routledge, Warne & Co., 1852); *The Cook's Guide and Housekeeper's and Butler's Assistant: A Practical Treatise on English and Foreign Cookery in all its Branches* (London: Richard Bentley, 1861); *The Royal English and Foreign Confectioner* (London: Chapman and Hall, 1862). See 'Famous Chefs', *British Journal of Catering*, 1 December 1888, p. 17.

[51] See Auguste Escoffier, *Auguste Escoffier: Memories of my Life*, trans. Laurence Escoffier (New York: Van Nostrand Reinhold, 1997).

[52] For example, see a review in *Illustrated Sporting and Dramatic News*, 1 November 1890, and numerous articles in the Savoy Hotel cuttings collection, Savoy Hotel, London.

While the notion of a 'celebrity chef' has connotations that make it unhelpful, not to say anachronistic, one can certainly acknowledge the existence of what a regular feature in the journal the *Chef* in the 1890s termed the 'celebrated chef'. The celebrated chefs that featured in this column tended to be employed in the worlds of elite private households or institutions, as well as grand state and official hospitality. For example, readers of the *Chef* were treated to short sketches, such as of Edward Arthur Gurney, who ran the kitchens of St Catharine's College Cambridge, and subsequently many large London railway hotels and university clubs.[53] However, the celebrated chefs' column also began to incorporate men who were much more explicitly embedded in the world of the restaurant. For example, a sketch of Gabriele Maccario, the head chef of the Circus restaurant in Oxford Street, highlighted his esteemed role in the world of Italian cookery.[54] A profile of Louis Peyre, formerly of the Grand Hotel at the Louvre and the Hotel Continental in Biarritz, described his arrival in London as a marvel, after he had restored the degraded reputation of the Charing Cross Hotel by modernizing its cuisine in the 1890s.[55]

The *Chef* clearly intended recognition of a select number of renowned chefs to be part of a broader project to assert the status of the professional cook. Significantly, this trade paper deployed the term 'chef' in a restricted sense, hoping to distinguish the expert from the run-of-the-mill cook. Here the emphasis was less on the artistry and creativity of the chef that featured in romanticized narratives of Soyer and others, and more on a more hard-headed desire for professional recognition and respectability. Many of those who placed advertisements in the *Chef*, seeking positions, internalized the self-image of chefs as presented by the paper. Although never explicitly articulated, the distinction between a professionalized chef and the more workaday cook was undoubtedly gendered. This is not to say that such assumptions went entirely uncontested. In a vigorous defence of her position, one writer calling herself 'Isobel' argued in an editorial to the *Chef* that 'man, who is a smoking and drinking animal with course and blunted susceptibilities, has not the same keen discriminating sense of taste that a woman has, and so his dishes and sauces have not the subtle aroma and flavour which only a woman's palate can discern'.[56] But for some readers, like 'A Mere Man', a sensitive palate was not enough to elevate women in the profession. Rather, 'the inventive

[53] 'Celebrated Chefs: Edward Arthur Gurney', *Chef*, 15 August 1896, p. 1.
[54] 'Celebrated Chefs: Gabriele Maccario', *Chef*, 18 April 1896, p. 1.
[55] 'Celebrated Chefs: Louis Peyre', *Chef*, 1 May 1897, p. 1.
[56] 'Correspondence: Female Cooks—to the Editor of the *Chef*', *Chef*, 14 March 1896, p. 6.

faculty is precisely one of the qualifications which distinguish the chef from the mere cook. The ability to invent new dishes, to concoct new sauces, to devise new garnishes, and to prepare new menus is the characteristic of the true chef,' and on this basis, as 'Isobel' admitted, 'women are out of the hunt'.[57] Pointing to the additional responsibilities of the chef to control numerous servants and direct operations, the writer added that 'the administrative powers of a man are imperatively required' over a woman's.[58]

The most obvious way of asserting status and providing welfare was through the creation of formal associations. The venerable United Friendly Society of Cooks and Confectioners appeared to struggle for much of its existence, its membership in 1889 being little more than 156 members. An article in the *British Journal of Catering* in that year attributed this 'monstrous state of affairs' to the relative scarcity of 'genuine British Cooks' and the fact that those who did exist were 'too modest to obtrude their claims to the dignity of their profession'.[59] Interestingly, the article suggested the response was not to adopt exclusionary initiatives, but rather to have British cooks 'take their foreign brothers by the hand and join issue for the good of the art which is world-wide, and not confined to nations'.[60] Indeed, the United Friendly Society itself proposed the creation of an amalgamated union of British and foreign cooks in order to create a body that would 'control the profession of cooks of this country and raise the standard of them as a class'.[61] While the inclusive sentiments of this proposal were commendable, a more cynical observer might see here a rather thinly veiled attempt to raise the status of British chefs by allying themselves with the superior status enjoyed by their foreign-born counterparts. Significantly, these aspirations to professional status, unlike those articulated in the *Chef*, did not make a verbal distinction between chef and cook. This was probably a wise decision, given the complex hierarchies of different types of cooks to be found in a single kitchen of a large restaurant.[62] In addition to a head chef, there were stove cooks, pastry cooks, head cooks, larder chefs, roasting chefs, sauce chefs, and vegetable maids. In less rarified establishments, these highly calibrated

[57] 'Correspondence: Female Cooks—to the Editor of the *Chef*', *Chef*, 21 March 1896, p. 6.
[58] *Ibid.*
[59] 'Original United Friendly Society of Cooks and Confectioners', *British Journal of Catering*, 15 May 1889, p. 13.
[60] *Ibid.* 14.
[61] 'Amalgamation of Cooks', *British Journal of Catering*, 15 May 1889, p. 14.
[62] See, for instance, 'Situations Vacant', *Chef*, 11 January 1896, pp. ii–iii.

hierarchies were undoubtedly less prevalent. In smaller establishments, the term chef was hardly used.

As the restaurant sector expanded in the late nineteenth century, and some individual establishments became larger and more sophisticated, it became increasingly necessary for proprietors to delegate some of their responsibilities to managers. It probably comes as no surprise that the most organized management structures were in place in the Lyons chain restaurants.[63] In smaller-scale establishments, managerial functions were less clearly demarcated. However, the increasing ubiquity of restaurant managers is testified to by the regular appearance of the term in articles in the trade press and in job advertisements. These sources reveal some of the particular challenges faced by, and qualities required of, the restaurant manager. Managers often needed to have some facility with more than one language in order to cope with foreign-born waiting and kitchen staff. When the Duval Restaurant opened in Charing Cross in 1894, it employed a bilingual Frenchwoman as manager.[64] Managers were likely to be the first people to experience the hostility of waiters complaining about wage reductions and longer hours.[65] They were also on the front line when dealing with troublesome diners, especially those who refused to finish up sufficiently quickly or were drunk.[66] Conversely, the manager of the Frascati restaurant possibly created a rod for his own back when he invited anyone with a complaint to address it to him, as he endeavoured to perfect everything.[67]

The increasing importance of the manager, and the extent of his or her responsibilities, is revealed in a series of articles on various aspects of 'Business Management' that appeared in the pages of the trade journal the *Restaurant* in 1909 and 1910. Topics covered in the paper included the engaging and managing of staff, securing provisions and kitchen equipment, bookkeeping and accounts, and the composition of the bill of fare.[68] Efficient management was often an aspiration rather than a reality. The author of one article in the series, 'The Economy in Small Things', chided managers (at least outside the larger establishments) for

[63] 'Feeding Half-A-Million Daily', *Organiser* (December 1910), 459–65.
[64] 'Chops and Changes', *Caterer*, 15 December 1894, p. 550.
[65] These complaints are discussed in Chapter 3.
[66] 'A London Restaurant at Midnight', *British Journal of Catering*, 1 March 1888, p. 189.
[67] 'The Restaurant Frascati', *Era*, 31 August 1895, p. 16.
[68] All citations in the *Restaurant*: 'How to Start a Restaurant' (August 1909), 8; 'The Economy in Small Things' (September 1909), 34; 'Kitchen Equipment' (November 1909), 79; 'Keeping Accounts' (December 1909), 106–8; 'Kitchen Accounts' (January 1910), 130–1; 'Bill of Fare' (February 1910), 151–2; 'Engaging and Managing the Staff' (March 1910), 175–6.

neglecting proper bookkeeping and carelessness in the buying of excessive amounts of food that was then wasted.[69] Nevertheless, in larger restaurants, the manager was a permanent fixture by the Edwardian period, his presence linked to the increasing tendency to divide restaurants into various departments for the purposes of accounting and administration. It was certainly the case that managerial positions were important for those who saw the restaurant as a career, not merely a job. Former waiters, as we have seen, might become managers, and managers in restaurants overseas (and indeed some proprietors) took up managerial positions in London before going on to own their own establishments. Managerial positions also offered a particular opportunity for women. In 1897, an advertisement in the *Caterer* specifically sought a manageress for a restaurant with a licence.[70]

Having secured staff, restaurant proprietors also obviously required provisions, both food and equipment. Restaurant expansion took place at the same time as the food retail sector grew and became more complex.[71] Some aspects of securing food for restaurants seemed almost timeless, not to say clichéd. In 1891, the *Caterer* insisted that, if a restaurateur was to secure the best food for his restaurant, he would need to visit the markets every day at five in the morning when they opened.[72] If this gave the restaurant owner very little opportunity for a full night's sleep after the exertions of the night before, he might have been relieved to read an article in 1912 that maintained that restaurant and hotel people did their business at Leadenhall market between eight and ten in the morning.[73] However, by the Edwardian period, restaurant owners and managers were often conflicted about whether to obtain their supplies locally or through specialist distributors. If bread was not baked in restaurant kitchens, it was probably secured from local bakeries, although even here there was a shift towards larger-scale provision.

[69] 'Business Management: The Economy in Small Things', *Restaurant* (September 1909), 34.

[70] 'Engagements open', *Caterer*, 16 August 1897, supplement.

[71] On the expansion of this sector, see A. St John Adcock, 'London's Food Supply', in George R. Sims (ed.), *Living London* (3 vols; London: Cassell and Co., 1901–3), vol. iii, sect. 2, pp. 293–9. For a study of one aspect of food provisioning, here focused on the first half of the nineteenth century, see Robyn S. Metcalfe, *Meat, Commerce and the City: The London Food Market, 1800–1855* (London: Pickering and Chatto, 2012). Cf. Gergely Baics, *Feeding Gotham: The Political Economy and Geography of Food in New York, 1790–1860* (Princeton: Princeton University Press, 2016).

[72] 'Restaurant Marketing', *Caterer*, 15 April 1891, p. 150.

[73] 'Men in the Markets', *Restaurant and Hotel Review*, 12 April 1912, p. 206.

For example, the Empress Bakery in Whitechapel supplied 120 of the largest hotels and restaurants in London with bread in the 1880s.[74]

The increased proliferation of frozen and canned goods also impacted on their decisions. The availability of canned goods obviously increased dramatically in this period, but it is difficult to establish how far they became a notable presence in restaurant kitchens and storerooms, as opposed to the pantries of domestic households. At times of rising meat prices, it seems possible to speculate that restaurants on tight budgets may have had increased recourse to canned meat.[75] Many restaurateurs still insisted on fresh meat, rather than frozen, and in one case in 1910 took the purveyors to court for fraud for supplying them with frozen meat.[76] At this time, constant references in the trade press to rising meat prices suggested the tension between maintaining quality and keeping costs down. Restaurateurs also complained about wholesalers supplying them with contaminated or rotting food. For instance, in 1898, health inspectors investigated '117 unsound haddocks' sold by Billingsgate 'Bombaree' (that is, salesmen to a local fried fish shop).[77] Few restaurateurs had recourse to the expedient used by restaurant behemoth Spiers and Pond, which possessed its own slaughterhouses at Deptford and Islington. The firm had a dedicated meat manager, who attended cattle markets and purchased live cattle that were then slaughtered at its facility.[78] That said, even small-scale restaurants were now integrated into much larger economies of scale, positioned at the lower end of a chain that ran through the centralized cold storage chambers erected in markets like Smithfield, the gargantuan refrigerators at the Victoria Docks (with a holding capacity of 200,000 carcasses), and the global trade routes that were vital to a nation dependent on importing food.[79]

Technological innovation that underpinned the new economies of scale in food supply and distribution also found their way into provisioning the restaurant kitchen. Even a superficial perusal of the trade press in the 1890s reveals advertisements for, and reviews of, not merely more quotidian culinary implements (pots, pans, steamers, glassware, dishes, and knives), but also a variety of labour- and cost-saving appliances including

[74] *Hotel Review and Catering & Food Trades' Gazette* (June 1886), 58.
[75] One commentator in 1892 argued that rising meat consumption was increasingly being satisfied by canned meat, but did not make clear whether this assertion applied to restaurants or household consumption. See 'Caterer's Notebook', *Caterer*, 15 December 1892, p. 493.
[76] 'Cases in Court: Alleged Breach of a Meat Contract', *Restaurant* (May 1910), 228.
[77] 'Unsound Fish', *Food and Sanitation*, 12 February 1898, p. 702.
[78] 'The Restaurant Business', *Caterer*, 15 December 1890, pp. 460–1.
[79] 'Cold Storage of Meat in London', *Caterer*, 15 September 1894, p. 384.

stoves and refrigerators. By 1912, it was possible for one author in the *Restaurant and Hotel Review* to assert that refrigeration, although it had been commercially exploited for no more than thirty years, had become increasingly ubiquitous. It declared that 'no large hotel-keeper or restaurant proprietor considers himself properly fitted out until he has some form of refrigerating appliance'.[80] Modern vapour compression refrigerators were presented as more cost effective than the old-style insulated box or chamber filled with ice. Somewhat disconcertingly, though, the author of the article felt obliged to provide a dictionary definition of refrigeration ('briefly, the maintaining of low temperatures') and to explain the link between colder temperatures and the inhibition of bacterial growth on food.[81] The need to convey such basic information suggests that not all restaurants had yet embraced either the scientific knowledge, or the cost advantages, of the modern refrigerator.

By contrast, restaurants with more capital available eagerly adopted technological innovation, not merely to reduce costs in the kitchen but also in order to attract customers.[82] From the 1890s, many restaurants used electricity to light their dining rooms, as well as to cook their food.[83] At Neal's in the City, electricity was used to power a service lift connecting the dining room with the kitchen below, thereby reducing the disruption to diners caused by waiters carrying dishes and platters up and down stairs.[84] Myriad other new appliances reflected both the ingenuity and the unapologetic commercialism of the age. The trade press contained invitations to restaurateurs to purchase an ox-tongue holder (used to prevent the tongue wobbling during carving), a potato-peeling machine, a trap to prevent gases from being released from the kitchen to the dining room, and a device for chopping spinach (the latter clearly not a conspicuous success, since it apparently led to a suit brought against the Holborn Restaurant for personal injuries suffered by a diner who found a needle in his dish).[85] Advertisements for appliances in the trade press were

---

[80] 'Refrigeration for Hotels and Restaurants', *Restaurant and Hotel Review* (July 1912), 381.

[81] *Ibid.*

[82] For the dissemination of technological innovation more broadly in this period, see David Edgerton, *Science, Technology, and the British Industrial 'Decline', 1870–1970* (Cambridge: Cambridge University Press, 1996).

[83] For the impact of electric lighting in London, see Desmond Young, 'Lighting London', in Sims (ed.), *Living London*, vol. ii, sect. 2, pp. 274–80; and, in relation to the City of London, see Chris Otter, *The Victorian Eye: A Political History of Light and Vision in Britain, 1800–1910* (Chicago: University of Chicago Press, 2008), 243–51.

[84] 2 May 1914, Restaurant Files, box M–P, London Cuttings, Bishopsgate.

[85] 'The Late Food and Cookery Exhibition', *Hotel Review and Catering & Food Trades' Gazette* (February 1887), 31; 'Mabbott and Co.'s Catalogue', *Restaurant* (October 1909), 70; 'The Furnishing and Equipment of Hotels and Kindred Establishments', *Tourist and*

supplemented by special exhibitions of state-of-the-art products—for instance, the one held at the Royal Agricultural Hall in 1898.[86] Manufacturers also offered restaurant owners a variety of cleaning detergents and pest killers. One American hotelier extolled in the pages of the *Caterer* the virtues of pulverized borax for removing cockroaches from kitchens and storerooms.[87] Another, slightly more salubrious, import from the United States was the cash register, which not only helped expedite payment by customers, but also allowed proprietors to uncover fraud among their employees. A 1912 advertisement by the American giant the National Cash Register Co., which claimed to provide complete records 'in total and detail of all sales', specifically promised to record 'what was sold in your absence'. The advertisement, significantly, opened with the arresting appeal 'Do you get all your profit, Mr Restaurateur?'[88]

In the longer term, the appliance that most fully registered the intersection of the expanding restaurant sector with modernity was the telephone, which not only facilitated easier contact with food and kitchenware purveyors, but also allowed customers to book tables and request special menus. Already by the turn of the century, an increasing number of restaurants that advertised in newspapers, journals, and theatre programmes included (in addition to their postal address) a telephone number.[89] Even Newnham-Davis, who prided himself on the personal touch in his relations with restaurant proprietors, managers, and chefs, recorded that he used the telephone to make a booking at the Savoy. When told there was space only in a supplementary room, Newnham-Davis insisted that Monsieur Echenard, the manager, come to the telephone. The manager informed the colonel that he would do what he could, but, interestingly, Newnham-Davis still felt it necessary, having 'switched off the telephone', immediately to take a cab to the Savoy to secure his table and pick the menu.[90]

Traveller, and Hotel Review, 7 June 1884, p. 17; 'An Amusing Exhibition of Cookery', *Hotel Review and Catering & Food Trades' Gazette* (February 1887), 32.

[86] 'Special Souvenir Supplement to the *Caterer*', *Caterer*, 15 November 1898, pp. 535, 545, 554–5.

[87] 'A New Cockroach Destroyer', *Caterer*, 16 March 1885, p. 63.

[88] 'Advertisement', *Restaurateur* (August 1912), 2.

[89] For example, see the advertisements in the following: 'Restaurant Frascati', *Pall Mall Gazette*, 22 March 1897, p. 3; 'Romano's Restaurant', and 'Berkeley Restaurant', *Pall Mall Gazette*, 24 May 1897, p. 3; programme, Tivoli, 22 July 1904, cup. 1247 ccc. 5, William Edmonds Collection, British Library; programme, Oxford Music Hall, 1908, ACC 3527/2, Lyons Archive, London Metropolitan Archives [hereafter LMA].

[90] Nathaniel Newnham-Davis, *Dinners and Diners: Where and how to Dine in London* (London: Grant Richards, 1899), 73–4.

Convenience and comfort became increasingly important to securing customers in what became a highly competitive market. In addition to electric lighting, restaurants introduced various forms of ventilation, revolving doors, and plate glass windows (the latter aligning the restaurant with that most modern feature of *fin-de-siècle* metropolitan consumption, the department store, and distancing it from the opaque windows of the traditional chophouse). Restaurant interiors were regularly updated and improved. For example, after a disastrous fire, the Bay Tree was refurbished, with the inclusion of new facilities such as an oyster bar and billiard rooms.[91] Restaurateurs not only endeavoured to raise their establishments to a standard that matched the expectations of customers. They also sought ways to isolate the novelty and distinctiveness of their particular restaurant. Many restaurants had a signature dish. Galt's in Cheapside was known for its turtle soup, while at the Dolphin, also in the City, the owners sold oysters that they had farmed themselves in Essex.[92] Some restaurants drew attention to novel features within, or the general opulence of, their interiors. At Magog's in Cheapside, there were stained-glass windows and a clock with movable figures.[93] Both the Tivoli restaurant and the Hotel Cecil in the Strand had dining rooms decorated in what purported to be Indian style.[94] The Holborn Restaurant was renowned for the succession of increasingly ornate dining rooms, which were the outcome of a series of remodellings (supplemented by fireproof floor boards and Edison electric lighting) that took place in the 1880s and 1890s.[95] The Holborn was also said to be the first restaurant to introduce music at the *table d'hôte*.[96] While some high-end restaurants had orchestras or bands, some others could opt to provide more novel forms of musical entertainment. For instance, in 1912, restaurant proprietors could avail themselves of the Harper Electric Piano, which, sold either with or without slot attachment, 'pleases the patrons and increases trade'.[97] Other restaurants sought patrons through offering supplementary services. The St Paul's

[91] 1 January 1890, Restaurant Files, box A–B, London Cuttings, Bishopsgate.

[92] 'Turtle Soup for the Million: A New Cheapside Enterprise', November 1903, Nobel Collection, C.23.1, Guildhall Library, London; 25 November 1885, Restaurant Files, box C–F, London Cuttings, Bishopsgate.

[93] 'The Cheapside Clock', 8 April 1876, Restaurant Files, box M–P, London Cuttings, Bishopsgate.

[94] 'The New Tivoli Restaurant', 8 August 1888, Restaurant Files, box T–Z, London Cuttings, Bishopsgate; 'The Great Caravanserai: A Ramble over the Hotel Cecil', *Westminster Budget*, 8 May 1896, p. 5.

[95] 'Extending the Holborn Restaurant', 13 October 1894, Restaurant Files, box G–L, London Cuttings, Bishopsgate.

[96] See 'The Holborn Restaurant', *Era*, 5 October 1895, p. 16.

[97] 'Trade Card Index', *Restaurateur* (April 1912), 32.

Café and Restaurant adopted a series of initiatives to attract customers, including (in 1884) not only its popular sixpenny fish dinners, but also the provision of rooms where men could receive a shave or haircut, and a lavatory for ladies in the basement.[98]

Competition also necessitated publicity and advertising.[99] Discussions in the trade testify to the necessity of attracting the attention of potential customers, even if the initiatives suggested were sometimes outlandish and unrealized. A paper on 'the Science of Advertising' presented at the annual Coffee Tavern Conference in 1888 recommended that an eating house might project a dissolving view on the wall outside, a series of pictorial advertisements presented in rapid succession, in which 'business and beauty combined and eminent men are sandwiched between gastronomic proclamations'. The speaker suggested, for example, 'a lovely scene on the Rhine is followed by the invitation to "try our excellent porkpies and German sausages." A portrait of Gladstone. Then perhaps Irish stew, 3*d*. a plate. A view of the Cobden Hotel succeeded by "short cakes"', the latter suggestion provoking 'loud laughter' among the audience.[100] An article in the *Hotel* in 1895 proposed that London restaurants adopt an attention-grabbing novelty found in some New York and San Francisco restaurants, in which businessmen were served lunch by waitresses wearing New Woman outfits: 'surely...the heroine of Du Maurier would prove a draw'.[101] If such arresting ideas were not transferable to London, it is still the case that restaurateurs did seek imaginative ways to draw attention to their establishments. James Harris put a portrait of himself over the entrance to his sausage and pork house on Oxford Street 'with eyes that glance up and down the busy street, in quite a business like way, as if in quest of customers'.[102] Slightly more technologically advanced, the Café d'Italie used an electric light in a glass drum projected over the front door to call attention to the restaurant and inform customers 'that *table d'hôte* meals can be had there'.[103] A display of live turtles in one

---

[98] 'The St Paul's Café and Restaurant', 12 March 1884, Restaurant Files, box Q–S, London Cuttings, Bishopsgate.

[99] For a general survey, see Thomas Richards, *The Commodity Culture of Victorian England: Advertising and Spectacle, 1851–1914* (Stanford: Stanford University Press, 1990). For a contemporary reflection of the range and significance of advertising practices in this period, see Thomas Russell (ed.), *Advertising and Publicity* (London: Educational Book Co., 1911).

[100] 'The Annual Coffee Tavern Conference', *Refreshment News*, 15 September 1888, p. 5.

[101] *Hotel*, 25 December 1895, p. 20.

[102] 'Watchman's Notes', *Refreshment News*, 24 November 1888, p. 4.

[103] Cuttings, 'Dinners and Diners: The Café d'Italie', September 1899, Norman Collection, 101b, London Guildhall Library.

restaurant window was accompanied by the sign 'tomorrow we are to be made into turtle soup'.[104] The trade press urged restaurants to adopt artistic window dressing to entice customers, although complaints about mouldy English restaurant windows never seemed to go away.[105]

Many restaurants relied on long established forms of publicity, notably the man with the sandwich board who walked up the street advertising a dining room, or the distribution of a bill of fare to local businesses. This latter expedient reflected a broader symbiotic relationship between restaurants and other businesses, since menus often featured advertisements placed by a variety of retailers (including tailors and hatters, sellers of alcohol and aerated drinks) and services (including hotels and, in one case, a Turkish bath).[106] 'The Science of Advertising' speaker, sceptical about the value of handbills (which he felt were seen as a nuisance and liable to be thrown away), argued that it might be better instead to produce small cards in the colours of a local football club or stamped out in the shape of a cup and saucer or a meat chop.[107] He also suggested the benefits of advertising in different languages (namely, French and German) to attract patrons from overseas. Restaurants also obviously advertised in newspapers, and in published guides to London intended for both domestic and overseas visitors. As early as the 1870s, the *International Travellers' Journal* advertised a number of establishments said to be frequented by 'foreigners' and which catered to their particular needs and tastes. In the case of one house, the Wiener Bier Halle und Restaurant in the Strand, the advertisement pointed to its German, French, and English kitchen, which presumably offered a hybrid menu.[108] In the next decades, those restaurants with name recognition, such as the Trocadero, Langham Hotel, Holborn Restaurant, Frascati's, Hotel Cecil, and Florence Restaurant (to name a few), created their own publicity machine, publishing in-house souvenir booklets containing illustrations of their splendid buffet, dining, grill, and coffee rooms (and, in some cases, reading and smoking rooms,

---

[104] 'Restaurant Window Displays', *Caterer*, 15 October 1898, p. 513.

[105] See, for instance, 'Window Dressing', *Caterer*, 16 August 1886, p. 224, as well as related complaints in City chophouses mentioned in the previous chapter.

[106] See, for instance, menu, Restaurant Exeter Hall, 1892, item No. 1892–124, Buttolph Collection of Menus, New York Public Library. There was concern about the disfiguring effect of advertisements on menus, which were seen as an affront to more refined sensibilities. See 'Advertisement Menu', *Caterer*, 15 July 1885, p. 175.

[107] 'The Annual Coffee Tavern Conference', *Refreshment News*, 15 September 1888, p. 5.

[108] See advertisements in the *International Travellers' Journal* (January 1873), 7. Restaurant advertisements (including phone numbers) later appear in the London food guide by Newnham-Davis, *Dinners and Diners*.

courtyards, and gardens) for the purpose of distinguishing themselves from the competition.[109]

Of course, restaurant managers and owners were sometimes obliged to accompany their pursuit of ever-increasing numbers of customers with the necessity of excluding diners deemed to be undesirable. In this context, an intriguing document is to be found in the archives of J. Lyons and Co. Ltd. This takes the form of a list of 'persons to be Refused Admittance', most probably to the Trocadero Restaurant. The list, dating from 1898, comprised thirty-two individuals (including one woman) all identified by names, or at least surnames. In some cases, the name was accompanied by a short description of the previous offence in the restaurant, or other indication that elements of the individual's prior history may have failed to match the scrupulous standards of respectability that Lyons liked to represent. One of 'the Brothers Brown' was identified as a dangerous thief, the other as having 'no money to spend'. Ryley, Appletree, Fraser, and Piper had all served a term of imprisonment. Closer to home, a Mr Murray had apparently been 'drunk, [and] created a disturbance', as had someone identified (in an indication that Lyons' emphasis on self-discipline and probity applied across the social spectrum) as 'Rev. Young'. Someone called Townsend had been found fighting in the buffet, while George English used 'filthy expressions' in the same part of the restaurant. Other individuals were merely labelled as 'loafer' or 'undesirable', while Gordon Keyvett was deemed 'impossible to satisfy'.[110]

Even if a restaurant was able to bring in (desirable) customers and see off its competitors, the provision of public eating could still be a risky affair. The fortunes of individual restaurants inevitably matched ebbs and flows of the wider economy, although the period often identified as the so-called Great Depression of the late nineteenth century actually coincided with the expansion of the restaurant sector. Commenting on the official statistics supplied by the Board of Trade, the *Caterer* pointed out that, while 1893 might be marked as a year of 'gloom if not disaster' in many trades, the depression had not been as severely felt by restaurant keepers as it was by other businesses. Indeed, the number of bankruptcies among

[109] *Souvenir of the Trocadero* (London, 1901), Food and Drink Box, 34/127/13, Museum of London; *The Langham Hotel Guide to London Prepared for the Use of Visitors* (London, 1881); Frederick Leal, *Holborn Restaurant Illustrated* (London: Holborn Restaurant, 1894), D 93.2 London Collection Pamphlets, Box 323/38, Bishopsgate; [Frederick Leal], *The Restaurant Frascati*, with illustrations by Horace Morehen (London: Spottiswoode and Co., 1894), D 93.2, London Collection Pamphlets, Box 322/6, Bishopsgate; *The Hotel Cecil* (London: Hotel Cecil, 1896), D 93.1 London Collection Pamphlets, Box 323/35, Bishopsgate; *The Florence Restaurant* (London, c.1900), D 93.2 London Collection Pamphlets, Box 323/18, Bishopsgate.

[110] J. Lyons and Co. Reference Book, ACC 3527/186, p. 13, Lyons Archive, LMA.

restaurants and coffee houses gazetted in 1893 was twenty-five, a decline from twenty-eight the previous year.[111] Even a well-capitalized business with clear profit margins, in a period of general economic prosperity, faced the potential catastrophic risks of fire, a far from negligible hazard in establishments that employed open ranges on stoves in their kitchens. Both the trade and national press regularly reported fires that consumed a number of well-known London restaurants.[112] Some entrepreneurs used fires as an opportunity to renovate and improve their premises, but inevitably lost money in the interim.[113]

If the risk of fire had been a perennial problem in London, some of the inconveniences the restaurant faced were much more novel. The processes of urban expansion and modernization, of which the enlarged restaurant sector of the late nineteenth century was itself a product, sometimes placed dining establishments in conflict with the prerogatives of metropolitan transportation. Some restaurateurs, like Mr Tenchio mentioned earlier, were obliged to leave their premises, forced out by the expansion of rail lines and stations. However, overall the development of suburban rail lines benefited restaurants in the urban core, since daily commuters required lunch at places in proximity to their offices. By contrast, the regulation of street traffic often proved to be a more taxing issue for restaurant owners. In 1901, two solicitors wrote to the Chief Commissioner of the Metropolitan Police on behalf of a Mrs Baker, proprietor of an eating house on the Harrow Road in Paddington. Their client's business was highly dependent on the custom of carmen, whose horse-drawn vehicles were still responsible for the conveyance of goods and people around the city. She was therefore suffering a severe loss of business when the police ordered these carmen not to stop outside her restaurant, but to move on in order not to block traffic. Mrs Baker insisted that she had done everything to prevent any such obstruction, by employing someone to

---

[111] 'Caterer Notebook', *Caterer*, 15 February 1894, p. 60.

[112] Throughout the period, references to fires appeared in the press. See, for instance, 'Fire at Brompton', *The Times*, 7 January 1863, p. 7; 'City Restaurant, Milk Street', 6 March 1875, Restaurant Files, box C–F, London Cuttings, Bishopsgate; 'Ruttermann's Restaurant', 11 December 1878, Restaurant Files, box Q–S, London Cuttings, Bishopsgate; 'Simpson's', *Caterer*, 15 March 1898, p. 141. For a very early example, see 'Saturday March 8...Excise Office Coffee House', 8 March 1794, Restaurant Files, box C–F, London Cuttings, Bishopsgate.

[113] For instance, the Old Burton Tavern and Restaurant seemed to be a money pit, as it went through several changes of management, upgrades, and auctions in the 1880s and early 1890s. See 'The "Old Burton"', 29 December 1880; 'The Old Burton Tavern and Restaurant', 3 November 1883; 'Ye Old Burton Tavern', 22 March 1884; 'Ye Old Burton Coffee House', 2 April 1888; 'The Old Burton', 8 November 1890; 'Cheapside-Old Established Tavern', 12 December 1891; 'Sale by Order of the Mortgagees', 12 March 1892, all in Restaurant Files, box M–P, London Cuttings, Bishopsgate.

look after the cabs while the carmen were inside her dining room.[114] The police, while sympathetic to Mrs Baker, a widow with children, declared that, since there were a number of similar establishments on the same road, any dispensation to her would have to be applied to her neighbours, which would make the problem of street congestion even worse.[115] Two years later, a representative of the Carmen's Trade Union petitioned the Home Office to request that police take charge of cabs for forty-five minutes, while the men who drove them had the opportunity to have their meals.[116] Not surprisingly, the Home Office turned down this request, although it did hope that future official enquiries into London street traffic might consider expedients such as the creation of designated stands to accommodate carmen while they took refreshment.[117] It would be too easy to reduce Mrs Baker's story to the conflict between ordinary citizens (whether business people or workers) and the regulatory structures of the state. In fact, it tells us more about the restaurant's place in a complex pattern of commercial forces that could be both complementary and competing. If Mrs Baker's eating house was floundering, it was less because of petty officialdom and more because she was obliged to defer to the commercial pressures of neighbouring (and undoubtedly rival) establishments and the needs of businesses to move goods and people through the increasingly crowded streets in the metropolis.

While Mrs Baker's modest establishment was likely to have been typical of restaurants whose narrow profit margins made them particularly precarious, the restaurant sector more generally proved to be one characterized by instability, and even regular failure. Press cuttings in the Bishopsgate Library are a testimony to the regular presence of restaurants on the auction block.[118] Size, longevity, and initial capitalization were no guarantees against restaurant closure (see Figure 2.1). In 1890, Lucas's Luncheon and Dining Salon on Parliament Street in Westminster closed,

---

[114] Letter to the Chief Commissioner of Police from Bourgognes and Greatbach, 4 March 1901, MEPO/2/520, TNA.

[115] Metropolitan Police Report, Paddington F Division, 4 March 1901, MEPO/2/520, TNA.

[116] Deputation from the Trade Union Congress Parliamentary Committee, 'Street Stands for Carmen', attached to Letter to the Commissioners of Police, 18 February 1903, MEPO/2/520, TNA.

[117] Reply to Deputation, by Mr Akers Douglas to Trade Union Congress Parliamentary Committee, February 1903, MEPO/2/520, TNA. In the era of the motorized cab that followed, this issue was resolved in part by the creation of the designated, now iconic, green taxi refreshment cabin.

[118] See Restaurant Files, London Cuttings, Bishopsgate. For the broader context of bankruptcy in the nineteenth century, see V. Markham Lester, *Victorian Insolvency: Bankruptcy, Imprisonment for Debt, and Company Winding-up in Nineteenth-Century England* (Oxford: Oxford University Press, 1995).

Figure 2.1. Unidentified restaurant with signs in window stating 'premises closing down', 1890. (Reproduced with permission of the London Metropolitan Archives, City of London)

after Mr Lucas had occupied the premises for thirty years.[119] By contrast, the Daily, which opened in the City in 1877, was already on the auction block a year later.[120] Despite elaborate refitting and redecoration in 1888, the Tivoli on the Strand had closed by 1891.[121] Even a high level of name recognition and reputation for quality could not save Webster's, a well-known City restaurant, from coming to the auction block in 1889, when its proprietor died.[122] A major cause of restaurant closure was the expiry of the lease, although some establishments certainly succumbed to bankruptcy or insufficient profit, as in the case of Jules Charles Gaillard mentioned earlier.[123] Nevertheless some restaurants were sold as going

    [119] 'Lucas's High Class Luncheon and Dining Salon', 22 February 1890, Restaurant Files, box G–L, London Cuttings, Bishopsgate.
    [120] 'A New City Restaurant', 18 August 1877, and 'Licensed City Restaurant', 19 June 1878, Restaurant Files, box C–F, London Cuttings, Bishopsgate.
    [121] 'The New Tivoli Restaurant', 8 August 1888, and 'The Tivoli up for Sale', 29 April 1891, Restaurant Files, box T–S, London Cuttings, Bishopsgate.
    [122] 'For Absolute Sale', 15 June 1889, Restaurant Files, box T–Z, London Cuttings, Bishopsgate.
    [123] See nn. 8–10; on profit loss a few years earlier in another part of the city, see 'Great Eastern Coffee Palace', 19 May 1883, Restaurant Files, box G–L, London Cuttings, Bishopsgate.

concerns. The Mercantile restaurant on Leadenhall Street, which also belonged to Mr Webster of Webster's fame, was auctioned in 1889 as 'an independent business done at large profits', its attractiveness presumably enhanced by its possession of a 'valuable lease' and the fact that its success had been achieved despite conducting trade 'during short hours' and remaining closed on Sunday.[124] Many restaurants closed in one location, only to reopen somewhere else. In 1892, the lease expired on the venerable Jerusalem Coffee House situated in Cowper's Court in Cornhill, but the establishment relocated to the Billiter Buildings.[125] Some restaurants remained in the same location, but changed name. The Ye Three Cups in the City, of *The Pickwick Papers* fame, demolished in 1889, was rebuilt as the Clarence Hotel, but then became Coltman's in 1906, and later the Clarence in the interwar period.[126]

Running a restaurant in late Victorian and Edwardian London was an occupation beset with a dizzying mix of risk and reward, as the contrasting financial histories of Steffano Gatti and Jules Charles Gaillard, with which this chapter opened, reveal. As a business enterprise, the restaurant could be aligned with broader narratives of expansion and increased sophistication in the metropolitan economy more generally. Prestigious restaurants secured capitalization through recourse to the stock exchange. Dining rooms were increasingly overseen by specialized managers, reflecting a divorce of ownership and control that marked the emerging 'managerial revolution'. Restaurant proprietors and managers resorted to specialized agencies to find staff and also sought efficiency and increased comfort for their customers by the use of modern technology. Those restaurant proprietors and managers (and even cooks) who sought social recognition, and not merely financial gain, looked to schemes (executed and unrealized) to establish their status as professionals.[127] Irrespective of contemporary debates at the national level about the virtues of free trade and the increasing authority of local and national government, the restaurant remained emblematic of an ongoing commitment in Victorian and Edwardian culture to the practice of free enterprise and the sustenance

---

[124] 'For Sale by the Direction of Executors', 15 June 1889, Restaurant Files, box M–P, London Cuttings, Bishopsgate.

[125] 'City of London', 16 July 1892, Restaurant Files, box G–L, London Cuttings, Bishopsgate.

[126] '25th Anniversary, Four Million Lunches Served in 25 Years at the Clarence Restaurant', *City Press*, 17 July 1931, n.p., Noble Collection, Guildhall Library, London.

[127] For the late-nineteenth-century preoccupation with professional status, see Harold Perkin, *The Rise of Professional Society: England since 1880* (London: Routledge, 1989); Daniel Duman, 'The Creation and Diffusion of a Professional Ideology in Nineteenth Century England', *Sociological Review*, 27 (1979), 113–38.

of a robust commercial domain.[128] That said, there was something distinctive about the restaurant as a business enterprise. The regular appearance of eating houses on the auction block highlights the frustratingly peculiar status of the restaurant in the urban landscape, ubiquitous yet ephemeral, vital yet transient. The fluidity and complexity of the restaurant was also characteristic of those who worked within it. This was particularly true of waiters, the nature of whose work underlined their impermanency (not to say indeterminacy) in the labour market, even as they established a prominent place in the popular imagination. It is to this intriguing contradiction surrounding the waiter that we now turn.

[128] For works that emphasize the continued centrality of the market (albeit as a political, ideological, and legal construct rather than a natural and neutral phenomenon) in late Victorian and Edwardian Britain, see Trentmann, *Free Trade Nation*; Paul Johnson, 'Market Disciplines', in Peter Mandler (ed.), *Liberty and Authority in Victorian Britain* (Oxford: Oxford University Press, 2006).

3

Waiting in the Restaurant

In *The Town Traveller* (1898), George Gissing's classic depiction of some of the more deracinated figures who populated the late-nineteenth-century London imaginary, we are introduced to the character of Polly Sparkes.[1] Polly is an unattractively greedy, petulant, and confrontational figure, an imperious social climber who inflates her own standing in the lodging house where she is an ungrateful tenant. She treats her fellow lodgers with withering contempt and cruelly flaunts an expensive gold watch chain in front of her landlady and a potential suitor. However, Polly nurses a secret sense of shame in the form of her estranged father, whose ostensibly inferior status is a source of acute embarrassment to her: 'And Mr Sparkes was a waiter, had been a waiter for some thirty years, and would probably pursue the calling as long as he was fit for it' (p. 52). While Mr Sparkes saw nothing to be ashamed of in his occupation, Gissing nevertheless portrays him as 'a disappointed, even an embittered man', and, in so doing, provides one of the more memorable renderings of the London waiter as an abject and distressed figure in the urban landscape, a trope that was not uncommon in literary and popular cultural texts of the period, and was often grounded in the reality of the grim life of waiters.

Mr Sparkes's character was weak, compromised even further by the fact that (against his better judgement) he continues to work in an establishment that has been converted from an old chophouse into a modern restaurant, after a young man 'with new ideas' took over the business. He grows more despondent the more he talks about the change, adding with doleful self-reproach: 'If I'd been half a man I should have left' (p. 56). True, the new Chaffey's 'remained English, flagrantly English, in its viands and its waiters', but its atmosphere was degraded by the 'large hall, painted and gilded and set about with mirrors, furnished with marble tables and cane-bottomed chairs—to

---

[1] George Gissing, *The Town Traveller* (London: Methuen, 1898). Subsequent references are in the text.

all appearances a restaurant on the Franco-Italian pattern', according to Sparkes (pp. 53–4). He also disliked the new clientele: 'his "thank you, sir" had the urbanity which had become mechanical, but more often than not he sneered inwardly, despising himself and those upon whom he waited' (p. 55). Gissing gives some sense that the waiter's life, at least for Mr Sparkes, was not all despondency and gloom. Sparkes himself concedes that the transformation of his place of employment has provided him with higher wages and increased tips. When he decides to write to Polly to criticize her behaviour and 'way of carrying on', he reveals that he has been 'a respectable and a saving man' and has been able to put away a not inconsiderable sum of money (indeed 'there may be more than you think for', he tells her) (p. 60). Polly is taken by surprise by this disclosure, which causes her to reflect that 'Chaffey's head-waiter had long held a tolerably lucrative position, whilst his expenses must have been trivial; so much the better for her' (p. 61). Underneath the premise of the disaffected, disrespected, and ineffectual waiter, Gissing hints at the possibilities of personal security and advancement that were available to those who waited at tables in London's restaurants. Such ambivalent understandings of the waiter feature in myriad other sites, and reveal the complex status of the waiter in the labour market, and in the cultural formations of London, at this time.

The London waiter could be represented as an object of pity and even abjection, and seen as a marginal, melancholy figure. Certainly, there were waiters who were exploited or, at the very least, seriously undervalued. However, it might be more useful to see the waiter as a key social actor in a metropolitan environment characterized by the power of commercial and capitalist forces. If these forces could render the waiter a degraded victim of exploitation, they also offered the opportunity for him to benefit from an economy that was remarkably open and dynamic. In particular, the heterogeneity of public eating, and the transnational nature of the restaurant service economy, created opportunities for mobility and even advancement. The rapid growth and diversity of the restaurant sector also provided the context for the emergence of the waitress in the closing decades of the nineteenth century.

The London waiter is most obviously a representative of the increased size and sophistication of the service sector in late-nineteenth-century Britain. However, incorporating restaurant servers into the broader narratives of employment and labour history in this period is far from straightforward. While a dualistic vision of capital and labour became increasingly significant in political discourses after the 1880s, historians have long been alert to the insufficiency of this binary as a description of how British society operated.[2] In particular, while the opportunities for social mobility among some sections of society (notably the very poor) were scant, there was a considerable amount of movement across the frontier between the upper reaches of the working class and the lower middle class. Waiters, whose working lives encompassed the possibilities of both social and geographical mobility, might be seen as a particularly arresting example of these more dynamic understandings of class.[3] Indeed, the ability of some waiters to convert gratuities into savings might suggest it is better to consider them, not so much as workers, but rather as small entrepreneurs.

Given this, it is perhaps not surprising that the waiter possesses an ambiguous status within the history of trade unionism. In the last four decades of the nineteenth century, the traditional craft unions had already achieved acceptability of collective bargaining as a legitimate aspect of employment, at least in the eyes of progressive opinion. The expanding boundaries of organized labour, particularly its increasing reach to both unskilled and female workers, was dramatically demonstrated in the 1880s by two London-based labour disputes: the 1889 Dock Strike and the 1888 Match Girls' Strike. While most unions exploited a relatively cooperative industrial-relations environment to demand higher wages and improved working conditions, the provision of mutual insurance benefits (especially prior to limited introduction of old age pensions and national insurance in 1908–11) played an important role in attracting and retaining members. Waiters and waitresses were not untouched by these broader developments. However, even when they chose to organize (and on some occasions even to strike), the nature of their employment distinguished them from those for whom organization and action came more readily.[4] The fact that some waiters' unions were organized on an international, rather than only a national, basis further added to their distinctiveness. The demand of organizations representing waiters for both a living wage and, simultaneously, the right to retain their individual tips is but just one example of the awkward fit between the working lives of

---

[2] For a forceful articulation of this point, see Jose Harris, *Private Lives. Public Spirit: A Social History of Britain, 1870–1914* (Oxford: Oxford University Press, 1993), 8–9.

[3] For acknowledgement of the 'vast and unnumbered race who worked for themselves and others on a catch-as-catch-can basis', see Ross McKibbin, 'Why Was There No Marxism in Great Britain?', *English Historical Review*, 99 (April 1984), 299–300. However, McKibbin does not include waiters in his discussion of the sections of the working class that existed in an 'occupational world of chance and quick-wittedness' outside collectivist politics.

[4] This may also explain the absence of waiters (and indeed the service sector more generally) from standard histories of organized labour in Britain. For example, see Alastair J. Reid, *United We Stand: A History of Britain's Trade Unions* (London: Allen Lane, 2004).

restaurant servers and the conventional strategies and discourses of trade unionism. This chapter highlights the particularity (if not singularity) of those who waited on restaurant tables, even as it presents them as emblematic of wider metropolitan identities and practices.

If the bitterness of Gissing's Mr Sparkes is rooted in the pressures of new forms of dining, the character of the melancholy waiter featured in several other cultural texts from this period. In the satirical column 'On Waitin'', published in the *British Journal of Catering*, one Alec Finch, 'a professional waiter', describes erratic pay as but one example of the oppression common in his trade: 'sometimes [waiters] hain't pade at all, but has to pay for the privilege of waitin'', referring to a system by which they paid restaurant proprietors for their position, in exchange for keeping the tips that diners left them. Moreover, waiters had to share tips with assistants or pay 'taxes' to other members of staff 'which guv'nors is heither unawares on, or winks hat'. In this environment, 'it's the waiters as is weak, and the guv'nors make the terms, wich they naturally does to their best advantage in consekvence of the competishun', from the large pool of waiters (both foreign and domestic) looking for work. According to Finch, the system was made worse by the fact that the waiter had no place to air his grievances, the remedy for which, to him, was clear: 'The waiters of this 'ere kuntry must combine to form hinstitooshuns, and guv'nors must 'elp the hinstitootshuns, two; if guv'nors will 'elp the waiters, waiters 'elp the guv'nors.'[5]

If this caricature was aimed at a trade audience familiar with the subject, references to the frustrated and underappreciated waiter were also to be found in texts with a broader public exposure. *Robert; or, Notes from the Diary of a City Waiter* (1885), written originally for *Punch*, offers an exaggerated rendering of the inexpert handling of the formal tone that was clearly associated with waiters by the broader public. This particular Robert (the term was widely used to refer to English waiters) is seen as pretentious and supercilious, but also constantly put upon. He receives pitiful tips, feels under pressure from more effective foreign waiting staff, and baulks at having to deal with a thoughtless public. Because the waiter in the reputable eating house had to have knowledge of fine wines and rarified menus, and donned formal dress, the diners confused wealth with knowledge (see Figure 3.1).[6] Those who worked in these environments

    [5] Alec Finch, 'On Waitin'', by 'The Waiter', *British Journal of Catering*, 1 May 1888, p. 255.
    [6] John Thomas Bedford, *Robert; or, Notes from the Diary of a City Waiter* (London, 1885), 112.

Figure 3.1. From *Robert; or, Notes from the Diary of a City Waiter* (1885), illustration by Charles Keene. (Reproduced with permission of the Bishopsgate Institute)

were not necessarily beneficiaries of them, evidenced, according to Robert, by the often small tips left by the diners. Frustrations ensued when diners failed to pay attention to the hard work that went into the meal's preparation and demonstrated more interest in business matters (Robert was, after all, a City waiter).[7]

---

[7] *Ibid.* 121.

In the music hall song 'Waiter, Waiter' (1895), the diners were more than just inattentive, they were rude. Among a catalogue of abusive encounters, the waiter recalls how

> a fat old girl came in last week
> And ordered a mutton pie
> She looked at it, and smelt at it,
> then pitched it in my eye.
> She told me the crust was hard,
> And the meat was bad,
> They want too much for money
> They nearly drive me mad.[8]

The diner was not only represented as combative, but might also be seen as irritatingly demanding. In 'A Waiter's Tale of Woe' (1897), the waiter tries to tell his plaintive story about a failed romance, but is constantly interrupted by diners requiring service, and therefore the song dramatizes the inability of the waiter to have any privacy.[9] In both cases, audience members were meant to sympathize with the waiter by singing the chorus in songs about his ill-treatment inflicted by diners, thus underpinning the theme of social isolation common in music-hall song.

There is no doubt that the complaints of the fictional Robert would have been shared by many actual waiters. Judging from the commentary and letters that feature in the trade and general press, waiters appeared to be in a state of constant dudgeon about their lives. As with other categories of workers, there were the inevitable complaints about poor working conditions, long hours, and inadequate wages. This was particularly true of those employed in the cheap dining rooms that burgeoned in the City. One writer, who had been driven by temporary hard luck to join 'the waiting fraternity' at a squalid Cannon Street dining room (whose dimensions he calculated as being 10 feet by 30 feet with a 7-foot ceiling), complained about 'the constant ingress and egress of diners, the clamour of the hungry to be served, the sickly steam from the dinners, and the constant struggling up and down the narrow central passage with loads of plates'.[10] Likening the experience of serving to jostling for space on an omnibus, he was further burdened by the need to keep a sharp eye open 'that none should slip out without paying'. This scrum (from twelve to two o'clock) required 'a dogged endurance to which a march over the

---

[8] Tom Huntley, 'Waiter, Waiter' (London: London Music Publishing, 1895).

[9] Albert Perry and Steve Leggett, 'A Waiter's Tale of Woe' (London: Francis, Day & Hunter, 1897).

[10] 'A Waiter's Experiences', *Caterer*, 15 September 1885, p. 237. First appeared in *Pall Mall Gazette*.

burning sands of the Soudan must have been mere child's play'. To add insult to injury, he was cheated out of his tips by a fellow waiter and forced to endure the meals provided by his employer.[11] This amounted to 'a dirty plate of adulterated gravy or discoloured hot water, in which a lump of fat was swimming about, called on alternate days roast beef and roast mutton', an unappetizing fare that (in his opinion) had to be endured by waiters at other cheap dining places.[12] If City waiters such as these thought they could take solace in having the rest of their day to recover and recuperate from the lunchtime melee (given that most City restaurants closed early), their paltry pay often obliged them to work as evening waiters elsewhere.[13]

Those requiring a comprehensive or consolidated list of the grievances (petty or more serious) felt by waiters would do worse than to reference an editorial in the first issue of the *Waiters' Record*, published in February 1900. Clearly, there was an element of special pleading here given that the publication was the organ of the Amalgamated Waiters' Society. The society was obviously not entirely oblivious to the benefits of highlighting the worst cases of exploitation, in order to bolster its campaign to improve wages and conditions. Nevertheless, its catalogue of complaints undoubtedly incorporated genuine sources of disaffection: The waiter

> has to spend long busy hours in rooms full of smoke and foul air. He has no time to think, and the lack of reflection on his part is one of the greatest obstacles to improvement of his condition. Very often waiters have to work from 16 to 18 hours per day, and on account of bad arrangements they seldom have sufficient time to eat their meals properly. Generally they have to gulp them down at odd moments, and they are usually either too hot or too cold.[14]

The long working hours also meant that they often suffered from varicose veins and swollen feet, as well as ill health more generally.[15] The claim by the *Waiters' Record* that the bedrooms of waiters, who had been offered accommodation by their employers, were often badly ventilated was endorsed by London County Council (LCC) inspectors' reports—for example, an investigation into 'the alleged insanitary condition of the sleeping apartments for waiters and others' in the basement of

---

[11] For a similar case, see 'Caterer's Notebook', *Caterer*, 15 June 1897, p. 295.

[12] 'A Waiter's Experiences', *Caterer*, 15 September 1885, p. 237. First appeared in *Pall Mall Gazette*.

[13] 'Work and Wages in Hotels and Restaurants', *Good Words* (1892), 756.

[14] 'Waiters' Grievances', *Waiters' Record* (February 1900), 2.

[15] Quoted from the Amalgamated Waiters' Society manifesto. 'The Wail of the Waiters: Contentment of the City', *Daily Mail*, 24 September 1897.

(the suitably named) Robert's restaurant in Lambeth's York Road.[16] The editor of the *Waiters' Record* went so far as to speculate that 'the mortality among waiters is very great indeed', adding that 'it is lamentable to find that suicide, especially of youths, figures very prominently as the cause of death'.[17] The editorial may have been vaguely histrionic, but those who wrote to the paper afterwards used it as a starting point to talk about their own exploitation, some of which had to do with wages. In a letter to the editor about his time at the Hotel Cecil, one waiter calling himself 'Napkin' described a very arbitrary system, in which his pay for evening work was steadily reduced from 7s. 6d. to 5s. to 4s., the change owing (he believed) to the arrival of a new head waiter. While he and other waiters were initially able to end their shifts after dinner, under the new head waiter they had to stay two or three hours longer after dinner had finished.[18] The veracity of cases like this in the *Waiters' Record* appears to be borne out by press reports of similar arbitrary regimes. In a case reported in the *Weekly Chronicle*, the attempt by the proprietor of 'one of the best known', if unnamed, West End hotels to reduce wages led to a mutiny by the waiters, who 'broke the mirrors, threw the china and glass about' the dining, coffee, and smoking rooms. In this case, they were invited back by the proprietor, who promised their previous wages, but not all such cases ended in mutual satisfaction.[19]

If the Amalgamated Waiters' Society's case for reform was bolstered by the testimony of individual waiters, it also attempted to substantiate its claims by naming individual establishments that it felt were particularly egregious. What amounted to a waiters' hall of shame was published in the March 1900 issue of the *Waiters' Record*, a list of thirteen separate restaurants, next to which were itemized the particular deleterious conditions found within. For example, Anderton's Hotel in Fleet Street, known by its waiting staff as the Dogs' Hole, was singled out for poor accommodation provided for its workers, the Palmerston restaurant in Old Broad Street for fining its waiters for being late, and the Freemasons' Tavern (owned by Spiers and Pond) in Great Queen Street in Covent Garden for wages of only 15s. a week with hardly any rest time.[20]

Where waiters had particular justification in drawing attention to the esoteric drawbacks of their occupation was in regard to the conventions of employee liability and the practice of deductions. Novelist Morley Roberts

[16] Sanitation report, complaint no. 37, 26 March 1903, Register 1, LCC/Ph/Reg/5/2, London Metropolitan Archives [hereafter LMA].

[17] 'Waiters' Grievances', *Waiters' Record* (February 1900), 2.

[18] 'Correspondence', *Waiters' Record* (April 1900), 3.

[19] 'General News', *Weekly Chronicle*, 25 August 1888, p. 7.

[20] 'Waiters' Conditions', *Waiters' Record* (March 1900), 1.

reported the convention by which, if a diner left the restaurant without paying his bill, the waiter 'loses the money, not the employer'.[21] A survey of work and wages by C. H. d' E. Leppington, Fellow of the Royal Economic Society, highlighted the particular disadvantages of this convention for those waiters employed under the so-called cheque system.[22] This system required the waiter, at the start of his day's work, to pay a deposit of between £2 and £5 to the proprietor to cover the value of the orders he was likely to receive during the day, and for which, in exchange, he was given a number of cheques. On taking an order from a diner, the waiter would hand in a cheque to the proprietor or clerk to an equivalent amount. Leppington claimed that, if the value of the orders exceeded the value of the deposit, 'the waiter must pay in more money before he receives the dishes'. Whether the waiter incurred further loses during the 'settling time' at the end of the day was not made clear. However, Leppington observed that, 'if the customer goes away without paying, the waiter must bear the loss'. To underline his point, Leppington relayed a specific case in which a customer, after enjoying a sumptuous dinner, informed the waiter that he was unable to pay, and 'must go to borrow it from a friend'. He offered to take the waiter with him, chartering a cab for the purpose. On arriving at the friend's house, the diner disappeared through a door and made his escape, leaving the unfortunate waiter with, not only the dinner to pay for, but also the cab fare, 'which might be considered, under the circumstances, as insult added to injury'.[23]

Formalized deductions suggested an affinity between late-nineteenth-century waiters and the conventions of early industrial employment cultures in which workers were required to take on a heavier burden of the operating costs in a more direct sense of paying for clothing and the use of equipment (practices that the various Truck Acts passed during the century tried to eliminate or mitigate).[24] This was especially true in cases where waiters had to pay for breakages—what was often referred to as 'glass money'. In 1897, the *Caterer* listed the deductions incumbent on waiters working in an (unnamed) 'large commercial establishment'. Out of a basic weekly wage of 10s., 3s. were deducted for 'glass money' and 3d. for the newspapers that they supplied to the guests.[25] The waiters were also required to compensate the porter, the plateman, and the

[21] Morley Roberts, 'Waiters and Restaurants', *Murray's Magazine*, 7 (1890), 538.
[22] C. H. d' E. Leppington, 'Work and Wages in Hotels and Restaurants', *Good Words*, 33 (1892), 755.
[23] *Ibid.*
[24] An intervention aimed at waitresses came only at the end of the century; see *Bills, Public &c.*, 'Waitresses Bill', 1898, Bill 244.
[25] 'Hors D'Oeuvre', *Caterer*, 15 February 1897, p. 100.

attendant in the servant's hall, each 6*d.* per week. After all the deductions had been made, the waiter was obviously left with approximately half his wages. However, the extent of deductions at this house may not have been representative, for the *Caterer* also reported that the Amalgamated Waiters' Society was intending to intervene 'in this unfortunate matter'.[26] Waiters were vulnerable to the myriad ways in which proprietors sought to limit costs and preserve profits in even the most quotidian aspects of restaurant work. In some cases, waiters received no wages at all. Leppington reported that foreign waiters in particular were entirely dependent on tips from customers, and even this was subject to a percentage cut enacted by their employers.[27] Roberts described 'a well-known West-end establishment' in which all that the waiters 'make is given them by the customers'.[28] Moreover, he also noted that waiters at this restaurant were required to pay 9*s.* a week for their board and the privilege of waiting.

As a consequence of having to endure these conditions, some waiters found it difficult to maintain respectability and supplemented their meagre living through fraud and theft.[29] While it is possible that the trade attracted poorly trained and inefficient workers, it is certainly the case that representations across a variety of sources portrayed the waiter as morally degraded. In an 'amusing sketch' that appeared in the *Echo* signed by 'About Town', the author lamented that the usual rules of mathematics were not applied to making up the diner's bill, recalling one instance in which the waiter overcharged him by half a shilling (a sum that the waiter may have added in lieu of a tip) for lunch at a City restaurant. When the diner pointed out that the sum was wrong, the waiter's disingenuous expression of surprise 'was worthy the study of a character painter'.[30] For good reason, then, the bottom of an 1882 menu from the Holborn Restaurant instructed: 'Gentlemen are respectfully requested to examine

---

[26] *Ibid.*   [27] Leppington, 'Work and Wages', 754.

[28] Roberts, 'Waiters and Restaurants', 538.

[29] For a broader context of nineteenth-century crime, see Clive Emsley, *Crime and Society in England, 1750–1900* (New York: Longman, 1987; repr. 1996). Crimes committed by employees in the workplace have received less attention than the crimes committed by shoppers, particularly female ones. See Tammy Whitlock, 'Gender, Medicine, and Consumer Culture in Victorian England: Creating the Kleptomaniac', *Albion*, 31/3 (1999), 413–37; for comparative studies of the USA and France, respectively, see Elaine S. Abelson, *When Ladies Go A-Thieving: Middle Class Shoplifters in the Victorian Department Store* (Oxford and New York: Oxford University Press, 1989); and Patricia O'Brien, 'The Kleptomania Diagnosis: Bourgeois Women and Theft in Late Nineteenth Century France', *Journal of Social History*, 17/1 (1983), 65–77.

[30] Reprinted in 'London Restaurants', *British Journal of Catering*, 1 November 1887, p. 53.

their Bills before paying the waiter.'[31] Attempts to inflate the bill were understandable—if not justified—because waiters were so poorly remunerated 'that they had to swindle the public in order to make up their wages', explained Paul Vogel at a meeting of the Amalgamated Waiters' Society. In reporting on the meeting, the *Caterer* commented that the audience was composed of waiters of all nationalities, conjecturing that their poor command over the English language made them unaware that their character was being maligned.[32] However, many knew from direct experience how morally suspect some of their fellow-waiters were, and were themselves the injured party. In one case, waiter Jean Pierzo robbed another waiter, Antonio Roncoroni, of the Cavour restaurant, of £160, a large sum for a waiter and possibly the man's life savings. Before the incident, Roncoroni had taken pity on Pierzo, who was then destitute and out of work. Supplying him with daily board and lodging without remuneration was clearly not enough, however. When Roncoroni discovered 'his room stripped of his valuables' and Pierzo gone, he went to Charing Cross rail station, 'thinking the accused might try to get away by the first Continental train', obviously pointing to the mobility of this workforce. Roncoroni then proceeded to Victoria station, where he found the man 'walking up and down the platform waiting for the booking office to open' and handed him over to the police, although not without first striking him repeatedly over the head with his stick.[33] If the case confounded hasty associations between criminality and foreign waiters (Roncoroni was, after all, the victim), the confusion persisted. A 1911 report on the workings of the Aliens Act accused unemployed waiters of regular recourse to criminality, prompting the trade paper, the *Restaurant*, to respond by asserting that, 'just as women of a certain class, when at the police court, usually describe themselves as actresses, so do criminal aliens conceal their want of any honest occupation by usurping the term, "waiter"'.[34] While such defence of the waiter was commendable, the allusion to popular understandings of prostitution here was as likely to reinforce associations between foreign waiters and crime as it was to confound them.

In the fevered imagination of some writers consumed with the waiter's underworld, his shady activities extended not merely to fraud and theft, but even to murder. At the centre of an 1880 short story, deliciously entitled 'The Romance of the Café D'Italia', that appeared in *All the Year*

[31] Menu, the Holborn Restaurant, 1 April 1882, A3 Food and Drink, 134/127/1, Museum of London.
[32] 'Caterer's Notebook', *Caterer*, 15 April 1898, p. 165.
[33] 'Law: Base Ingratitude', *British Journal of Catering*, 1 December 1887, p. 93.
[34] 'Trade Topics: The Foreign Waiter', *Restaurant* (August 1911), 290.

Round is a French waiter (albeit bearing the non-Gallic name of) Gustav Mas, who works at a small restaurant near Leicester Square, owned and staffed by Italians.[35] The story begins with the testimony of James Johnson, a member of the Stock Exchange. Johnson relates how he went to dinner with his colleague Reginald Richards at the Café D'Italia. During dinner, part of their conversation is overheard by Mas, who grows agitated to the point that, in the middle of dinner, he 'dropped a plate which he was bringing to us, and, as he stooped to pick up the pieces, we both noticed that he trembled very much and that his face was very white . . .'.[36] The waiter then returns, ostensibly to bring the men coffee, but he then proceeds to stand behind Richards, forcing his neck backwards and 'in a moment, cut[s] his throat from ear to ear'. The motive for Mas's crime is never fully established (it is possible that he has been roused to violent anger by overhearing Richards's slighting of a mutual female acquaintance), but the description of him possibly draws attention to the physical and mental burdens of the waiter's life. He is characterized as having, despite being only 40 years old, the appearance of 'a man fully twenty years above that age'.[37] Although he was a tall, muscular fellow, 'he had no strength or spirit to hold himself upright . . .'. He had 'great black eyes, marvellously mild for a murderer, you would say, with a wistful, weary look in them as of a tired over-worked animal; and big bony hands clasped upon his knees'.[38] Mas's debasement is registered in relation not merely to his body, but also to his clothes: 'He wears still [during the trial] his waiter's dress—a threadbare suit of seedy black, with a shirt that once was white, and round his neck, instead of a tie, a silk shoe-lace tied in a bow with its tag of brass dependent.'[39]

Violence was a motif in other uncongenial understandings of the waiter, but, in these cases, as victim rather than perpetrator. In an 1886 case brought before the Westminster Police Court, as reported in the *Caterer*, a waiter, A. Tinelli, found himself on the sharp end of an encounter with Mr Charles Harris, a self-described commission agent, who entered a Pimlico restaurant owned by one Innocent Rampazzi, and proceeded to order an array of items, including two bottles of the best port wine in the house.[40] Based on Harris's shabby appearance, Tinelli, having informed Rampazzi that 'the customer did not look quite the sort of gentleman to indulge in so expensive a repast', asked Harris to settle the bill, which amounted to 11*s*. 6*d*.[41] After Harris was pressed for payment, and it became clear he had no means to pay, the waiter informed him, 'if you

[35] 'The Romance of the Café D'Italia', *All the Year Round* (August 1880), 353.
[36] *Ibid.* 353.　　[37] *Ibid.* 353.　　[38] *Ibid.* 354.　　[39] *Ibid.* 354.
[40] 'Dining on Credit', *Caterer*, 15 June 1886, p. 186.　　[41] *Ibid.*

come here for a good dinner, and you refuse to pay, you have come to the wrong place'.[42] Harris responded by leaping up and striking Tinelli in the face, before he was taken to the police station. The shadow of violence hung over the waiter in more tragic circumstances. Another court case, reported on by the *Daily Mail* in 1899, related to one Mr Thomas Keddie, who worked at the Crystal Palace for fifteen years as a waiter before he was discharged 'owing to change in the catering'. At the age of 52, he found himself superfluous: 'all his efforts at getting another situation being futile, on account of his age.' A widower with grown married sons, 'somewhere, he found himself alone in the world'. With the few shillings he had left, he paid his rent and, in an act of desperation, tried to end his life by cutting his throat, an impassioned cry for help that proved to be ineffective. During Keddie's court hearing in which he was charged with attempted suicide, the police court missionary remarked that he was a 'very respectable and industrious man' while the chief clerk added that 'he did not look too old for the work of a waiter'.[43] Following his remand in the infirmary, the court promised that 'an attempt will be made to get some work for him when he recovers', but whether or not this gesture led to re-employment is unknown. These two cases, the reporting of which blended the discourses of violence with literary conventions of either farce or melodramatic tragedy, were obviously extreme, not to say esoteric. The representations and realities of the degraded waiter were much more likely to encompass poor working conditions, long hours, meagre pay, inadequate lodging, and bad food, rather than a bloody nose or a hospital bed. However, all in all, the anonymous writer in the *Caterer* might be forgiven for (referencing a famous stanza from Gilbert and Sullivan's *Pirates of Penzance*) asserting that 'the waiter's lot, any more than the policeman's, is not always a happy one'.[44]

For every case of disenchantment or degradation, there were clearly large numbers of waiters whose lives were characterized by satisfaction, and even success. Even some of the stories of waiters' misfortunes discussed previously could lend themselves to a more congenial reading by a slight adjustment in perspective. While the amateur waiter at the cramped

---

[42] *Ibid.*

[43] 'The Old Waiter's Despair', *Daily Mail*, 25 March 1899, p. 6. Police court missionaries were the precursors to modern probation officers, although the alternatives they offered to punitive sentencing continued to work within the parameters of a discretionary and moralized justice system, rather than its more modern and bureaucratic variant. See Sascha Auerbach, '"Beyond the Pale of Mercy": Victorian Penal Culture, Police Court Missionaries, and the Origins of Probation in England', *Law and History Review*, 33/3 (August 2015), 621–63.

[44] 'All About Waiters', *Caterer*, 15 June 1886, p. 179. The stanza in question is from the number 'When a Felon's not Engaged in his Employment'.

Cannon Street dining room was rightfully chagrined by being short-changed on his tips, we should not forget that his more experienced colleague stood to benefit from such conventions.[45] Likewise, the story of waiters Jean Pierzo and Antonio Roncoroni is a compelling reminder that one man's misfortune could be another man's gain.[46] Even without recourse to exploiting their co-workers, waiters did not necessarily despair and nor did they require pity. While their jobs clearly lacked security, waiters were able to benefit from working in a field of employment characterized by flexibility, opportunity, and mobility.

For a start, finding initial employment and moving between positions was facilitated, not merely by the constant turnover of staff in London's restaurants, but also by the existence of established conventions and informal networks. A sampling of advertisements from an 1879 issue of the *Hotel and Tavern Advertiser* taken out by waiters provides a glimpse into their working lives. One self-described 'Head Waiter', an Austrian, aged 32 and single, advertised his need for a situation, noting his fifteen years' work experience and fluency in French, German, and English.[47] Like-wise, an Italian waiter, aged 27, noted that he spoke four languages and listed the numerous hotels in which he had worked, in both England and Ireland.[48] Other waiters highlighted other details that they thought relevant for employment—for example, one German waiter noted his height while another mentioned that he was a teetotaller, an advantage in a trade where it was not unusual for aggrieved employees to filch drink, as well as food. Potential employers were then able to contact prospective employees through the newspaper. In some cases, this system was even more elaborate, with the creation of what were effectively employment agencies, which not merely solicited applications from waiters looking for work, but also collected references and offered employers yearly subscriptions. The British and Foreign Hotel Servants' Agency in South-ampton Row was one such organization that promised to save employers both time and trouble by 'making enquiries into servants' characters' and then sending to them 'only those of good character and ability'.[49] In return for a subscription, the agency allowed them up to ten servants annually, as well as a copy of the *Hotel and Tavern Advertiser*, whose 'help wanted' columns allowed them to find prospective staff without the help of a middle man. Although this obscure newspaper was short-lived, it was an early example of what other more enduring ones, such as

---

[45] 'A Waiter's Experiences', *Caterer*, 15 September 1885, p. 237. First appeared in *Pall Mall Gazette*.

[46] 'Law: Base Ingratitude', *British Journal of Catering*, 1 December 1887, p. 93.

[47] *Hotel and Tavern Advertiser*, 8 November 1879, p. 1.   [48] *Ibid.*   [49] *Ibid.*

the *Caterer*, continued to do, which was to create networks, matching prospective employer and employee. The offices of these agencies appear to be relatively ubiquitous: there were at least two agencies on Baker Street alone. Edward Stuart Humpheries recalled that in 1904, when he was 15, he went to the Baker Street Domestic Agency for an interview, and got a job as a page at the Almancks Club in Berkeley Street. After losing this job (owing to repeated lateness), he turned to Hunts' Domestic Registry Office, also located in Baker Street, which found him a job as a still-room boy at the Union Club in Trafalgar Square, a position that confined him to the basement where he did kitchen work (and which he again lost). Returning to Hunts', he found another job at a private hotel in Dover Street as a waiter.[50]

Given their mobility compared to domestic workers, waiters were in a more privileged position, and many were keen to assert the dignity they derived from their labour. The traditional 'Robert' found in old-fashioned taverns and chophouses was described by one E.J.C., a waiter at the Sussex Hotel in Leadenhall Street, as 'civil to all, servile to none' in the pages of the *Caterer* in 1885.[51] If a court case from 1895 is anything to go by, the waiter's sense of self-worth was retained through the changes that took place in the trade in the late nineteenth century. In this particular case, one head waiter at the Strand restaurant took a diner to court when he felt the latter had wounded his *amour-propre*. The offending diner was a retired army captain, who, after calling the waiter 'a slave', was charged at Bow Street court with causing a disturbance. In a sympathetic report of the case, the *Caterer* noted that, in a thirty-year career, the waiter had never been called such a term, and it shared his outrage, declaring that the offending diner must have been 'very far gone in liquor' if he was unable to distinguish between a slave and a waiter.[52]

While some waiters made considerable efforts to distance themselves from servitude and assert the traditions of 'la grand manière',[53] a handful of others had a broader, more ambitious vision, regarding waiting as but one step on a ladder that eventually led to management, or even ownership. This class of waiter, with 'the advantage of his parents' means, for starting off with a good education', 'will be able to enter thoroughly into every part of the catering business—working for a sufficient time in the

[50] Edward Stuart Humpheries, 'Childhood: An Autobiography of a Boy from 1889–1906', TS 361, Special Collections, Burnett Archive, Working Class Autobiographies, Brunel University Library.

[51] 'Waiters—As They Were, Are and Should Be: No. 1 As They Were', *Caterer*, 15 September 1885, p. 240.

[52] 'Caterer's Notebook', *Caterer*, 16 September 1895, p. 392.

[53] 'The Foreign Waiter Question Resuscitated', *Caterer*, 15 June 1888, p. 236.

kitchen, cellar, and office', noted the *Caterer*.[54] Certainly, this was true of Oscar Philippe, who started his working life as a waiter, eventually rising to become proprietor of the fashionable Cavour restaurant in Leicester Square. As testament to his success, it was reported at his death in 1907 that his estate was valued at £98,873, a not insubstantial sum that nearly approximated that of the businessman turned politician Joseph Chamberlain, who died seven years later.[55]

While Philippe's status was fully established by the turn of the century, another man's career trajectory was just beginning, that of Mario Gallati. After working as a kitchen helper and a waiter in a pastry shop in his hometown of Broni in Lombardy, in 1899, the 10-year-old Gallati found work as a *commis* (or under waiter), moving between Milan, Nice, Germany, and Switzerland, before arriving in London.[56] It was there, according to his autobiography, that he secured increasingly more interesting and remunerative employment, especially at the Queen's Restaurant in Leicester Square, which was at that time, in 1905, 'the rendezvous of many theatrical and musical celebrities'. His experience at the Queen's made an undeniable impression on him—he described it as 'a magical place'—and there he rose from *commis* to *chef de rang*, which involved waiting at tables and serving the famous people of the day.[57] The character of the place provided a model for him more than forty years later, when he opened what became one of the most fashionable restaurants in the post-war period, the Caprice in St James's. However, there were interruptions to his career in London, notably in 1909, when he was conscripted into the Italian army. On returning to London over two years later, he found work at Romano's as *chef de rang*, and then at the Ivy, where he stayed for twenty-eight years, during which time he became manager and learned all aspects of running a restaurant. By his own account, long experience, thrift, ambition, opportunity, and a perfectionist's eye for detail helped pave the way for his eventual success as proprietor.

Gallati's story shares several details with that of the life of German-born waiter-turned-entrepreneur O. R. Goring, who first went to work in the 1880s as a waiter in two Weimar and Frankfurt hotels, both of which were

[54] 'About Waiters and Waiting', *Caterer*, 15 March 1899, p. 115.

[55] 'Trade Topics', *Restaurant* (February 1911), 47. Philippe's death was in 1907, and his estate was mentioned in this newspaper in 1911. Joseph Chamberlain's estate was valued at over £125,000. See Peter T. Marsh, 'Joseph Chamberlain', *Oxford Dictionary of National Biography*, <http://www.oxforddnb.com/view/article/32350?docPos=2> (accessed 22 February 2014).

[56] Mario Gallati, *Mario of the Caprice: The Autobiography of a Restaurateur* (London: Hutchinson and Co., 1960), 15–30.

[57] *Ibid.* 43.

said to cater to visiting European royalty.[58] Like Gallati, Goring clearly benefited from the internationalism of the trade, as well as the links between serving elites on the Continent, and then in London, where in 1893 he found work as an 'extra waiter' at the Hotel Metropole. He went on to manage two hotels in Southend, where presumably he built his savings and gained experience. Wanting to be his own boss, Goring grasped the opportunity in 1905 to renovate a London club that became the Harrington Hotel in South Kensington (whose success was owed, in part, to the opening of the underground railway), and that, within two years, allowed him to buy the Cromwell Hotel, before opening the perennially fashionable Goring Hotel in Victoria in 1910. Given their overlapping geographies and chronologies, one wonders whether Goring and Mario Gallati knew one another. Certainly, they both sought a similar route of entry into the London restaurant trade—namely, by making use of employment agencies. While Goring relied on the German-run Boden employment agency, Gallati made use of his aunt in Milan, who contacted, on his behalf, an agency that 'sent young Italians to Britain as waiters, kitchen-hands, and house servants'.[59]

Waiters were also able to benefit from a not inconsiderable network of mutual aid and self-improvement organizations. By providing workers with a safety net in times of need, these bodies helped their members to assert their respectability and that of their trade.[60] One of the earliest of its kind, the London United Waiters' Provident Society, was founded in 1866, and was still in operation three decades later, when James Bailey, Tory MP for Walworth, a former hotelier (of Bailey's Hotel in Kensington), presided at their annual dinner in 1895.[61] While membership figures for this society appear to be lost, in that year 300 members received sick fund benefits.[62] A similar society, the City Waiters' Provident and Protection Society, was begun in 1867, and offered sickness, old age, and death benefits, and gave advice 'in times of difficulty to protect the members in all things that are lawful and just'.[63] According to its prospectus, the society

---

[58] O. G. Goring, *Fifty Years of Service* (1960; repr. London: Goring Hotel, 1984), 12–13. O. G. Goring was the son of O. R. Goring and was himself a prominent figure in the London restaurant and hotel world in the first half of the twentieth century.

[59] Gallati, *Mario of the Caprice*, 33.

[60] On another set of transient workers and mutual assistance networks, see Brenda Assael, *The Circus and Victorian Society* (Charlottesville: University of Virginia Press, 2005), ch. 4; for a general survey, see Simon Cordery, *British Friendly Societies, 1750–1914* (Basingstoke and New York: Palgrave Macmillan, 2003).

[61] 'Caterer's Notebook', *Caterer*, 15 November 1895, p. 488.

[62] 'Waiters' Column', *Caterer*, 15 November 1895, p. 523.

[63] 'Prospectus of the City Waiters' Provident Society', *City Waiters' Provident Society Journal*, 1 September 1867, p. 1.

aimed to provide the public with 'a respectable class of professional waiters' and, to that end, it accepted only waiters 'of good character and who are in a good state of health', on the recommendation of other members. Moreover, its members were required to have a minimum of two years' experience in the 'profession', as stated in the society's rulebook.[64] For an entrance fee of anywhere between 3*s.* 6*d.* and 7*s.* 6*d.* (depending on age), membership thereafter cost 2*s.* per month. After twelve months, the member could draw on weekly contributions of 10*s.* in cases of illness, £10 at death, or £5 at the death of a member's wife.[65] By the 1870s, the society had extended compensation to include a pension fund.[66] Two decades later, it launched an employment agency and, in the winter of 1894, started a distress fund 'whereby members in extreme circumstances had been assisted with clothes and money'.[67] At its annual festival in 1895, it announced that its yearly subscriptions amounted to approximately £300, suggesting that, if members paid upwards of 2*s.* monthly, then they numbered nearly 250.[68] By 1910, membership had dwindled to 162 waiters and, four years later, to 147.[69] Even before 1910, it remained a small-scale operation, much more akin to the City guilds on which it was modelled. By contrast, the Hotel Employees' Society, founded in 1877, had sufficient membership and resources (possibly on account of its international status: it proclaimed itself 'the largest trade union in the world') to be able to offer impressively high rates of compensation. In 1892, it provided sick pay amounting to 5*s.* daily for members of ten years' standing, and 2*s.* daily for new members. The success of the Hotel Employees' Society was testified to by the eagerness of several hotel proprietors to become honorary members.[70]

By the turn of the century, waiters' organizations were supplementing their usual programme of self-improvement with a more extended engagement in politics. Wages were a major issue, and in 1894 this took the form

---

[64] Rule no. 4, 'Rules of the City Waiters' Provident Protection Society' (London, 1867), FS 15/998, The National Archives [hereafter TNA].

[65] 'Prospectus of the City Waiters' Provident Society', *City Waiters' Provident Society Journal*, 1 September 1867, p. 1.

[66] Rule no. 2, 'Rules of the City Waiters' Provident and Pension Society' (London, 1877), FS 15/988, TNA.

[67] 'Odds and Ends', *Caterer*, 15 February 1894, p. 97.

[68] 'The Waiters' Column', *Caterer*, 15 June 1895, p. 277. The monthly subscription rate was 2*s.* in 1867, 2*s.* 2*d.* in 1877, and between 2*s.* 2*d.* and 2*s.* 8*d.* in 1898, thus indicating that in 1895 it was probably upwards of 2*s.* For the 1877 rate, see rule no. 17 in 'Rules of the City Waiters' Provident and Pension Society' (London, 1877), FS 15/988, TNA. For 1898, see 'Odds and Ends', *Caterer*, 15 December 1898, p. 635.

[69] Assets and Liabilities Valuation for the City Waiters' Provident and Pension Society, 21 December 1914, FS 15/998, TNA.

[70] 'Caterer's Notebook', *Caterer*, 12 December 1892, p. 492.

of a demand put to the LCC for a minimum weekly wage of 30*s*. Many waiters believed that the LCC had the power to help their cause, since its licensing committee was in charge of granting music and dancing licences to music halls and theatres (some of which had restaurants).[71] Societies such as the International Waiters' Union urged it to include a 'fair-wage' clause that would become part of the licence.[72] However, the LCC's response was that it had no authority to enforce such a provision. Faced with this setback, another society, the Waiters and Waitresses and Licensed Victuallers' Employees Union, pledged that six of its members would run as candidates at the next election of the LCC licensing committee in order to change opinion on the subject.[73] Such tactics intensified four years later, when the newly formed Amalgamated Waiters' Society tried to sway an LCC election by issuing a manifesto that invited fellow workers to vote only for candidates who supported the 'fair-wage' clause.[74] Paul Vogel, the honorary secretary of the Amalgamated Waiters' Society, saw the subject of wages as a stepping stone to a larger set of demands that would ultimately improve the waiter's lot. The following year, he urged the LCC to abolish all public caterers and take over the ownership of 'public houses and such like establishments, and work them for the benefit of employees and the community', a demand the normally sympathetic *Caterer* sardonically called 'modest'.[75] Despite backing the Progressive Party in the 1901 LCC election, Vogel and his union were unable to change the LCC's decision, possibly because the Amalgamated Waiters' Society, at this point, had no more than 400 members.[76] As the *Waiters' Record* lamented, 'how can a general win a battle without soldiers?'[77] Indeed, Vogel himself conceded the inability of his society to attract more members, but attributed this to the unwillingness of some waiters to risk losing their jobs through such an affiliation.[78]

Vogel's attempts at political agitation were not directed only at the LCC. In 1895, when he was honorary secretary of the Waiters and

---

[71] On the LCC and theatrical licensing, see Susan Pennybacker, ' "It Was not what she Said, but the Way in which she Said it": The London County Council and the Music Halls', in Peter Bailey (ed.), *Music Hall: The Business of Pleasure* (Milton Keynes: Open University Press, 1986), ch. 6; on the limits of the LCC's authority in this period, see John Davis, 'London Government, 1850–1920: The Metropolitan Board of Works and the London County Council', *London Journal*, 26/1 (2001), 47–56.

[72] 'Caterer's Notebook', *Caterer*, 15 September 1894, p. 392.

[73] 'Chops and Changes', *Caterer*, 15 December 1894, p. 562.

[74] 'Caterer's Notebook', *Caterer*, 15 March 1898, p. 117.

[75] 'Waiters on the War Path', *Caterer*, 15 May 1899, p. 218.

[76] *Waiters' Record* (March 1901), 1.

[77] *Waiters' Record* (November–December 1901), 2.

[78] Paul Vogel to Mr Bodkin, 'The Living Wage for Waiters and the LCC Licensing Committee', *Waiters' Record* (November–December 1900), 3.

Waitresses and Licensed Victuallers' Employees Union, he petitioned the Home Secretary, Henry Asquith, asking for the inclusion in the new Factory and Workshop Bill of a clause providing protection for workers in hotels, restaurants, taverns, and coffee houses, in matters relating to working hours, conditions, and accommodation.[79] When this initiative failed, a mass meeting of the Amalgamated Waiters' Society was held in Trafalgar Square in 1900, at which Vogel appealed to the government to reconsider the clause in the bill.[80] He also demanded that employees in hotels, restaurants, and other like establishments be included in the Compensation Bill, which provided benefits for workers who had suffered accidents. In a manoeuvre perhaps designed to shame the government into submission, he pointed to the bad practices of the House of Commons' Kitchen Committee, which, he said, refused to see a deputation on the question of the wages it paid its own waiters.[81] Vogel even sought out the help of the celebrated pioneer Labour MP Keir Hardie, although apparently to little effect.[82]

There were still other attempts to stretch the scope of legislation to include waiters, as with the various Shop Hours Bills that were proposed from the 1880s. Waiters did eventually come under the scope of the Shops Act of 1912, which made meal times and weekly half holidays compulsory for those 'employed in any retail trade or business for the sale of refreshment or intoxicating liquors'.[83] The law had a mixed, not to say controversial, reception, particularly among City waiters.[84] Under the new law, they were required to take a meal break at some point during their busiest period from noon to three, thus reducing the possibility of getting tips.[85] This was exacerbated by another clause requiring them to leave work at 1.30 p.m. at least once a week. Problems were also anticipated by small eating house proprietors who had only one waiter. As one owner complained, 'my waiter must sit down at certain hours and be off duty at certain hours; that means I am not allowed to be away for more than six hours, as I cannot afford to keep another waiter'.[86] In the light of the Act's insufficiencies, shortly after its introduction, it was referred to a Standing

---

[79] 'Waiters' Column', *Caterer*, 15 March 1895, p. 136; 'Caterer's Notebook', *Caterer*, 16 April 1895, p. 152; 'A Bill', *Waiters' Record* (June 1900), 2.

[80] 'Waiters and the Factory Acts', *Caterer*, 15 May 1900, p. 236.   [81] *Ibid.*

[82] 'A Bill', *Waiters' Record* (August 1901), 2.

[83] PP, Shops Act 1912, 2/3 Geo. 5 *c*. 3; 'The Shops Act and the Trade', *Restaurant* (May 1912), 245.

[84] See discussions in *Restaurant* (April 1912), 184; (May 1912), 243–8, 288; (June 1912), 320–1; (July 1912), 384–5; (October 1912), 604.

[85] 'Trade Meeting in the City of London', *Restaurant* (March 1912), 246.

[86] 'Small Establishments and the Shops Acts', *Restaurant* (May 1912), 288.

Committee for revision and proposed exceptions.[87] Predicting the potential pitfalls of the legislation, the *Restaurant* warned that, 'from the time
the new legislation was introduced to its Royal assent, the only representations made to the Government were put forward by the Incorporated
Association of Hotels and Restaurants', which was 'wholly concerned with
the interests of licensed establishments, and mainly with those of licensed
hotels', thus reflecting only a fraction of the interests (notably big business) that defined the trade.[88]

If the impact of collective organization and official intervention might
seem underwhelming, it should not be forgotten that some waiters did
achieve some success in ameliorating their position through recourse to
the courts. In a case brought before the Westminster County Court in
1897, an 'extra waiter' brought to court a restaurateur, demanding that he
be paid £4 10s. in unpaid wages for five weeks' work. Typically, these
types of waiters had to return to the restaurant the following day to receive
their daily wage, but in this case the wages were not forthcoming.
According to the *Caterer*, when the court decided in the waiter's favour,
the verdict was 'warmly applauded by a little crowd of garçons who
gathered at the back of the Court to hear this cause célèbre', a small
victory for a group whose existence was even more precarious than that of
the regular waiter.[89]

Whatever the benefits waiters accrued from organizational or collective
initiatives and legal action, ultimately it was in the more routine aspects of
their working lives that they saw the greatest potential for gain and
advancement. Perhaps no part of their job offered the greatest yardstick
for measuring this than the issue of gratuities. Extensive interest in the
tip, from both those engaged in the restaurant trade and the wider public,
reflected how public eating exposed the challenges of an enlarged
public sphere. The conventions and practices surrounding tipping varied,
as did the attitudes of both employers and diners towards their use. It
was generally not a convention to add a service charge to a bill of
fare, so tipping was left to the discretion of the individual customer.
A notable exception was the Paragon Restaurant in the Strand, which in
1889 advertised one-shilling dinners with 'attendance included', adding
that 'the total absence of fees to waiters and of other extra charges so
commonly made in London restaurants' pleased their customers greatly.[90]

---

[87] See PP, *Reports to the Secretary of State for the Home Department on the Shops Act
(1912), as It Applies to Refreshment Premises*, v. 26 (1912/13).

[88] 'Trade Topics—City Trade and the Shops Act', *Restaurant* (May 1912), 243.

[89] 'The Waiters' Column', *Caterer*, 15 April 1897, p. 216.

[90] Handbill, Paragon Restaurant, 1889, Evanion Collection 4207, British Library.

Some dining rooms actively precluded tipping. In an article in 1881, the *Caterer* noted that, in contrast to many City dining-room keepers, Messrs Reed Brothers abolished tips from their Cheapside establishment, and paid their waiters a wage.[91] The management of the Atlantic Dining Rooms in Westminster made clear its policy by announcing 'no gratuities allowed' on the bottom of an 1887 handbill, after informing the public that meals were served 'with civility and prompt attention'.[92] In a second article on the subject of waiting for the *Caterer*, E.J.C., the City waiter mentioned earlier, observed that 'there is a certain section of the public to whom tipping has become such a habit, that they really make its abolition rather difficult, even when the strictest endeavours are made to get rid of it'.[93] The use of the term 'habit' obviously testifies to the ubiquity of tipping in London restaurants in this period. The restaurateur Henry Roberts (of Bertram and Roberts), when pressed as to the possibility of abolishing the system of tipping waiters, declared that 'we should be willing enough, but it is a too generous public which keeps up the practice, and ever will; and as years go on the practice seems to me to increase'. He argued that those proprietors who forbade all tips were imposing a 'useless restriction':

> Perhaps it is that the diner feels generous after a generous dinner, or perhaps he thinks that the waiter has a wife and family depending upon him, or perhaps he is nervous and wonders what the waiter will think of him; but whatever it is, the waiter gets his tip all the same.[94]

This is not to say that diners might not have been perplexed by the pecuniary and social implications of adding additional remuneration for their meal. Most immediately, there was the question of how much was an acceptable tip. Pioneer restaurant reviewer Nathaniel Newnham-Davis urged his readers to be generous:

> I have always found that a shilling for every pound or part of a pound, or a shilling for each member of a party brings a "thank you" from the waiter at any first-class restaurant. I should be inclined to err a little on the liberal side of this scale.[95]

Frustratingly, in his collection of restaurant reviews published in *Dinners and Diners: Where and How to Dine in London* (1899), Newnham-Davis

[91] 'Waiters' Fees', *Caterer*, 15 April 1881, p. 71.
[92] Handbill, Atlantic Dining Rooms, 1887, Evanion Collection 4147, British Library.
[93] 'Waiters—As They Were, Are, and Should Be: No. 2 As They Are,' *Caterer*, 16 November 1885, p. 307.
[94] 'An Interview with a Famous Restaurateur', *Caterer*, 8 December 1885, p. 337.
[95] Nathaniel Newnham-Davis, *Dinners and Diners: Where and How to Dine in London* (London, 1899), xx–xxi.

detailed the bills from the restaurants he visited, but rarely revealed how much he tipped, with the exception of the Holborn, where he paid his waiter 1 shilling for a 12-shilling dinner, to which the waiter replied ' "Thank you" very heartily'.[96] Like a lot of prescriptive literature, it might be possible that the author's insistence on leaving a generous tip tells us what was not occurring rather than what was. Moreover, he was primarily dining in fashionable establishments. Further down the restaurant hierarchy, there is no equivalent to diners offering recommendations about what to tip, but, as a general rule, Leppington noted that 'the tips given are much smaller in amount, but greater in number and the pence mount up'.[97] In modest City dining rooms, one journalist, quoting from the experience of 'A Clerk', suggested in 1883 that it would probably be appropriate to tip a penny on receiving a plate of meat and potatoes 'of the poorest kind' costing 10*d*. Failure to do so, the author insisted, would risk being insulted or chastised, so it was probably wise 'to submit to this extortion'.[98] Morley Roberts claimed that it was possible to establish a 'tariff of politeness', by which the amount left as a tip determined the degree of acknowledgement and gratitude displayed by the waiter.[99] If a penny tip was pocketed in 'contemptuous silence', 2*d*. induced 'a reluctant "thank you"', and 3*d*. the addition of 'a smiling "Sir"', it might require as much as 6*d*. for the diner to be 'bespattered with servility and bowed gracefully to the opened door'. A full half crown, Roberts averred, was likely to 'kill the waiter with apoplexy', or to give the impression that the diner was 'intoxicated and incapable of counting money'.[100] Unfortunately, Roberts does not specify the cost of the meal itself to which this tipping scale would apply, but he does imply that there was an expectation that diners should leave a substantial, but not extravagant, tip.

Moreover, diners did not merely have to wrestle with the question of how much to leave, but also with the fact that they might need to reward multiple members of staff. An anonymous commentator in the *Tourist and Traveller, and Hotel Review* in 1884 pointed out that, in London taverns, the 'waiter-in-chief' made few demands on the diner with regard to tipping, but it was also necessary to leave something for the 'functionary who has looked after you' and even the carver, who needed to be 'conciliated with a modest offering', if the diner was to be guaranteed the choicest cut of the joint.[101] Faced with all these requirements and

[96] *Ibid.* 20.   [97] Leppington, 'Work and Wages', 755.
[98] 'City Clerks and their Dinners', 10 October 1883, Restaurant Files, box A–B, London Cuttings, Bishopsgate.
[99] Roberts, 'Waiters and Restaurants', 540.   [100] *Ibid.*
[101] *Tourist and Traveller, and Hotel Review* (October 1884), 64.

complications, some sympathetic observers argued that tips should be eliminated altogether and replaced with a fair wage, a plea that was echoed in the following decade, as we have seen.[102]

In itself, the amount left as a tip by the diner was no guarantee of return to the waiter. Many restaurants operated the so-called tronc system under which all the tips received by the entire waiting staff were pooled and then divided each week according to an agreed scale of payment.[103] Based on their interviews with members of the hotel and restaurant trade for a report on waiting as a vocation, Miss K. I. M. Medley and Ernest Lesser noted in 1911 that 'the head waiter naturally receives the largest share, and the rest of the staff are paid in accordance with the positions they occupy'. These others included the 'young commis', the casual waiter who was engaged for an evening's work, and, if the establishment was large enough (as in a hotel, club, or palatial restaurant), the floor, smoking-room, and coffee-room waiters.[104] In practice, there was much that could go wrong, as occurred at one anonymous but 'well-known' Strand restaurant in 1897, when the head waiter, 'who by virtue of his office was treasurer of the whole of the waiters' tips', absconded with one week's collection, which amounted to £22. As the *Caterer* reported, instead of dividing the tips with his fellow waiters (his own share amounted to £3), he 'distributed the money amongst the "bookies" at Kempton Park, and the tips he received there not being so good as those of the restaurant, he had nothing better to show his colleagues on his return than an empty cashbox'.[105] Fortunately for the men, the head waiter repaid the money with the help of some friends, but not without first being brought before the Bow Street magistrates. Even when the money was shared, there was still much scope for discontent. Recalling his career as a waiter that spanned at least fifty years, Albert Thomas wrote in 1944 that 'the pool system is not a success; the heads got a lot, the workers very little'.[106] In some cases, it was the proprietor who took for himself the lion's share of the pot, leaving his staff out of pocket.[107] Based on his seventeen years in the trade, another waiter observed in 1895 that in the large hotels he knew of cases where the

---

[102] See, e.g., 'Waiters and Waiters' Tips', *Caterer*, 15 August 1887, p. 267.

[103] Based on the French system, 'le tronc' indicated a wooden box where tips were collected. For a comparative study, see Patricia Van den Eeckhout, 'Waiters, Waitresses, and their Tips in Western Europe before World War One', *International Review of Social History*, 60/3 (2015), 349–78.

[104] Miss K. I. M. Medley and Ernest Lesser, *An Inquiry into the Waiter's Calling* (London: Apprenticeship and Skilled Employment Association, 1911), 11–12.

[105] 'Caterer's Notebook', *Caterer*, 15 June 1897, p. 295.

[106] Albert Thomas, *Wait and See* (London: Michael Joseph, 1944), 27. Special Collections, Burnett Archive of Working Class Autobiographies, Brunel University Library.

[107] 'Waiters and Waiters' Tips', *Caterer*, 15 August 1887, p. 267.

waiters 'go for a whole week and not make 1*s*. in tips'.[108] Moreover, there were inevitably many waiters who regarded their tips as insufficient to maintain even their most basic needs. The 'extra waiter' who appeared at Westminster County Court in 1897 (as mentioned earlier) earned tips amounting to approximately 2*s*. 6*d*. daily, but the restaurant keeper for whom he worked provided no meals. Since it usually cost the waiter between 1*s*. 6*d*. and 2*s*. to go out for his dinner, he told the court that he was left with roughly 6*d*. at the end of the day.[109]

The potential inequities of tipping for the waiter might seem to be reinforced by the fact that many waiters were entirely dependent on tips for remuneration. A correspondent for the *Weekly Chronicle* in 1888 pointed out that London waiters 'as a rule are paid no regular salaries' and relied entirely on gratuities they received from the public. While the writer, who called himself a 'Friend of Robert', implied that this system might soon give way to one based on fixed salaries, he nevertheless insisted that remuneration solely through tips was 'not such a precarious way of living as it seems at first'. He cited an example of a waiter in a 'first class restaurant' who, 'besides paying a premium for being allowed to wait there, pays an assistant out of his own pocket, and then makes a clear profit of £200 per annum out of the gratuities he receives', an amount approximating to what a senior civil service clerk might make in this period.[110] We might consider the possibility that those waiters who paid to wait at tables referred to earlier did so with the clear expectation that they would receive tips that would be sufficient to make a livelihood. It was certainly the case that, at the Monico on Shaftesbury Avenue in 1894, waiters, who received no salaries and indeed paid between 3*s*. and 4*s*. a day for the privilege of serving, were given free meals and 'the permission to keep any "leavings"'.[111] One observer reckoned that these tips approximated to 1*s*. 6*d*. to 2*s*. for each pound of their takings, 'and as some take home from £12 to as high as £20 a day, their earnings are decidedly good'.[112] While the raw figures for tips are not necessarily helpful, given the vagaries of the cost of living and the individual circumstances of the waiter, there is sufficient testimony, in both contemporary reportage and subsequent memoirs, to suggest that many waiters found their tips to be, at the very least, satisfactory, and sometimes more. Albert Thomas wrote that 'a sovereign or half a sovereign used to be a fair tip for

---

[108] From *Tit Bits*, repr. in 'Waiters' Tips and Wages', *Hotel*, 14 August 1895, p. 24.
[109] 'The Waiters' Column', *Caterer*, 15 April 1897, p. 216.
[110] 'Correspondence', *Weekly Chronicle*, 29 September 1888, p. 8; *Tempted London: Young Men* (London: Hodder and Stoughton, 1888), 42.
[111] 'The Café Monico', *Caterer*, 15 January 1894, p. 26. [112] *Ibid.*

services rendered', adding that 'in the posh hotels (where I regret to say English waiters were seldom engaged) the tips were much larger'.[113] Thomas himself appears to have been largely employed in more modest establishments, but still recorded that he was able, on 'a good night', to take home 10s., which allowed for 'a supper, theatre, several drinks, and a cigar'.[114] Critically, the tipping system demonstrated the complex and fluid nature of the waiter's employment, serving sometimes as another source of grievance and disaffection, but also offering the possibility of a not insubstantial financial reward.

If discussions of tipping suggest the need to look at the subject from multiple perspectives, which encompass both disaffection and satisfaction, the issue of foreign waiters may also benefit from taking a similar approach. In anticipation of an argument to be emphasized in Chapter 5, the status of foreign waiters in London demonstrates that, while sometimes discomforting, cosmopolitanism could also be seen as rewarding for both workers and consumers. London's positioning in an international labour market also provides further testimony to the importance of recognizing the intersection between the local and the global when analysing British society and culture in this period. This is not to deny that by the end of the century references to waiters who travelled to London from overseas become increasingly framed in pejorative terms, coloured by a growing nativist and exclusionary sentiment. As early as 1886, one correspondent for the *Caterer* complained that 'it is manifestly unfair of English restaurateurs and hotel-keepers to employ so many foreigners, to the exclusion of those who are not only their own countrymen, but equally as good, if not better waiters'.[115] The notion that the population of foreign waiters was large (and indeed growing) provoked one of the first of many collective responses from within the trade. A month later in the same paper it was noted that 'the increased and increasing employment of foreign waiters has put the native "Robert" on his mettle', and, in response, the Central Waiters Union was established, 'for the exclusive supply of English waiters "who thoroughly know their business"'.[116]

The problem of foreign waiters came to be viewed in increasingly racial terms, with one correspondent writing in 1889 on the 'waiter question' that 'it is high time that the pauper aliens were warned off the course in the race for life in this country'.[117] Such tensions heightened in the 1890s as

[113] Thomas, *Wait and See*, 26–7.   [114] *Ibid.*

[115] 'All about Waiters', *Caterer*, 15 June 1886, p. 179.

[116] 'Gastronomic Items', *Caterer*, 15 July 1886, p. 198. A few years later, the less specialized English Hotel, Restaurant, Club, and Tavern Servants Union was founded on similar principles. See 'Editorial', *British Journal of Catering*, 1 December 1889, p. 10.

[117] From the *People*, repr. in 'The Waiter Question', *Caterer*, 15 March 1889, p. 157.

part of a broader anti-alien sentiment. The fact that London seemed hospitable to workers from abroad drove some members of the trade to make their individual voices heard. In an open letter that appeared in *Tit Bits* and the *Hotel*, one anonymous waiter complained about working at an unnamed restaurant under 'one German who got promoted to manager. The first thing he did was to shorten our wages, give us longer hours, and bad food.'[118] This might not have seemed as bad a case as the one a few years later at a 'well-known' City restaurant, where a newly appointed German manager 'immediately started discharging all British waiters, in order to replace them by his own countrymen, a course which, we should add, is explicitly acknowledged in the "character" given to the discharged men'. The article cited the claim by the secretary of the Amalgamated Waiters' Society that it was now 'common practice' for new managers 'to surround themselves with waiters of their own nationality'. The author, referencing colonial secretary Joseph Chamberlain's contemporary efforts to bolster the economic and political ties between metropolitan Britain and the white settler populations of the dominions, concluded that it was 'curious' that, 'while we are all talking so much about imperialism and Greater Britain, it should happen that in the City of London, under our very noses, Englishmen are being turned out of employment to make room for foreigners'.[119] For this reason the organization that represented City waiters, the City Waiters' Provident Society, drew attention to 'the invasion of foreign waiters' in the City in particular as a means to rouse support for the group and increase its membership.[120]

Theirs was a refrain that was heard outside the portals of the City. One 'Englishman' who had worked for twenty years at a first-class West End restaurant explained, in an editorial in the *Evening News* in 1909, that 'the only reason of so many foreigners being employed in hotels and restaurants is that the men who first started or modernized them were foreigners themselves; they pushed forward their own countrymen'.[121] For this writer, the solution was to make British directors or proprietors aware of good English waiters who could then become managers, a call that was part of a larger initiative in this period that led to the founding of the Loyal British Waiters' Society, whose object was 'securing positions for Britons only', and whose membership amounted to nearly 900 in 1910 when it was created.[122] The society's official organ, the *Restaurateur*, founded in

[118] From *Tit Bits*, repr. in 'Waiters' Tips and Wages', *Hotel*, 14 August 1895, p. 24.
[119] 'Caterer's Notebook', *Caterer*, 15 April 1899, p. 148.
[120] 'The Waiters' Column', *Caterer*, 16 December 1895, p. 571.
[121] From *Evening News*, repr. in 'English and Foreign Waiters', *Restaurant* (October 1909), 70.
[122] 'The Loyal British Waiters' Society', *Restaurant* (March 1911), 96.

1912 and discontinued in April 1914, helped to 'promote the welfare of British waiters, supplying their services for temporary and permanent employment', for example by running wanted advertisements, announcing training opportunities and trade meetings.[123] While 'British' waiters and 'English' waiters were terms that were largely interchangeable, the correspondents' pages of the *Restaurateur* showed that this regular elision left open the possibility of confusion. One correspondent, identified only as 'Taffy' from Cardiff, might well have been troubled by a predominantly English element in this nominally British organization and sought clarification. In response, the editor of the *Restaurateur* reassured 'Taffy' that 'the fact that you are a Welshman need not prevent you from joining' the Society.[124]

The growing clamour to exclude foreign waiters manifested itself at the organizational and political level. While more established unions and improvement societies increasingly resorted to xenophobic rhetoric, exclusionary waiters' unions were also set up throughout the period. Obviously this hostility to foreign waiters was bolstered by concerns that, because foreign waiters seemed to be reliant on tips, they were threatening those who sought to procure for waiters a formal standard wage.[125]

The negative connotations surrounding foreign waiters also found their way into popular culture. The association of the foreign waiter with espionage and treachery was a popular motif in middlebrow novels. An early example was C. Forth's *The Surprise of the Channel Tunnel: A Sensational Story of the Future* (1883), in which French soldiers disguise themselves as not merely bootmakers and milliners, but also pastrycooks and waiters, in order to create a bridgehead for a larger invading army that pours through a tunnel under the Channel. Waiters also featured in the notoriously fevered invasion-scare melodramatic novels and short stories of William Le Queux. In these breathlessly hysterical fables of German invasion and British unpreparedness, German waiters are singled out as spies (they overhear things, after all). In *The Invasion of 1910* (1906), his best-known work, first serialized in the *Daily Mail*, the largest daily circulating paper, Le Queux imagines a war in which the Germans launch a naval attack on Britain that leads to a land invasion. Upon penetrating the capital, 'undoubtedly the objective of the enemy', the 'alien lawless' unleash disorder in every quarter.[126] In the background, secretly helping

---

[123] *Restaurateur* (March 1912), 5.
[124] 'Answers to Correspondents', *Restaurateur* (January 1913), 32.
[125] See, e.g., 'The Wail of the Waiters: Englishmen Give Place to the Swiss', *Echo*, 17 August 1900, in Norman Collection, London Guildhall Library [hereafter LGL].
[126] William Le Queux, *The Invasion of 1910* (London: Eveleigh Nash, 1906), 280.

this army, are German waiters, clerks, bakers, hairdressers, and private servants who are really spies. Their efforts go unnoticed, as 'we had, ostrich-like, buried our heads in the sand and refused to turn our eyes to the grave peril that for so long threatened'. In one of the novel's most dystopian scenes, 'London awoke to find herself a German city'.[127] By provoking moral outrage and fear, the novel implicitly made the case for introducing compulsory military training, a demand made by Lord Roberts and the National Service League (Roberts advised Le Queux on this novel).[128]

These xenophobic associations reached a climax in the summer of 1914. German and Austrian waiters faced popular intimidation, and then official coercion. At the outbreak of the First World War, one correspondent for the *Evening News*, calling himself 'A Patriot', urged readers to boycott all hotels and restaurants where German and Austrian waiters continued to be employed.[129] 'Publish a list', the writer demanded, 'and let the man in the street know, and if knowing, he still trades with the King's enemies . . . let him be treated as a pariah.'[130] If such tirades made individual waiters uncomfortable, then police intrusion in their lives presumably felt like a more direct attack. The numerous cases brought before magistrates' courts suggest the climate of fear and suspicion surrounding these men, whose own voices remain largely silent in the record. Although the exact number of these cases is difficult to establish, the *Restaurant* reported that in August 1914 alone there were at least four cases involving the arrest of German waiters, on charges ranging from failing to register with the police to possession of a revolver.[131] An article in *The Times* in that month made reference to another case involving a waiter recently charged with espionage.[132] Once billeting in hotels began, the fear of espionage heightened. In October 1914, the House of Commons drew attention to the problem of British General Staff officers billeted in several London hotels staffed by Germans and Austrians and urged these officers to 'be on their guard' against the dangers of 'being improperly overheard or [having] their correspondence being secretly opened' by these foreign waiters.[133] Fearing association with the enemy,

---

[127] *Ibid.* 395.

[128] Roger T. Stearn, 'William Tufnell Le Queux', *Oxford New Dictionary of National Biography*, <http://www.oxforddnb.com/view/article/37666> (accessed 4 April 2014).

[129] From *Evening News*, repr. in 'Banish the Teuton', *Restaurant* (September 1914), 471.

[130] *Ibid.*

[131] 'Alien Waiters in the Courts', *Restaurant* (September 1914), 472. Though the cases were published in September, the charges were made in the previous month.

[132] 'The Spy Peril', *The Times*, 26 August 1914, p. 5.

[133] 'Waiters as Spies', *Restaurant* (October 1914), 510.

some restaurants, such as the Vienna Café in New Oxford Street, prominently floated a Union Jack high above their premises.[134] Those restaurateurs interested in further asserting their patriotic credentials could apply to the Publicity Department at Whitehall in order to obtain a special recruitment and service card specially designed to be put in the windows or on the walls of their establishments.[135] In this climate, the *Catering Trade Worker*, a newly founded international trade paper (which printed articles in four languages and was the official organ of the Amalgamated Union of Hotel, Club, and Restaurant Employees), urged German and Austrian waiters in London to become naturalized British citizens: 'the full cost should not exceed £3/17/6', it estimated, adding opportunistically, 'if you come to us'.[136]

Clearly there were some native-born waiters who felt that their position was extremely vulnerable. However, if we shift our perspective on the issue of the 'foreign waiter' towards other elements within the restaurant trade, and to those who dined in their establishments, we see a very different picture. Those that employed foreign-born waiters, or encountered them in the dining room, regularly commended them for their professionalism, culinary knowledge, and cosmopolitan sophistication. Their skilfulness emerged from a system on the Continent that was underpinned by 'very decided notions . . . as to how a waiter should be trained'. By contrast, the English waiter 'has taken up the profession as a makeshift', wrote one *Caterer* columnist on the art of waiting.[137] Foreign waiters, especially from Germany, Switzerland, and 'perhaps some parts of Italy . . . begin as lads when quite young, and an imperative phase of training consists of the travelling probation'.[138] Echoing this comment, another writer waxed lyrical about German waiters who have 'seen the world', adding that they 'made the tour of the Continent before they find themselves in Great Britain, and this cosmopolitan experience has rendered them deft and generally more adaptable than the untravelled waiter'.[139] Writing of the Swiss waiter, another correspondent observed that he is generally 'the son of a large hotel proprietor or some other person in good position, and has only come to England to learn the language and tastes of those who are his best customers at home', underlining not merely the nature of transnational dining, but also serving.[140] As many commentators noted,

[134] 'Round Table', *Restaurant* (October 1914), 530.   [135] *Ibid.*

[136] 'Naturalisation', *Catering Trade Worker* (September 1914), 3. The Amalgamated Union of Hotel, Club, and Restaurant Workers was formed from a combination of the well-established International Caterers' Union and the newer National Union of Waiters. See *ibid.* (February 1913), 6.

[137] 'The Art of Waiting', *Caterer*, 15 August 1893, p. 354.   [138] *Ibid.*

[139] 'German Waiters', *Caterer*, 15 September 1890, p. 339.

[140] 'The Caterer's Notebook', *Caterer*, 15 November 1890, p. 417.

the cosmopolitanism of these waiters was evident from their linguistic dexterity, or 'polyglot accomplishments',[141] as one put it, which appealed to visitors from abroad, particularly those staying at large West End hotels, who 'prefer being attended to by a man who can use their respective languages; and hence the waiter who speaks two or three dialects must be preferred by the managers of these mammoth hotels to the [English Robert] who only uses his mother tongue'.[142] Another quality attributed to the foreign waiter was his high standards of personal hygiene and self-presentation. One authority lauded him for 'keeping up a presentable and cleanly appearance, both when on and when off duty. As a rule, the same cannot be said of the average English knights of the napkin.'[143]

Perceived by many as urbane, chic, and unsoiled, these foreign waiters had reason to be optimistic about their working lives. Not only did they have an approving audience, but many also had important social and professional structures that protected their hard-earned status. As we have seen, Mario Gallati's aunt contacted on his behalf an employment agency that sent young Italians to work in London's restaurants, and his experience was probably not atypical. In his study of work and wages in 1892, Leppington (whom we previously encountered) estimated that foreign waiters have 'some half dozen clubs or unions with employment registries attached, and these clubs have established relations with employers, to whom they guarantee the character of the servants they supply'. Moreover, he added, 'these unions combine the functions of social club, employment registry, and friendly society; and one at least of them lets furnished sleeping rooms to its bachelor members at a moderate rent, with the general comfort and cleanliness of which I was much impressed'.[144] Certainly this generalization rang true for one observer noting the presence of a tight-knit 'little colony off Tottenham Court Road', consisting of German and Austrian restaurants, half of which were combined with waiters' employment agencies.[145] One writer for the *Tourist and Traveller, and Hotel Review* criticized this state of things some years earlier, mentioning that, while the German Union of Waiters possessed a clubhouse at 84 Charlotte Street near Fitzroy Square 'for the use of its

---

[141] 'Odds and Ends', *Caterer*, 15 July 1892, p. 281.
[142] 'The English versus Foreign Waiter Question', *Caterer*, 15 October 1887, p. 340.
[143] 'The Waiters' Column', *Caterer*, 15 June 1896, p. 304.
[144] Leppington, 'Work and Wages', 756.
[145] 'Foreign London at Dinner: The Resorts of our Permanent Visitors', 1897, Norman Collection, LGL.

members in the Metropolis', 'it is strange that at home we have nothing corresponding to it'.[146]

In addition to these grass-roots networks, foreign waiters also stood to benefit from the help meted out by the Geneva Society in Shaftesbury Avenue, which, founded in 1880, was the largest and most well-established sick fund society of its kind.[147] With chapters in different cities, the Geneva Society and similar clubs, such as the Helvetia, also offered an important safety net of employment: 'A waiter who belongs to one of them is almost always assured of work; if he leaves London and goes abroad he still gets the advantages of fees paid here in the foreign branches', Morley Roberts wrote. With their membership dues, workers were given references with a special stamp to assure the hirer that he was not 'bestowing employment on an undeserving man'.[148] Such a system was vital for maintaining some level of coherence within a group of itinerant workers whose movements ranged widely. If we recognize that employment in London restaurants was part of an international labour market, then we also need to remember that there were also opportunities for native-born waiters to work overseas. For example, in 1893, one correspondent for the *Caterer* said he 'was glad to hear from an important New York caterer that it was the native Londoner who is considered in New York the best waiter'.[149]

On one occasion the modishness that was positively associated with the foreign waiter intersected with another novel feature in the restaurant scene in this period. In 1894, the *Caterer* reported that the soon-to-be-opened St Martin's Lane branch of the Duval Restaurant would be 'managed under the direct supervision of French experts, and served by French women'.[150] The opportunities for employment and advancement created by both the dramatic expansion of the restaurant sector in the late-nineteenth century and its essential heterogeneity also led to the creation of a new phenomenon at the turn of the century: the emergence of female waiting staff. The rise of the waitress provides another example of how the practice of public eating intersected with broader social and cultural changes, notably the increased prevalence of heterosociability and the dramatic expansion of the public sphere for women.

It is likely that women waited on tables at earlier points in the century, particularly at family-run establishments. An article on London eating

---

[146] 'Hotel Notes and Trade News', *Tourist and Traveller, and Hotel Review* (December 1885), 304.

[147] 'Notes by the Secretary', *Waiters' Record* (March 1901), 2.

[148] Morley Roberts, 'Waiters and Restaurants', *Murray's Magazine* 7 (1890), 544.

[149] 'Catering Notes from Paris', *Caterer*, 15 March 1893, p. 111.

[150] 'Chops and Changes', *Caterer*, 15 December 1894, p. 550.

houses in 1837 noted the 'remarkable attention' devoted to diners at Hancock's in Rupert Street 'by the waiters—two most active, neat-handed and tidy females'.[151] In particular, the female server at Hancock's was lauded for her astonishing capacity for remembering complicated and lengthy orders submitted by over fifty diners, and for her ability to complete her duties with 'no dawdling or hesitation'. Interestingly, the female staff at Hancock's were accorded the appellation 'waiters' or, on one occasion, 'waiting-maids'.[152] The term 'waitress' was in widespread use by the 1840s and 1850s, but it was used loosely and inconsistently, being applied to women who undertook a number of service functions in a variety of hostelries, and even to domestic servants who served dinner in family homes.[153] By contrast, by the 1880s, contemporaries tended to reserve the term for the growing number of women employed in waiting at tables in restaurants.

If attention was bestowed on the waitress, then it came from a variety of quarters, not least from within the theatre world, where her humble existence took on a larger-than-life quality. In music-hall song, she was often cast as an object of affection to employers and male customers alike. 'The Waitress' Love Letter' (1894) is sung from the point of view of Bill Brown, the manager of a restaurant that employs a waitress called Clara Clay. Clay writes Bill a letter, using a menu, but her feelings for him get mixed up in the jumble of words listing the dishes, causing the manager to be amused and even encouraged: 'my love can never swerve. You are just my own (hors d'oeuvre). Of my love I will not boast. You're my own (soft roe on toast)!' The menu closes with a salacious invitation (referring ostensibly to restaurants that also offered accommodation) to 'come and see me soon (Good beds)...Do be kind! (There are no fees of an-y kind)'.[154] In this particular rendering of music hall *double entendre*, the waitress seems to be less a person who carries a meal, and more the dish itself, laid out for male delight.

If 'The Waitress' Love Letter' permitted the (albeit objectified) waitress a (bawdy) voice, the popular song 'The Girl at the A.B.C.' (1898) articulated the perspective of the male diner, whose infatuation with

[151] 'London Eating-Houses', *Chambers's Edinburgh Journal* (June 1837), 174.
[152] *Ibid.*
[153] That said, one self-described 'Old Playgoer' made mention of the 'waitresses at the night oyster-rooms'. See 'The Orange Girl', in Albert Smith (ed.), *Gavarni in London: Sketches of Life and Character* (London: David Bogue, 1849), 47; Charles Selby, the actor–playwright, also referred to a 'damsel in attendance' called Sarah who waited at a 'humble dining establishment'. See Tabitha Tickletooth [Charles Selby], *The Dinner Question, or how to Dine Well and Economically* (London: Routledge, 1860), 144.
[154] 'The Waitress' Love Letter' (song), written by R. Morton, composed by W. G. Eaton (London: Francis, Day and Hunter, 1894).

a waitress is specifically directed towards the female staff at the light refreshment establishment, the Aerated Bread Company. The song appears to ventriloquize the sensibilities of an elite patron, who is slumming it somewhat, in his patronage of an institution that was undoubtedly frequented by many of the very same lower-middle-class patrons who were to be found in the music hall. He describes how, despite his snobbish Uncle Dick's reproach, he visits the A.B.C. to see a 'smart little waitress', 'her name's Ar-a-bel-la Be-lin-da- Clark... though I've christened her A.B.C.'. His desire for his uncle's approval of his match leads him to take Dick to the A.B.C. for lunch. When they are waited on by A.B.C., the waitress in question, Uncle Dick then falls for her and warns his nephew: 'take her, lad, quick, or your old uncle Dick will marry that girl at the A.B.C.'[155] By portraying both nephew and uncle as smitten, the song suggests that the possibility of having multiple suitors was an occupational hazard for these waitresses. That the name she is given by the nephew is the same as the place where she works also suggests that, in the popular imaginary, the waitress was an icon for the company and that part of the appeal of taking a meal there was in being waited on by her.

Waitresses could potentially cross class boundaries in popular fiction as well. In the serialized novel 'Peggy of Lyons: A Romance of the Famous Tea-Shops' (1910), the protagonist, Lady Margaret, the daughter of a Scottish peer, assumes the identity of a working girl in need of a job, which she finds at 'the great catering firm' Lyons.[156] Peggy, as she now styles herself, has fled to London in search of her suitor, John Strong, a man of whom her father disapproves. What follows is a series of chance encounters and separations that eventually resolve themselves in the betrothal of the two young lovers. Securing a job for herself at Lyons serves to justify Peggy's move to London and accords her financial independence from her father. Added to the allure is that posing as a waitress proves to be something of a novelty, particularly in the context of a light refreshment room: 'Yes, she, Lady Margaret Arnould, was going out to earn her living by waiting on men and women who also worked for their living', she tells herself haughtily.[157] Lady Margaret subsequently takes employment as a salesgirl for a West End milliner (thereby entering the domain of fashion, another critical site for the intersection of consumption, female objectification, and modern urban sensibility). But, significantly, the serialization

[155] 'The Girl at the A.B.C.' (song), written by W. E. Imeson, composed by W. G. Eaton (London: Francis, Day and Hunter, 1898).
[156] Miles Fairfax, 'Peggy of Lyons: A Romance of the Famous Tea-Shops', *Week-End*, 31 March 1910–15 September 1910.
[157] *Ibid.*, 7 April 1910, p. 752.

retained its original title, 'Peggy of Lyons', suggesting the high level of recognition associated with Lyons in this period.

In a review of the novel that appeared in the *Restaurant*, one correspondent noted that, while much attention had been given to the waiter in fiction, the waitress by contrast received little. However, with 'Peggy of Lyons', its author Miles Fairfax 'seeks to make good this neglect so far as it concerns the waitress of the popular restaurant of today'. Given the narrative details, from the waitresses' earnings to the round of duties they carried out, the *Restaurant* writer added, the 'story has elements of *vraisemblance*'.[158] Entering into the world of the Lyons waitress may have involved more than just passing interest for some; it also allowed apparently privileged access into the lives of single working women employed in a distinctly modern metropolitan space.

There is no doubt that fictional works like 'Peggy of Lyons' reflected the existence of a broader fascination with the waitress as emblematic of an increasingly heterosocial urban environment. In particular, extensive attention was accorded to the apparent ubiquity of waitresses in the light refreshment chains (as opposed to elite West End restaurants that continued to rely on waiters) that spread across the metropolis at the end of the century. An 1890 article devoted to waitresses in *All the Year Round* noted that Spiers and Pond, with its thirty branches in London mostly situated in or near underground and railway stations, employed about 2,000 waitresses.[159] A particular source of fascination was the waitress's uniform. At Spiers and Pond's Duval Restaurant, one reporter in 1888 waxed lyrical about 'the waitresses in their black gowns and white aprons, collars, and caps'.[160] Similarly, an undated photograph (probably from the 1890s) of a Lyons waitress features her wearing a snug-fitting black dress with white cuffs and a white collar, on which is fastened a white apron. Her hair is tucked neatly underneath a lace and linen white cap in 'the regulation Lyons fashion—that is to say, in neat rolls set carefully back over their forehead', as her fictional counterpart, Peggy, explains.[161] One waitress interviewed by the *Daily Mail* in 1896 admitted 'neatness means a lot...and to tell you a little secret of the profession, I think most girls know they look young and fresh and sweet in the white frilled caps'.[162]

[158] 'The Waitress in Fiction', *Restaurant* (May 1910), 221.
[159] 'Waitresses', *All the Year Round* (May 1890), 461; *Post Office London Directory for 1890* (London: W. Kelly and Co., 1891), 1967.
[160] 'Restaurant Waitresses', 8 December 1888, Restaurant Files, box C–F, London Cuttings, Bishopsgate.
[161] Miles Fairfax, 'Peggy of Lyons: A Romance of the Famous Tea-Shops', *Week-End*, 21 April 1910, p. 806.
[162] From *Daily Mail*, repr. in 'The Life of a Waitress', *Chef*, 22 August 1896, p. 7.

Another photograph, probably intended for publicity purposes, emphasized the dazzling full-length white aprons worn over the uniform, which further underlined Lyons's commitment to hygiene and efficiency. If they recalled contemporary images of the nurse, the uniform of the Lyons waitress also accorded with modern conceptions of an ordered, rationalized workforce. For Lyons waitresses also wore a circular broach affixed to the collar, which displayed a number that they were required to write on each customer's bill (see Figure 3.2).

If the allocation of a number to the waitress suggested the depersonalizing consequences of Lyons's insistence on streamlined efficiency, the testimony of many of his female employees (albeit recovered from the decidedly partial context of the firm's own archive) presented narratives steeped in pride and corporate identity. A certain Miss Nell Bacon, 'through whose hands 500,000 girls have passed into public service', rose through the ranks from waitress to teashop executive, and finally Chief Superintendent. In an unpublished reminiscence deposited in the Lyons archive, she recalled that she was initially employed at the first Lyons house, at 213 Piccadilly, where 'waitresses worked 74 hours a week

Figure 3.2. Lyons waitresses wearing the standard uniform worn between 1897 and 1916. (Reproduced with permission of the London Metropolitan Archives, City of London)

and thought nothing of it. The Teashop Staff were happy crews. The customers were our friends and we looked forward to seeing them every day, though my strong Suffolk accent used to amuse them.'[163] Presumably waitresses were expected to 'bandy a few words of small talk' particularly with men who 'just looked in for a little chat', as dramatized in 'Peggy of Lyons'.[164] This 'light chaff' likely created a congenial atmosphere that kept the men coming back. In her reminiscences, Nell Bacon testified to the fact that 'the majority of our customers [in the 1890s] were men'.[165] Clearly, some restaurant owners deliberately selected comely young women as a means to attract male diners. The *Caterer* reported in 1895 that 'pretty girls are eagerly taken as waitresses in certain restaurants and cafés, no matter how ignorant of their duties they may be'. One café manager defended his decision to advertise for twelve young ladies 'who must be . . . pretty' by insisting that 'the young fellows will go where there are the prettiest girls to wait upon them'.[166] Nevertheless, while waitresses offered the possibility of a parasexual frisson for male diners, it is also the case that they were indicative of an increasingly heterosocial restaurant scene. Bacon herself noted that women and children were regular customers on 'matinee days'.[167]

If employers and diners accorded the waitress a largely positive welcome to the public culture of the metropolis, many women themselves were attracted to the occupation, not least because it compared favourably to alternative employment, notably domestic service. The waitress at an underground railway station encountered by the *All the Year Round* correspondent declared that she would rather be a waitress than a governess, on the grounds that she would have more leisure and more independence.[168] A preference for waitressing over domestic service was lamented by some householders, who complained, as did one lady in her provincial paper, about the difficulty of finding domestic servants in London: 'it is useless to apply at registry offices for there are no servants to be had. We are told that Lyons' refreshment and tea shops has [*sic*] absorbed all

[163] Miss Nell Bacon, 'My Days with Lyons', TS, n.d., ACC 3527/231, Lyons Archive, LMA.
[164] Miles Fairfax, 'Peggy of Lyons: A Romance of the Famous Tea-Shops', *Week-End*, 28 April 1910, p. 837.
[165] Miss Nell Bacon, 'Nippy No. 1', TS, n.d., ACC 3527/231, Lyons Archive, LMA.
[166] 'The Waiters' Column', *Caterer*, 15 July 1895, p. 325. For another example of the intersection of commerce, female sexual allure, and male spectatorship, see Peter Bailey, 'Parasexuality and Glamour: The Victorian Barmaid as Cultural Prototype', *Gender and History*, 2/2 (1990), 148–72, repr. in Peter Bailey, *Popular Culture and Performance in the Victorian City* (Cambridge: Cambridge University Press, 2003), ch. 7.
[167] Miss Nell Bacon, 'Nippy No. 1', TS, n.d., ACC 3527/231, Lyons Archive, LMA.
[168] 'Waitresses', *All the Year Round* (May 1890), 461–2.

parlour maids who are available, and of course, just now the busy season has commenced.'[169] Waitressing also compared favourably to other non-domestic forms of labour, notably factory employment. Charles Booth observed that the daughters of the respectable working class 'shun the factories, many going to the City to become waitresses in tea-rooms'.[170] Waitressing was also preferable to office work, which required that women 'are shut up in small offices or small rooms. Their life never changes a fraction', as a waitress interviewed by the *Daily Mail* believed. By contrast, she said, 'we see new faces', adding brightly 'and get new ideas for dresses and bonnets from the women patrons'.[171]

The vocation of the waitress, while relatively attractive to many young women and glamourized in the discourses of popular culture, was, of course, not without its trials. Select Committees investigating shop hours and conditions provide extensive reportage of burdens endured by waitresses that replicate some of the grievances associated with their male equivalents. These included poor living conditions, inadequate meal hours, and bad food.[172] The testimony of a doctor called before the 1886 Select Committee on Shop Hours Regulation Bill also detailed the consequences for female health of the long hours that waitresses were often required to work.[173] Some waitresses highlighted problems specific to waitressing, notably the unwelcome attention of male voyeurs, a particular issue in establishments with limited space for washing and changing. Miss Emily Drake testified before the Select Committee on Shop Hours in 1892 that she and the other waitresses who worked at a refreshment house

[169] See 'Our Ladies' Column', by One of Themselves, *Evesham Journal*, 21 May 1898. The writer presumably lived in this locale outside the London season. For the broader context, see Lucy Delap, *Knowing their Place: Domestic Service in Twentieth Century Britain* (Oxford: Oxford University Press, 2011).

[170] Charles Booth, *Life and Labour of the People in London* (3rd ser., vol. 4; London: Macmillan, 1902), 145.

[171] From *Daily Mail*, repr. in 'The Life of a Waitress', *Chef*, 22 August 1896, p. 7. Cf. Jane E. Lewis, 'Women Clerical Workers in the Late Nineteenth and Early Twentieth Centuries', in Gregory Anderson (ed.), *The White Blouse Revolution: Female Office Workers since 1870* (Manchester: Manchester University Press, 1988). On popular representations, see Emma Liggins, ' "The Life of a Bachelor Girl in the Big City": Selling the Single Lifestyle to Readers of *Woman* and the *Young Woman* in the 1890s', *Victorian Periodicals Review*, 40/3 (2007), 216–38. More widely, see Jane Humphries, 'Women and Paid Work', in June Purvis (ed.), *Women's History: Britain 1850–1945* (London: University College London Press, 1995), 85–106.

[172] See, e.g., PP, *Report from the Select Committee on Shop Hours Regulation Bill* (1886), *Report and Special Report from the Select Committee on the Shop Hours Bill* (1892), *Report from the Select Committee of the House of Lords on Early Closing of Shops* (1901).

[173] Mr William Abbotts, MD to Sir James Fergusson, PP, *Report from the Select Committee on Shop Hours Regulation Bill* (1886), 101, l. 1965. In agreement was the author of 'Waitresses and Barmaids', *British Journal of Catering*, 1 September 1889, p. 7.

at Victoria station had inadequate washing facilities in a cellar, and 'we had to put up boards to keep the cellar-men and other people down below from looking through'.[174] A report by the *Lancet* on sanitation in shops that was included in the committee's findings drew attention to the intrusion into the waitresses' rest hours by the forewoman of a vegetarian restaurant who, between meal hours, distributed sewing among the waitresses 'and makes them work for her'.[175] Nor should we assume that the mention of waitresses before the Select Committees equates to widespread official concern about their condition. Indeed, waitresses came under the scrutiny of these committees only after their plight had been drawn attention to by a number of expert witnesses. One writer in 1886 pointed out that, while legislative action was being taken to help shop girls, 'why should waitresses have to wait for similar relief?'[176] By 1892, however, the Select Committee had specifically isolated waitresses for its inquiry, and a year later the Royal Commission Report on the Employment of Women reported in depth on their working conditions, leading at the end of the decade to proposed legislation dealing exclusively with them.[177]

In one notable and well-publicized case the grievances of waitresses became a public *cause célèbre*. Ironically, it was at Lyons, the establishment that showcased the waitress, that frustration with poor wages and conditions for waitresses spilled over into industrial action. In October 1895, probably as a consequence of the pressure felt by new financial investments and the desire to maximize revenue,[178] Lyons decided to reduce his waitresses' commissions from 5 per cent to 2½ per cent. These commissions, made from food ordered by customers plus any tips they left, constituted waitresses' wages; Lyons's waitresses earned no fixed salaries. When staff challenged the new policy, the management explained that new waitresses would be recruited on a 2½ per cent commission, which would rise to 5 per cent as they became more experienced. Meanwhile, behind the scenes, according to the standard history of Lyons, some more experienced waitresses were dismissed for minor offences, while new ones,

[174] Miss Emily Drake to Mr Provard, PP, *Select Committee on Shop Hours Bill* (1892), 227, l. 5485.
[175] 'Report of the "Lancet" Sanitary Commission on Sanitation in the Shop', in PP, *Select Committee on Shop Hours Bill* (1892), appendix 10, p. 247.
[176] 'Why Should Waitresses Have to Wait?', *Hotel Review and Catering & Food Trades' Gazette* (May 1886), 56.
[177] See PP, *Royal Commission on Labour: The Employment of Women* (1893); PP, Bills, etc., *A Bill to Amend the Law Relating to the Employment of Waitresses in Restaurants* no. 244, 9 June 1898.
[178] As is evidenced in Report of the Directors and Balance Sheet, 31 March 1895, ACC 3527/002, Lyons Archive, LMA.

earning a lower rate of commission, replaced them.[179] On 23 October, the waitresses at the Piccadilly and Strand tea shops walked out on strike, which, according to one reporter, was 'in the middle of the dinner hour', and they reconvened at St Andrew's restaurant in Bride Street, where they planned their strategy under the guidance of trade unionist Tom Mann, one of the leaders of the London Dock Strike of 1889.[180] A publicity campaign, under the slogan 'Lyons versus the Lambs', was launched in order to damage Lyons's reputation, and caught the attention of general and trade newspapers alike. Faced with such a vigorous response, the management quickly moved to offer a number of concessions, notably introducing salaries and abolishing the commission system altogether, a response that brought the strike to an end.

This apparent capitulation was warmly greeted by many, including the *Hotel*'s 'Looker-On', who said 'the commission system applied to waitresses, who are not saleswomen, is illogical in its reasoning and unfair in its working, and by thus opportunely abandoning it Messrs Lyons and Co. have gone a good way towards reestablishing themselves in favour'.[181] For the waitresses, however, Lyons's resolution may well have been something of a disappointment, for the commission system offered them opportunities lacking in other trades. Their objection was not to the commission system per se, but to the lowered rates that Lyons was attempting to enforce. Nevertheless, the ability of the waitresses, both to draw upon the popular good will, and to establish institutional support for their cause (the dispute led to the creation of a waitresses' union convened by the Women's Trade Union League), reveals the broader ability of both waiters and waitresses to avoid exploitation in this period.[182] Efforts at amelioration for those who waited on tables in London's restaurants were not confined to the high-profile female staff at Lyons. One month after the Lyons dispute had been settled, an 18-year-old coffee-tavern waitress appeared before Shoreditch County Court, suing her employer for being summarily dismissed for failing to get up at 4.30 in the morning. The young woman had been allowed a certain time off in the afternoon, but had been obliged to work until 12.45 the previous evening. The judge ruled in the waitress's favour, allowed her a full claim, and even awarded her 4s. expenses for attending court.[183]

[179] Peter Bird, *The First Food Empire: A History of J. Lyons & Co.* (Chichester: Phillimore & Co., Ltd, 2000), 44–5.
[180] 'A Novel Strike', *Hotel*, 30 October 1895, p. 17.
[181] 'The Looker On', *Hotel*, 6 November 1895, p. 19.
[182] 'Formation of a Waitresses Union', *Hotel*, 6 November 1895, p. 16; 'The Waiters' Column', *Caterer*, 15 November 1895, p. 523.
[183] 'Caterer's Notebook', *Caterer*, 16 December 1895, p. 539.

The redress offered to the Shoreditch waitress would suggest that waiters and waitresses could be beneficiaries of the increased regulation in the workplace that throughout the nineteenth and early twentieth centuries did much to alleviate the working conditions of labourers. Moreover, waiting staff also had a presence in the friendly societies and trade-union movements that, in different ways, sought to achieve a greater degree of security for members. In this sense, waiters and waitresses need to be accorded their proper place in the broader narratives of labour history. However, if the image of the alienated and disgruntled waiter to be found in the texts of popular culture was a misleading stereotype, it remains true that waiters and waitresses possessed characteristics that differentiated them from many other types of worker. In an age in which remuneration became more formalized, the continued reliance of waiting staff on commissions and tips (and the conventions of deductions) did create a distinctive, even idiosyncratic, working culture. Clearly, some elements of this workplace experience could be irksome. However, most waiters and waitresses appear to have benefited from a flexible form of remuneration that drew upon a broader culture that emphasized the free play of commercial forces and the strictures of self-reliance and self-improvement. This was even true of tipping, even if much of its operation remained something of a mystery to both waiting staff and those on whom they waited. The fluid labour market that allowed these workers considerable opportunity for reward and advancement also created a notable heterogeneity that they came to embody. The presence of waitresses and foreign waiters not merely underlines the association of London's restaurant scene with diversity. Taking the subject position of these particular social actors, rather than the strident, if unrepresentative, voices of a minority of nativists, reinforces a more congenial understanding of the lives and prospects of those who worked in restaurants. Far from being the source of moral panics, or being permanently fixed in the tropes of 'otherness', waitresses and foreign waiters draw attention to a more convincing narrative of cultural accommodation. More generally, the waiter's story is therefore part of a broader narrative about the late-nineteenth-century metropolis, one in which the free play of commercial forces and an increasing prevalence of cultural heterogeneity created as many opportunities as it did causes for anxiety and cultural pessimism. We would do well to remember, after all, that even Gissing's downtrodden Mr Sparkes had a little set by for a rainy day.

4

Health and Regulation in the Restaurant

Contemporaries in Victorian London confronted myriad risks in their daily lives, ranging from fires to sewer gases, from street crossings to railways. A sketch in *Punch* in 1900 relates the story of a man who takes refuge in a restaurant as an antidote to the enervating atmosphere of a journey on the underground. 'At the Bank I was staggering from sheer exhaustion, and was only just able to cross the road to this restaurant. But I feel better now!'[1] In fact, dining, or indeed working, in the restaurant did not necessarily offer respite from the perils of the urban environment. Diners could be subjected to food poisoning, resulting from the poor hygiene of either the restaurant kitchen or the people who prepared their food. Others got sick after eating food that had been adulterated. Restaurant workers suffered from a variety of ailments caused by unclean, cramped, and unventilated kitchens. Even those who did not enter the restaurant itself had good reason to complain about the negative impact of dining rooms on the urban environment, notably their production of noxious smells and suffocating smoke.

While such encounters with the less congenial aspects of the restaurant may have been unfortunate for the person afflicted, they might be felt to lack broader historical value. In fact, discussions that relate the restaurant to issues of hygiene and public health underline the significance of the restaurant to a developing urban culture in late-nineteenth-century London. A consideration of contemporary anxieties about adulteration and contamination draws attention to the chain that connected the consumer, not just to the restaurant, but also to the world of provisioning and supply.[2] Perhaps even more critically, the restaurant's potential as a site of pollution and disease ensured that it had a significant place in the activities and discourses of official regulation and inspection. Regulatory

---

[1] 'A Sleeping Partner', *Punch*, 10 October 1900, p. 254.

[2] In this regard, the history of the restaurant might intersect with the recourse among environmental historians to the concept of 'urban metabolism', in which cities are likened to organisms and considered in terms of inputs and outputs, although that is not the primary focus here. For 'urban metabolism', see J. R. McNeill, 'Observations on the Nature and Culture of Environmental History', *History and Theory*, 42/4 (2003), 5–43.

bodies such as the public health departments of the London County Council (LCC), individual boroughs, and the City of London became interested, not merely in the standards of hygiene to be found in restaurant kitchens, but also in the impact of restaurants on the wider urban environment. Indeed, inspectors seemed more aggrieved by the restaurant's contribution to air pollution than they were about rotting food or poisoned diners.

Considering restaurant inspection reinforces recent understandings of liberal governance in the late Victorian and Edwardian period, which emphasize pluralism and self-government. Inspection of restaurants was largely characterized by that same flexibility, sensitivity, and commitment to the prerogatives of self-regulation that were exhibited more widely in the official mind at this time. More critically, the official regulation of restaurants requires recognition of the power of commercial forces that has been absent from much of the scholarly literature on liberal governance but that has been a critical motif throughout this book. Moreover, if inspectors inevitably drew attention to the inadequacies of restaurant hygiene, the restaurant sector itself endeavoured to reassure customers that it had committed both effort and capital to maintaining the highest standards possible. In the case of temperance and vegetarian establishments, the restaurant was actively presented (by both proprietors and their allies in the wider reform movements) as a model modern urban space, in which not merely hygiene, but rational moral purity, could be ensured.

Falling ill after consuming contaminated food was a not entirely unexpected hazard in the world of public eating. One such perilous encounter with 'death in a pot' was reported in the *Anti-Adulteration Review and Food Journal* in 1882. When two friends dined at a restaurant on the Strand, one asked the other why 'he was not getting on with his dinner', to which he received the response that his fellow diner had been struck by a 'severe attack' of diarrhoea and sickness the night before. It then became apparent that both men had suffered the same unfortunate symptoms, perhaps not surprisingly given that they had eaten the same 'highly seasoned dish' the night before at the very same restaurant. The journal attributed this unfortunate occurrence to the poor hygiene of the restaurant's staff, and warned the proprietor who 'wink[s] at such unpardonable carelessness on the part of his assistants' that he was likely to ruin his business.[3] The fact that the journal did not seem surprised that the two gentlemen had returned to an establishment in which they had already succumbed to food poisoning raises interesting questions about the

---

[3] *Anti-Adulteration Review and Food Journal* (February 1882), 196.

prevalence of contamination and its associated hazards in London's restaurants in this period.

Holding restaurateurs to account for food poisoning was actually quite difficult. In a case brought before the King's Bench in 1911, an actor from Maidenhead, who was employed as an understudy at the Vaudeville Theatre during the autumn season, dined with another actor at Mr H. Appenrodt's restaurant in Piccadilly Circus. Both thespians claimed to have been taken ill after consuming potato salad at the restaurant, asserting that they were victims of ptomaine poisoning. In defence, the manager of the house explained that the salad was made with due care by his kitchen assistant, one Mrs Myer, who used a variety of ingredients including pickled herrings and cucumbers, gherkins, Spanish onions, capers, ham, boiled potatoes, and mayonnaise of egg and vinegar. A physician who acted as an expert witness cast doubt on the validity of the actors' charge. He said that their illness was not a result of Mrs Myer's slightly heady concoction, but stemmed from the diners' subsequent decision to retire to a public house, where their aperitif took the form of a robust glass of stout. The physician chastised the diners for their choice of after-dinner beverage. Coffee or peppermint liquor might have been a suitable accompaniment to a salad, he said, rather than a heavy ale that inevitably made digesting Mrs Myer's pickled onions more challenging than it should have been.[4] The distinction between food poisoning caused by the management and indigestion caused by the actors' poor judgement lay at the root of the case, which was decided in favour of Mr Appenrodt.[5]

It was much easier to hold restaurateurs to account for producing meals in palpably unhygienic premises. Contemporary reporting paid particular attention to the unsanitary dining room and kitchen. In spite of its usual advocacy for the restaurant business, the trade press often seemed to delight in revealing the failings of those in the sector who did not sustain the appropriate standards of cleanliness. These narratives echoed a combination of high-mindedness, indignation, and voyeurism found in reporting by social reformers in the same period. One writer calling himself 'Vegetarian' wrote to the editor of the *Vegetarian* newspaper in 1899, complaining of the squalor of the dining room in the newly opened Vegetarian Café Restaurant in Holborn, and the impossibility of finding a table

[4] 'Allegations against a Salad: Verdict for Mr Appenrodt', *Restaurant* (June 1911), 206.
[5] *Ibid.* In another case involving Gatti's Adelaide Gallery, the King's bench focused on the problem of one diner's illness from the mushrooms prepared in an omelette, and whether this was the result of the restaurant's negligence or the individual's constitution. 'Cases in the Courts: Alleged Poisoning by Mushrooms', *Restaurant* (February 1911), 53.

not 'showing the least traces of the last dinners, in the shape of crumbs, spilt fruit juice, etc.'.[6] Conditions like these may have led to the presence of 'a family of rats, snuggly at home behind a mirror' in an unnamed London restaurant, as reported in the *Caterer*, leading the unfortunate readers to fret about which particular establishment they might want to avoid in future.[7]

Other reporters were less concerned to single out specific establishments (named or otherwise) than they were to build a broader case that customers deserved protection from an unregulated industry that posed a more extensive challenge to public health. In a 1911 article entitled 'Restaurant Kitchens: A Growing Public Danger', printed in the short-lived *M.A.P.* (*Mostly about People*), the author argued that ptomaine poisoning and other dangerous illnesses arising from bad or improperly prepared restaurant meals were becoming all too common. Without naming names or revealing sources, the author complained about unprepossessing practices in many of London's restaurant kitchens that put even those diners with the strongest stomachs at risk. In busy kitchens could be found an abundance of grease, dirt, unclean utensils, and cooks and waiters who touched food and plates with dirty hands. Only a few restaurants kept a stock of clean cloths for wiping the plates and glasses. Recalling a complaint against one restaurant 'some years ago', he stated that the establishment received clean cloths only once a month, and the plates were wiped with rags that were used to wipe the floor. Adding to the evil combination of a dirty cloth in a dirty hand was the practice of breathing on plates and into glasses when giving them a final polish. The 'no waste rule' practised by some restaurants was evidence of the industry's further degradation and need for reform. According to the writer, those dishes served as entrées under a variety of different names were prepared from the remains that diners had left on their plates.[8] A similar observation was made in the popular *Strand Magazine* regarding some unnamed Soho eating houses, where soups were said to be composed of bits of bread left over from the dishes of previous customers.[9]

Even if most diners were to be spared the horrors of a squalid or unhygienic dining room and kitchen, there was no guarantee that the kitchen staff in the very same establishment were not subject to conditions that were substandard, or even close to unbearable. Monsieur Suzanne, the *chef de cuisine* to the Duke of Bedford, chastised clients of fashionable

[6] 'The Vegetarian Café Restaurant: To the Editor of the *Vegetarian*', *Vegetarian*, 26 August 1899, p. 408.

[7] 'Odds and Ends', *Caterer*, 16 September 1895, p. 396.

[8] 'Restaurant Kitchens', *M.A.P.* [*Mostly about People*], 28 January 1911, p. 118.

[9] 'Some Dining Places', *Strand Magazine*, 24 (1902), 191.

restaurants who, luxuriating in the artistically carved panels and gilded mouldings that surrounded them as they ate, might have been led to believe that 'the kitchen, in its construction and arrangements, would be on a par with the importance of the establishment—that space would not be spared, and ventilation be well secured'. Suzanne did not have a very high opinion of architects and builders, who, he believed, failed to register the 'novel requirements of the modern kitchen'. For, while the expansion of the restaurant sector led to the larger and better-equipped dining rooms that secured 'the ease and comfort of its habitués', the kitchen 'has been allowed to remain as it was originally, notwithstanding the larger number of customers entertained'.[10] Suzanne's particular attention was directed to the inadequacies of kitchen ventilation. In describing the problem, he pointed to the stifling atmosphere created by emanations arising from all sorts of viands in the process of cooking, intermingled with vapours from stockpots, the moisture of boiling vegetables, and steam from copper pots. The nausea-inducing odour of frying fat, fumes from the gas apparatus, and smoke from the fire further added to this unwholesome environment. Suzanne asked his readers to imagine a room about 8 yards square: at one end was a roasting grate where 'a scorching fire is blazing all day' and, at the other, a range composed of ovens, hot plates, and steamers. Adjacent to them were a hot closet, gas apparatus, charcoal stove, and grill. In the midst of 'this circle of fire' were eighteen or twenty men 'elbowing each other, and busy baking, frying, broiling, stewing, and roasting'. In these feverish conditions, it was little wonder that the health of the cook was seriously jeopardized.[11] To add to their suffering, these workers had to endure worse conditions when their managers fastened down kitchen windows, after neighbouring houses complained about smoke and bad smells wafting from them.[12]

Even if restaurateurs improved their own facilities and standards of preparation, they still faced the problem that the ingredients that their staff worked with might well have been contaminated at some point in the process of production, distribution, or supply. Public-health inspectors were regularly called upon to tackle what they termed 'unsound food' that was discovered at wholesalers, markets, and other distributors in London. References to putrid meat and fish, and rotting food infested with maggots, occur frequently in their reports. In 1911 and 1912, tuberculosis was identified in the carcasses of pigs imported from both Russia and China, and there were periodic discussions within the LCC about the need to

---

[10] 'Typical English Kitchens', *Caterer*, 15 April 1887, p. 117.   [11] *Ibid.*   [12] *Ibid.*

have a more rigorous and regular inspection of slaughter houses.[13] The Edwardian period also saw increasing concern about the spoiling and contamination of food that, while awaiting delivery, had been left on the street, where it had been exposed to the pollution of 'dogs and cats, human sputem, horse droppings, petroleum, lubricating grease, disinfecting oils, chemicals, and so on' derived from passers-by.[14] Moreover, scientific expertise in the area of botulism and other forms of germ contamination was becoming more sophisticated in this period, drawing greater attention to the dangers of spoiled food.

Fears of contamination were paralleled by concerns about the adulteration of foodstuffs.[15] Spiers and Pond were keen to publicize their investment in up-to-date technology and scientific improvements to maintain the appropriate hygienic standards for the food that was ultimately served in their restaurants. Their headquarters at Ludgate Hill incorporated temperature-controlled storage chambers, which guaranteed meat, fish, and dairy immunity from sudden changes of weather and problems of spoilage.[16] However, even they fell foul of the dangers of adulterated food and drink. In December 1893 alone, the firm faced several summonses for serving milk from which a proportion of the fat had been abstracted, 'so as to injuriously affect its quality, substance, or nature'.[17] According to the Sale of Food and Drugs legislation, it was an offence to sell milk that lacked the proper amount of cream, and offenders could be found guilty of fraud. In a case brought by the Camberwell vestry against the firm's Crystal Palace station restaurant, Spiers and Pond argued

---

[13] Annual Report of the Council (1911), v. 3, p. 67, LCC/Official Publications/18.7 (5) store; Annual Report of the Council (1912) v. 3, p. 76, LCC/Official Publications/18.7 (5) store. London Metropolitan Archives, [hereafter LMA].

[14] LCC Conference on Matters Relating to Public Health (1911), 19, LCC/Official Publications/791/72/25.0 store, LMA.

[15] For a brief commentary on the material and metaphorical aspects of food adulteration in the Victorian period, see Erika Rappaport, *A Thirst for Empire: How Tea Shaped the Modern World* (Princeton: Princeton University Press, 2017), 121–5. See also Michael French and Jim Phillips, *Cheated not Poisoned? Food Regulation in the United Kingdom, 1875–1938* (Manchester: Manchester University Press, 2000); Derek J. Oddy, 'Food Quality in London and the Rise of the Public Analyst, 1870–1939', in Peter J. Atkins, Peter Lummel, and Derek J. Oddy (eds), *Food and the City in Europe since 1800* (Aldershot: Ashgate, 2007); Sandra Morton, 'A Little of what you Fancy Does you . . . Harm!!', in Judith Rowbotham and Kim Stevenson (eds), *Criminal Conversations: Victorian Crimes, Social Panic, and Moral Outrage* (Columbus: Ohio State University Press, 2005); John Burnett, 'The History of Food Adulteration in Great Britain in the Nineteenth Century, with Special Reference to Bread, Tea and Beer', Ph.D. thesis, University of London, 1958; John Burnett, *Plenty and Want: A Social History of Diet in England from 1815 to the Present Day* (London: Scolar Press, 1979), 114–20, 240–67.

[16] e.g. 'A Visit to Spiers and Pond's, and what we Saw there', *Weekly Chronicle*, 8 December 1888, p. 8.

[17] *Food and Sanitation*, 16 December 1893, p. 390.

that, if there was any problem with their product, it was the fault of the milk contractor, who 'agreed to supply the defendants "new milk in good condition, pure and unadulterated, and in the same state as when taken from the cow"'.[18] The Lambeth magistrate, before whom the case was heard, argued that, even if the defendants obtained the milk in good faith, they were nonetheless personally responsible for it, and he fined them. Over the next years, the firm faced further summonses for this offence, on four separate occasions in 1895 alone.[19] Despite new additions, notably the introduction of specially constructed milk churns that caused the milk to be stirred, samples were still found to be impure, and more fines were imposed. In the same year, Messrs Pearce appeared before the Clerkenwell magistrates on similar charges, and lost their case on the grounds that it was illegal to pass off skimmed or diluted milk as whole milk.[20] So pervasive was the problem of adulterated milk that one correspondent for the journal *Food and Sanitation*, which frequently reported on the issue, commented that, over the last few years, 46 per cent of all coffee houses and restaurants had been found sufficiently inferior for their milk to warrant magisterial proceedings being instituted against them.[21] Nor was it only big restaurants that were the target of these investigations. For instance, Joseph Millis, restaurant keeper of a small establishment in Pimlico, was fined by the Westminster police court for adding boric acid 'for preservation purposes' to the milk instead of disposing of it.[22]

The Millis case suggested that small proprietors with limited profit margins were inevitably subject to the temptation of substituting ersatz ingredients or dishes in the food they served.[23] In two different cases in Lambeth, eating-house keepers Mrs Charlotte Lovell and Mr Joseph Richardson were each fined for adulterating foodstuffs on their premises, in their case coffee. What Lovell was passing off as coffee was in fact 70 per cent chicory. Her counsel pointed out that the challenge for modest establishments such as Mrs Lovell's was that their customers were unwilling to pay more than a halfpenny a cup, for which it was unrealistic to expect they might receive the authentic brew, which was usually sold for around four pence. The judge proved unsympathetic, pointing out that

[18] *Ibid.*

[19] *Food and Sanitation*, 26 January 1895, p. 27; 27 April 1895, p. 125; 13 July 1895, p. 207; 9 November 1895, p. 341.

[20] 'What is Skimmed Milk?', *Caterer*, 15 November 1895, p. 522.

[21] 'Correspondence: Coffee Houses and Restaurants', *Food and Sanitation*, 7 November 1896, p. 537.

[22] *Food and Sanitation*, 25 October 1896, p. 510.

[23] Indeed, official concerns about adulteration in this period tended to focus on fraud rather than health. See Jim Phillips and Michael French, 'Adulteration and Food Law, 1899–1939', *Twentieth-Century British History*, 9/3 (1998), 350–69.

'there was no reason why tradesmen should delude poor people by leading them to suppose they were selling an article at an impossible price'.[24] Such rulings suggest that the courts believed working people, no less than their more affluent peers, deserved not to be swindled, and were keen to maintain the good name of those engaged in the provision of public eating across the restaurant sector.

Because restaurants could be associated with illness, they inevitably came within the purview of the elaborate apparatus of public-health inspection and regulation that had emerged in London by the end of the nineteenth century. The expansion of the restaurant sector coincided with the consolidation, and growing confidence, of London local government.[25] From the 1890s onwards, the Public Health Department of the LCC became the dominant voice in this regard, but we also need to remember that there were sanitary committees attached to individual London vestries, and the City of London had its own semi-independent public-health apparatus (including up until 1897 its own Commission of Sewers). Inspectors and regulators often encountered the restaurant through the pursuit of longer-established public-health concerns, notably water supply, sewage, and smoke pollution. However, the 1891 Public Health (London) Act, which extended the powers of the inspectors to investigate conditions under which people worked, in its definition of workplaces, specifically included hotel and restaurant kitchens (a feature of the act that was confirmed in 1901).[26] Moreover, the dramatic expansion of the restaurant sector from the 1880s onwards ensured that it became more prominent in the discourses and activities of regulation. A conference on public health organized by the LCC in 1911, while it gave most attention to tuberculosis and measles in schools, water supply to tenement houses, and the disposal of the dead, dedicated a not inconsiderable part of its proceedings to 'places where food is prepared and exposed

---

[24] 'Coffee Shop House', *Food and Sanitation*, 18 April 1896, p. 189.

[25] Christopher Hamlin, 'Public Sphere to Public Health: The Transformation of "Nuisance"', in Steve Sturdy (ed.), *Medicine, Health and the Public Sphere in Britain, 1600–2000* (London: Routledge, 2002), 189–204; Michelle Allen, *Cleansing the City: Sanitary Geographies in Victorian London* (Athens, OH: Ohio University Press, 2008); Lee Jackson, *Dirty Old London: The Victorian Fight against Filth* (New Haven: Yale University Press, 2014); Bill Luckin, *Death and Survival in Urban Britain: Disease, Pollution and Environment, 1850–1950* (London: I. B. Tauris, 2015). For the expansion of local government in London more generally, see John Davis, *Reforming London: The London Government Problem, 1855–1900* (Oxford: Oxford University Press, 1988); Susan D. Pennybacker, *A Vision for London, 1889–1914: Labour, Everyday Life and the LCC Experiment* (London: Routledge, 1995).

[26] See, e.g., Notice to Abate Nuisance under the Public Health (London) Act 1891, to the Caledonian Hotel, 28 March 1895, 455/8, City of Westminster Archive Centre.

for sale'.[27] A delegate from Hampstead, one Dr McCleary, emphasized the necessity for stringent precautions being taken in places where food was prepared, insisting that this was particularly significant in the capital, because 'the greater proportion of Londoners are consuming food pre-pared in premises other than their own homes'.[28]

London's legislators regularly debated expanding or reforming legisla-tion that would have impacted on restaurant inspection, and at various points the powers of inspectors were extended. However, usually it was concluded that existing powers were sufficient, but they required more rigorous and thorough application. The annual reports of the LCC's Public Health Committee testified to the significance of restaurants within the scope of inspection. True, these reports are neither comprehensive nor consistent. In many cases, restaurants were not distinguished from the broader category of 'places where food is prepared for sale', and figures for inspection for some boroughs exist only for certain years, and for other boroughs they do not exist at all. Nevertheless, there are several occasions where the reports do isolate the number of restaurants inspected within the global figures for the number of workplaces that were scrutinized in each individual borough. For example, in the 1899 report, the Shoreditch Medical Officer of Health indicated that a total of 138 restaurants, coffee houses, and cookshops had been inspected, 93 of which had been 'found faulty' in one or more respects.[29] The 1901 report recorded that, of the 551 workplaces inspected in Holborn, 67 were restaurant kitchens. In that same year, two inspectors for Islington visited 25 restaurants (out of a total of about 1,600 places they inspected).[30]

Unfortunately, the statistical data available from the LCC's own records do not usually provide figures for the number of restaurants deemed unsanitary, nor is there routinely any reference to the particular problem that was being investigated. Nevertheless, the records of inspection and regulation illuminate the specific ways in which the restaurant related to the issue of public health, and testify to the increasing significance of public eating within the shaping and ordering of the late Victorian and Edwardian urban environment. While relations between inspectors and establishments they inspected could sometimes be fraught, public-health regulators generally seemed content that they had ensured improvement

---

[27] LCC Conference on Matters Relating to Public Health (1911), p. 19, LCC/Official Publications/791/72/25.0 store, LMA.

[28] *Ibid.* 20.

[29] Annual Report of the Medical Officer of Health (1899), 77, LCC/Official Publications/ 18.7 store, LMA.

[30] Annual Report of the Medical Officer of Health (1901), 74, LCC/Official Publications/ 18.7 store, LMA.

and sustained standards of hygiene in the restaurant sector. It is important to remember that the need for inspection was driven less by the impera- tives of surveillance and social control, and more by the need to respond to specific complaints raised by members of the public. As a consequence, inspectors went to restaurants to investigate a range of potential health hazards, encompassing rotting food, sewage, infestation, and contamin- ation. However, in the 1880s and 1890s, the major source of contention between inspectors and restaurants was to be over not the conditions in kitchens or dining rooms, but rather the restaurant's contribution to the broader issue of air pollution, notably the 'black smoke' phenomenon that had replaced drinking water and sewage as the main focus of anxieties about the toxicities of the urban environment.

This is not to deny that inspectors often encountered in restaurants public-health issues that echoed the concern with the supply of fresh water and the removal of human waste that had been central to the well- publicized evils and reform initiatives of the mid-nineteenth century. In the late 1870s and early 1880s, just as Joseph Bazalgette's monumental programme of sewer construction was reaching its completion, inspectors who entered restaurants still found evidence of poor hygiene created by substandard sanitation. In January 1879, inspectors discovered that a blocked drain on Lower Thames Street, combined with rotting fish, had created 'offensive odours' that had infiltrated a restaurant situated above.[31] Conversely, ineffective drainage of the kitchen of the Harp Tavern in Harp Lane in the City, investigated in December 1880, produced noxious smells that seeped into the post office with which it shared a party wall.[32]

Inspectors were concerned about water contaminated with sewage being used for cleaning and cooking purposes in restaurant kitchens. In the City, such incidents were often linked to water supply outlets that had survived from the district's premodern history. The inspector was trans- formed into an amateur archaeologist as he sought the cause of contam- ination in the subterranean wells, pumps, and basements that had originated in the City's medieval and even Roman past.[33] In May 1880, the Medical Officer of Health for the City of London's Commission of

---

[31] Report from the Sanitary Committee, 28 January 1879, p. 17, CLA/006/AD/05/ 22, LMA.

[32] Report of the Medical Officer of Health, 14 December 1880, p. 261, CLA/006/AD/ 05/23, LMA.

[33] In addition, there was always the possibility of stumbling upon the City's ancient burial grounds. For example, while renovation was being undertaken on the Chapter Coffee House in Paternoster Row in 1888, approximately 200 skeletons were discovered, possibly dating back to the Black Death. See 11 January 1888, Restaurant Files, box C–F, London Cuttings, Bishopsgate.

Sewers, William Sedgwick Saunders, found that the drinking and cooking water in an eating house on Ludgate Hill, polluted with urine and sewage, had been derived from a well situated in a neighbouring house in Fleet Street. The officer was able to ascertain that this was 'one of the old surface wells of the City, the existence of which was not previously known to myself or either of the Sanitary Inspectors'.[34] Five years previously, Sedgwick Saunders reported that inspectors regularly discovered ancient cesspits 'which lie hidden in all kinds of out-of-the-way places', not merely beneath residences and offices but also below restaurants.[35]

In a report prepared for the Medical Officer of Health for the LCC, on 'Preparation and Sale of Food in London', Dr W. H. Hamer pointed out that, in very many central London eating houses, the kitchen was situated in an underground cellar, the very same place where house drains were located.[36] Hamer recalled a visit to an eating house in the Strand in which the kitchen was in a cellar. The room was only 6 feet in height, and the sole ventilation was a small space situated under the grating of the pavement on the street outside.[37] To make matters worse, there was a trapped gulley, which communicated with the drain, situated at the back of the kitchen.[38] At one point, the cellar also served as a stable for a pony.[39] In what might have seemed a superfluous observation, Hamer concluded that 'under such conditions it is manifest that the cellar is not a fit place for use as a kitchen'.[40] In 1902, of the total of 155 kitchens inspected in the City of London, 76 were said to be situated in basements. The Medical Officer of Health identified this as 'a serious defect', but was pleased to report that, in more modern restaurants, it was not being repeated, since kitchens there were almost invariably located on the top floor.[41] However, seven years later, sanitary inspectors in Islington continued to bemoan the survival of basement kitchens. Openings intended to admit light and ventilation into the kitchens were much more likely to bring in dirt and detritus from the road above. Where there were no yards, kitchens were often used to store food and refuse, and the heat generated by cooking rendered 'this storage doubly offensive'.[42] A certain Mrs Young declared that the abolition of basement kitchens was ultimately

[34] Report of the Medical Officer of Health, 25 May 1880, p. 119, CLA/006/AD/05/23, LMA.

[35] Report of the Medical Officer of Health, 27 April 1875, p. 120, CLA/006/AD/05/18, LMA.

[36] *Preparation and Sale of Food in London* (LCC Official Publications, 1899), 11, LMA.

[37] *Ibid.*   [38] *Ibid.*   [39] *Ibid.*   [40] *Ibid.*

[41] Annual Report of the Medical Officer of Health (1902), 85, cited in Agenda Papers, Report of the Medical Officer of Health, 23 June 1903, p. 327, LCC/Min/10,046, LMA.

[42] 'Underground Kitchens in Restaurants', *Restaurant* (September 1909), 35.

the only solution. Since it was already forbidden to make clothing in insanitary places, it seemed even more necessary that the preparation of food should also be outlawed in any room 'through which it was impossible for a current of fresh air to pass'.[43]

In both old and new establishments, the perennial, not to say notorious, lack of space in metropolitan boroughs impacted on issues of hygiene and the restaurant. Inspectors were particularly concerned about the proximity of toilet facilities, for both workers and diners, to the places where food was prepared. In March 1891, a visitor to an eating house owned by one William Stockham at 71 Farringdon Street revealed that a toilet, without water, in a very defective and dilapidated condition, and 'smelling abominably', opened directly into the kitchen.[44] Other forms of poor hygiene were directly attributable to activities in the kitchen itself. In the 1880s, inspectors were concerned that failure properly to remove animal and vegetable refuse from taverns and restaurants might lead to cholera outbreaks. If food left to fester in kitchens was a health risk to workers and diners, transporting refuse away from the restaurant risked creating a nuisance for those living in the neighbourhood. In 1884, the removal of foul-smelling hogwash from Read's Dining Rooms in Cheapside sufficiently annoyed neighbours and passers-by that they appealed to the police to intervene.[45] What aggravated matters was that some restaurants retained refuse and fats, awaiting their collection by individuals and companies that made a living from recycling restaurant waste. In 1902, the LCC Medical Officer of Health investigated the premises of a Mr J. Podrotti in Wandsworth in order to establish whether he was operating as a 'fat melter'—in other words, someone who collected, and subsequently melted, kitchen grease, which was then sold to soap boilers or fish fryers.[46] The investigation proved inconclusive. However, the sale of restaurant waste was clearly a potentially lucrative enterprise. An article in the *Restaurant* described the activities of the venerable firm of Fred Squire and Sons. This company collected refuse and fats from restaurants and hotels in the early morning and then carried them, first by van and then by barge, from Paddington Basin, to its recycling factory in Middlesex.[47]

The unpleasant mephitic consequence of the removal of kitchen waste was part of a broader preoccupation of inspectors with the restaurant as a

[43] *Ibid.*

[44] Report of the Medical Officer of Health, 24 March 1891, p. 103, CLA/006/AD/05/035, LMA.

[45] Report of the Medical Officer of Health, 7 October 1884, p. 248, CLA/006/AD/05/28, LMA.

[46] Agenda Papers, 15 April 1902, p. 2, LCC/Min/10,048, LMA.

[47] 'By-Products of the Restaurant', *Restaurant* (March 1911), 88.

source of offensive odours. In the 1890s, inspectors were regularly called upon to intervene when the smells emanating from fried fish shops were the subject of complaint from neighbouring residences and businesses. In one case, on Farringdon Street, the smell of cooking fish was found to be 'of a disgusting and highly obnoxious character' and 'seriously prejudicial to health'.[48] In 1895, the fumes arising from boiling fat at Harris's Sausage and Onion Shop on Aldgate High Street produced what the inspector termed 'an intolerable nuisance' in the neighbourhood. The smell emanating from this establishment had apparently been so unbearable that it led to a member of the clergy threatening to leave his adjacent residence, and was also deemed unendurable by the owner of an abattoir across the street (whose sense of smell, one might have thought, would have been diminished by his line of work).[49] Sometimes putrid smells were combined with thick smoke. In 1904, LCC inspectors were perturbed by 'a pestilential odour' arising amid a cloud of smoke from the chimney of the Hans Crescent Hotel in Knightsbridge.[50]

Indeed, in the last two decades of the nineteenth century, smoke was to be the major bone of contention between London's public-health regulatory system and the restaurant sector. The authorities were concerned that the smoke arising from furnaces, fireplaces, or cookers was not being consumed internally, and was thus being discharged into the air outside. This created excessive amounts of free carbonic acid in the atmosphere, which contributed to respiratory problems and even death. The concerns of sanitary inspectors were bolstered by the complaints regularly submitted by individuals and businesses that were in proximity to the sources of escaped smoke. What made the problem particularly acute was the continued use of bituminous or 'soft' coal. Eating houses were not the only offenders here. The records of the City of London's Commission of Sewers, which remained responsible for investigating issues to do with air pollution up until 1897,[51] listed a variety of manufacturing, commercial, and financial premises (including, on one occasion, the Bank of England and a City post office) that were censured for allowing the escape

[48] Report of the Medical Officer of Health, 11 July 1893, p. 253, COL/PHD/AD/03/07, LMA.
[49] Report of the Medical Officer of Health, 22 October 1895, p. 294, CLA/006/AD/05/039, LMA.
[50] Letter from MA Bailliens Hamilton to Shirley Murphy, Medical Officer, 19 April 1904, LCC/Min/10,050, LMA.
[51] The Sewers Act of 1897 dissolved the Commission of Sewers, and its duties and responsibilities were transferred to the Corporation of London's Public Health Department in 1898.

of the black smoke associated with the burning of soft coal.[52] However, in the early 1880s, the inspectors asserted that 'the chief offenders have been the Restaurant keepers and the City Clubs'.[53] In February 1884, a list of repeat offenders that appeared in a report on smoke nuisance from the Medical Officer of Health included the Guildhall Tavern, Ruttermann's restaurant, and restaurants numbers 27, 28, and 30 Old Jewry. The report also recorded that Mr Joseph Thorn, manager of the People's Café, had been fined for 'negligently using a furnace'.[54] A report from July 1885 stated that notices under the Smoke Nuisances Act were required for a vegetarian restaurant at number 8 Queen Street, Cheapside, the Golden Fleece Tavern next door, a German restaurant at number 4 Bucklersbury, and Simpson's restaurant in Cheapside.[55]

In 1887, the Commission of Sewers welcomed an apparent tightening of the law under the terms of the Smoke Abatement (Metropolis) Bill, the Medical Officer of Health specifically referencing the problem of 'unconsumed smoke from restaurants, taverns, clubs, & against whom convictions have been most difficult to obtain'.[56] However, five years later, an extensive report on the Guildhall Tavern by the Medical Officer of Health, William Sedgwick Saunders, suggested that it was often still difficult to prosecute successfully restaurants that had committed smoke nuisances. The indefatigable Sedgwick Saunders went to the trouble of retrieving over a decade and a half's worth of records to reveal that he had reported on the Guildhall Tavern on no fewer than eleven occasions since 1878. Sedgwick Saunders was frustrated by the deficiencies of the law, because of which, in 'case after case', offenders had been able to escape convictions by deflecting their liability onto those who had constructed the furnaces, the incompetence of those employed to work them, or the use of poor-quality coal.[57]

However, such frustration did not blunt the zeal of the inspectors, who in some cases placed offending establishments under daily observation. W. J. Gellatly, responsible for inspecting the Cannon Street Hotel in late

[52] See, e.g., Extract from Report of the Medical Officer of Health, 8 January 1884, COL/PHD/AD/03/04, LMA.

[53] Report of the Medical Officer of Health, 19 June 1883, p. 151, CLA/006/AD/05/27, LMA.

[54] Report of the Medical Officer of Health, 5 February 1884, p. 35, CLA/006/AD/05/28, LMA.

[55] Report of the Medical Officer of Health, 14 July 1885, p. 194, CLA/006/AD/05/28, LMA.

[56] Report of the Medical Officer of Health, 10 May 1887, p. 200, COL/PHD/AD/03/05, LMA.

[57] Report of the Medical Officer of Health, 15 March 1892, p. 380, COL/PHD/AD/03/06, LMA.

1892, recorded that he had seen dense black smoke created by a furnace used for generating steam for cooking purposes emerge from a shaft on seventeen different days. He also recorded the exact times, to the minute, and the duration, of the offence.[58] Gellatly drew up a similarly detailed report on Ruttermann's restaurant located in London Wall two months later (in this case, taking the time to note the name of the person responsible for stoking the furnace).[59] What particularly vexed inspectors was that some of the most consistent polluters were well-known and profitable establishments. In the spring of 1895, notices were served on both Spiers and Pond in Water Lane and the Duval Restaurant on Wormwood Street.[60] In the latter case, on the basis of a report by the appropriately named Inspector Gathercole, legal proceedings were launched, the restaurant's proprietors having 'been repeatedly warned of their offence'.[61]

Sedgwick Saunders's preoccupation with the impact of restaurants on air pollution is most evident in an extensive memorandum he drew up in 1897 specifically dedicated to the subject of the 'smoke nuisance from City restaurants'.[62] He was candid about his frustrations with the legal loopholes, which he believed constituted the major obstacle to the successful implementation of 'a sanitary crusade for the annihilation of smoke'.[63] At one point in his report, Sedgwick Saunders appeared to distance himself from undue emphasis on the contribution of restaurants to the problem of smoke, pointing out that there were probably just as many fireplaces consuming soft coal in City offices as there were in City restaurants.[64] However, the fact that he had no intention of letting restaurants off the hook was definitively registered by the inclusion of what he termed 'a spot map' of the City, in which every restaurant, tavern, bakehouse, and other place where food was cooked for sale to the public was marked with a round dot (see Figure 4.1).[65] This was not a comprehensive mapping of public eating in the City. Sedgwick Saunders had mapped only the 614 establishments that gave off black smoke, deliberately excluding businesses such as the Aerated Bread Company (A.B.C.), which used gas stoves.[66] Three months later, a printed notice was

[58] Inspection Report on Smoke Nuisance, 22 November 1892, p. 463, COL/PHD/AD/03/06, LMA.

[59] Cited in the Report of the Medical Officer of Health, 10 January 1893, p. 3, CLA/006/AD/05/37, LMA.

[60] Report of the Medical Officer of Health, 7 May 1895, p. 139, CLA/006/AD/05/039; Report from the Sanitary Committee, 11 June 1895, p. 173, CLA/006/AD/05/039, LMA.

[61] Report of the Medical Officer of Health, 25 June 1895, p. 195, CLA/006/AD/05/039, LMA.

[62] Report of the Medical Officer of Health, 19 February 1897, p. 93, CLA/006/AD/05/41, LMA.

[63] *Ibid.* 94.   [64] *Ibid.*   [65] *Ibid.*   [66] *Ibid.*

delivered by hand to each of the 614 establishments marked on Sedgwick Saunders's spot map.[67] This notice reminded restaurant proprietors that the emanation of black smoke from their premises would be subject to legal sanction, but also recommended that the proprietor consider the construction of cooking ranges that used gas (or a mixture of gas and coke) as opposed to soft coal.[68] In September 1897, Sedgwick Saunders was happy to report that the notice had 'on the whole been attended with excellent results', and that complaints about black smoke had definitely decreased.[69] Nevertheless, prosecutions continued, as did requests for additional personnel to extend the monitoring of restaurants that failed to comply with the law.[70] From 1892, it appears that the LCC put increasing pressure on individual boroughs and the City to tackle the problem of black smoke. An LCC report from 1898 argued that this initiative, accompanied by a more rigorous implementation of the Public Health (London) Act of 1891, had led to 'very considerable improvement', with only isolated instances of nuisances from black smoke being now observed.[71]

While they were clearly dedicated to their task, it is important not to stereotype inspectors as self-righteous busybodies. Indeed, in their interactions with the world of London eating, inspectors were more likely to show themselves to be pragmatic. While the increased deployment by the LCC of women inspectors was no doubt a result of concerns about the particular consequences of overcrowded and unsanitary working conditions for women, most restaurant inspectors seemed largely uninterested in issues of moral hygiene. Scientific efficiency, by contrast, was undoubtedly valued. The reports of medical officers in the 1890s and 1900s show more evidence of specialist knowledge of the causes of public-health problems that arose from pollution or poor hygiene. For example, in 1899, the LCC's Medical Officer of Health investigated an outbreak of food poisoning among diners at a hotel in St Giles, in which thirty people developed gastroenteritis, and two deaths occurred. His report, based on the autopsy of one of the victims, provided a detailed identification and description of various bacteria, even though such comprehensive investigation failed to deliver any conclusive

---

[67] 'Smoke Nuisance from City Restaurants', 11 May 1897, p. 224, CLA/006/AD/05/41, LMA.

[68] *Ibid.*

[69] 'Smoke Prosecutions', 21 September 1897, p. 364, CLA/006/AD/05/41, LMA.

[70] *Report to the Sanitary Committee of the Commissioner of Sewers of the City of London* (London, 1895), 13–17, CLA/006/AD/07/06, LMA.

[71] Annual Report of the Proceedings of the Council, 31 March 1898, p. 115, LCC/Official Publications/28, LMA. This is not to say there were not intermittent cases of smoke nuisances into the 1900s created by taverns and restaurants. See 'Coal Smoke, City of Westminster', 12 November 1903, p. 313, COL/PHD/AD/03/10, LMA.

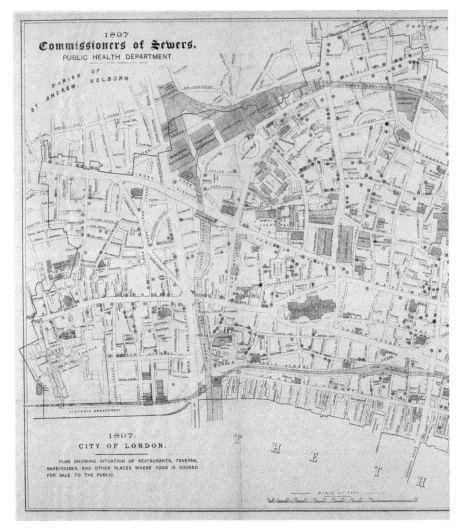

Figure 4.1. Public Health Department spot map from Wm. Sedgwick Saunders's investigation of places where food is cooked for sale (including restaurants) in the City of London, 1897. (Reproduced with permission of the London Metropolitan Archives, City of London)

results.[72] In September 1897, inspectors exploring black smoke pollution among restaurants in the City used photography in order to identify the offending establishments.[73]

[72] Annual Report of the Medical Officer of Health (1899), 79–80, LCC/Official Publications/18.7 store, LMA.
[73] 'Smoke Prosecutions', 21 September 1897, p. 364, CLA/006/AD/05/41, LMA.

Figure 4.1. Continued

It is also important to remember that many of the nuisances that inspectors investigated had been initially drawn to their attention by members of the general public. This was particularly true of complaints about smoke and food refuse. On one occasion, an inquiry into 'the insanitary state of affairs that prevails in many of the leading hotels and restaurants in the City and West End' was launched by the LCC after a plea for intervention from the Amalgamated Waiters' Society.[74] The society's

[74] Letter from Tom Morris, Chairman, AWS, to the Chairman, Public Health Committee, LCC, 7 November 1897, Papers Presented, LCC/Min/10,028, LMA.

chairman shared the testimony of several of his members who worked at the St James's Restaurant, in which they claimed the latrine used by staff adjoined the scullery where food was stored. The latrine was said to be in a 'filthy condition', and the stench arising from it made 'the assistants turn sick'.[75] He went on to insist that similar conditions prevailed at the Gaiety Restaurant and at the Trocadero. He raised additional concerns about the personal hygiene of those who worked as assistants to the cooks, who, he asserted, lived in common lodging houses and were dirty, not to say pestilential. 'It is', he declared, 'no uncommon thing to find men suffering from loathsome skin diseases engaged in cutting sandwiches, preparing salads, etc.'.[76] Clearly, the waiters' union was here attempting to bolster its own claims for respectability, by marking out a distinction between the 'clean, healthy men' it represented, and other categories of workers in the same establishment.[77] The LCC conducted a rigorous investigation, but ultimately found these complaints to be altogether unfounded.[78] Moreover, while perturbed by references to hands and arms covered with sores, it was determined that, unless these could be proven to be symptoms of an infectious disease, it was beyond their authority to act.[79]

Inspectors appeared willing to press their case only if they could establish, beyond doubt, that the law had been broken. Sedgwick Saunders also testified to the fact that magistrates were often highly reluctant to intervene in a manner that might interfere with 'the necessary methods of conducting business'.[80] Once again, it is important not to overstate the reach of official surveillance and regulation in late-nineteenth-century London, and to appreciate the continued ability of the commercial sector to set the agenda in economic and social development in the metropolis. In some cases, there may well have been some instances of collusion between inspectors and restaurant owners. There is a tantalizing reference in a complaint addressed to the LCC's Chief Sanitary Inspector in 1904 that poor hygiene at the East London Cake Company had been aggravated by an overly indulgent local inspector. As the complainant put it, 'no good telling the local sanitary officer for his [*sic*] is a great friend of Mr Bohs'.[81]

---

[75] *Ibid.*   [76] *Ibid.*   [77] *Ibid.*

[78] Letter from T. Hensman Munsey, LCC Vestry Clerk to the Clerk of the Vestry of St James, Westminster, 10 December 1897, LCC/Min/10,028, LMA.

[79] Papers Presented, W.A. Blaxland, Solicitor, 20 January 1898, pp. 1–3, LCC/Min/10,028, LMA.

[80] Report of the Medical Officer of Health, 19 February 1897, p. 94, CLA/006/AD/05/41, LMA.

[81] Letter from H. Brown to the Chief Sanitary Inspector, 3 March 1904, LCC/Min/10,050, LMA.

More usually, however, the relative absence of conflict between restaurateurs and inspectors was less a product of corruption, and more a reflection of a preference for pragmatism and accommodation on both sides. In 1896, the *Caterer* launched an indignant attack on the more arbitrary aspects of inspection. It conceded that, for the most part, restaurateurs were perfectly willing to live in harmony with the inspector, recognizing that the 'vigilance of this gentleman does much to reassure customers as to the cleanliness and order of the kitchen'. However, it protested that it was galling to have an inspector (especially when accompanied by a policeman) enter a restaurant during dinner and have the chef 'turn out the steaming soup in order that he may see whether the utensils are properly clean'. The customers would be kept waiting and the soup would be spoiled, but this appeared to matter little to the inspector, who 'thinks that he is doing a smart thing' in catching the restaurateur at the most inconvenient moment.[82] In fact, the records of inspectors suggest that they had little interest in catching off guard those engaged in the provision of food. The LCC's Assistant Medical Officer of Health insisted in 1899 that visits at 'unusual hours' to places where food was stored or prepared were unlikely to bring any rewards.[83] Moreover, most inspectors felt (at least in regard to kitchen visits and possibly less in regard to smoke pollution) that restaurateurs were generally amenable to making the changes they suggested. In 1902, an LCC report on the inspection of kitchens concluded that, 'speaking generally, the work required to be done to bring the various premises into line with modern sanitary requirements has either been completed or is in hand, and I am glad to be able to say that this result has been attained with the minimum amount of friction by the parties concerned'.[84] The relatively relaxed and temperate relationship between inspectors and restaurants stood in contrast to greater levels of official anxiety that characterized responses to issues of food hygiene in other domains of food preparation, notably the panics that surrounded the perceived association between, on the one hand, fried fish producers and Italian ice-cream sellers, and, on the other, the localized outbreaks of enteric fever, typhoid fever, and ptomaine poisoning that continued into the Edwardian period. Concerns about adulteration and poor hygiene were much more likely to focus on bakehouses than they were on the burgeoning restaurant sector.[85]

---

[82] 'Caterer's Notebook', *Caterer*, 15 April 1896, p. 170.

[83] *Preparation and Sale of Food in London* (LCC Official Publications, 1899), 12.

[84] 'Inspection of Kitchens and Restaurants, Tea Rooms &. &.', 29 September 1902, fo. 132b, COL/PHD/AD/03/10, LMA.

[85] See, e.g., Annual Report of the Medical Officer of Health (1904), LCC/Official Publications/18.7 (5) store; Annual Report of the Medical Officer of Health (1900), LCC/

Since 2000, historians have increasingly abandoned the notion of the emergence of a 'surveillance state' in late Victorian and Edwardian Britain. Instead of an emphasis on disciplining and controlling the population by means of impersonal modes of power, governance has been reimagined in neo-Foucauldian terms. The increasing reach of national and local government intervention in society is acknowledged, but it is presented as part of the commitment to maintaining a pluralistic society in which people could progress through self-regulation, as much as through external regulation.[86] Official attitudes to the restaurant have not found their way into this literature, but it would seem to endorse the view that inspection continued to be fashioned by a liberal culture of governance. Tom Crook's study of sanitary inspectors in the public sphere presents the culture of inspection as flexible and sensitive. Inspection was characterized not by anonymity and facelessness, but by sympathetic and interpersonal relations.[87] Crook's insistence that, 'at the very point where power·was performed and applied, inspection was a cautious and shrewd art, one which embodied various liberal sentiments', can certainly be extended to restaurant inspection.[88] However, Crook explains this preference for pastoralism over pedagogy in terms of official deference towards codes of privacy and morality and a culture of public accountability. In particular, he notes official sensitivity towards domestic privacy and the continued regard for the sanctity of the home. By contrast, official desires not to trespass on the prerogatives of businesses or trades receives no attention from Crook. Inserting the restaurant into the history of sanitary inspection is therefore an important reminder of the significance of commercial forces in shaping a complex liberal culture of governance, which balanced potentially competing requirements of social order, on the one hand, and freedom and pluralism, on the other.

Official Publications/18.7 (5) store; Annual Report of the Medical Officer of Health (1894), LCC/Official Publications/v.9, all in LMA.

[86] Notable examples would be Peter Mandler (ed.), *Liberty and Authority in Victorian Britain* (Oxford: Oxford University Press, 2006), 1–21; Chris Otter, 'Making Liberalism Durable: Vision and Civility in the Late Victorian City', *Social History*, 27/1 (2002), 1–15; Patrick Joyce, *The Rule of Freedom: Liberalism and the Modern City* (London: Verso, 2003); and, for a literary interpretation, see Lauren M. E. Goodlad, *Victorian Literature and the Victorian State: Character and Governance in a Liberal Society* (Baltimore: Johns Hopkins University Press, 2003).

[87] Tom Crook, 'Sanitary Inspection and the Public Sphere in late Victorian and Edwardian Britain: A Case Study in Liberal Governance', *Social History*, 32/4 (November 2007), 369–93. For a similar emphasis on flexibility and accountability, see Christopher Hamlin, 'Nuisances and Community in Mid-Victorian England: The Attractions of Inspection', *Social History*, 38/3 (2013), 346–79.

[88] Crook, 'Sanitary Inspection', 387.

If the culture of inspection regarded members of the public as 'active agents of self-government' (to be encouraged rather than coerced), restaurants already had a vested interest in getting their house in order.[89] Restaurants worked hard to reassure their customers. The notion that poor hygiene was prevalent, not to say universal, in the restaurant sector was challenged by spokesmen for the trade. At the time that sanitation inspectors were concerned with the problem of air pollution, many restaurateurs, including one Mr R. Woodin of the Whitehall Restaurant and Dining Rooms in Charing Cross, advertised 'large and well ventilated' dining rooms.[90] Some proprietors went further, offering material solutions to deal with the problem of London's 'smoky atmosphere'. In 1883, the manager of Spiers and Pond's new City restaurant in the Auction Mart notified potential patrons that the materials used to decorate the dining room were 'washable' and therefore less smelly than they might otherwise be.[91] The Avenue restaurant in Throgmorton Street boasted its use of 'sunburners' in their dining rooms, allowing vitiated air to be taken away at once.[92] Other new inventions used for eliminating odours were brought to the public's attention, such as 'Jennings' valve closet and trap' for the lavatory, whose ventilated soil pipes were hermetically sealed against impure air and allowed for the safe disposal of waste.[93] Kitchens, of course, were also repositories of unwholesome smells, as we have seen. Some restaurants publicized the fact that their kitchens were open for inspection to members of the public (see Figure 4.2).[94] On opening a fish restaurant in the Poultry in this period, Messrs Prince were keen to alert the public that their kitchen was situated on the fourth floor in order that 'the olfactory nerves of diners may not be offended by the objectionable odours which are there engendered'. With its ground floor devoted to receiving the supply of fish, and its dining rooms on the first and second floors, these pronouncements could only raise scepticism if deliveries had to be carried up four flights of stairs.[95] The increased recourse to kitchens on upper stories, observed, as we have seen, by the Medical Officer of Health,

[89] *Ibid.* 389.

[90] Handbill, 1887, Whitehall Restaurant and Dining Rooms, Evanion Collection 6642, British Library.

[91] 'The Auction Mart Restaurant', 1 December 1883, Restaurant Files, box A–B, London Cuttings, Bishopsgate.

[92] 'The Avenue Restaurant', 23 April 1881, Restaurant Files, box A–B, London Cuttings, Bishopsgate.

[93] 'The Furnishing and Equipment of Hotels and Kindred Establishments', *Tourist and Traveller, and Hotel Review*, 7 June 1884, p. 17.

[94] See, e.g., *The Florence Restaurant* (London, c.1900), D 93.2 London Collection Pamphlets, Box 323/18, Bishopsgate.

[95] 'A New Restaurant', *British and Foreign Confectioner*, 1 July 1881, p. 11.

MAIN KITCHEN.
Which is open for inspection to anyone who wishes to visit it.

Figure 4.2. Main kitchen, Florence Restaurant, *c.*1900, open for inspection to anyone who wishes to visit it. (Reproduced with permission of the Bishopsgate Institute)

is confirmed by reports of both the opening of new restaurants and improvements to existing establishments to be found in the trade and local press.[96]

Some restaurants did more than guarantee higher standards of hygiene. Some insisted that they could actively promote good health. Readers of the *Anti-Adulteration Review* in 1882 were advised that London might soon be receiving its own version of what was purported to be a 'Sanitary Restaurant' already existing in Paris. A correspondent for the journal detailed, in possibly fanciful terms, the attractions of an establishment

[96] See, e.g., 'The City Restaurant', 5 May 1866; 'Dining in the City (Old Excise Coffee-house)', 18 November 1876; 'A New City Restaurant (the Daily)', 18 August 1877; 'Prince's', 22 June 1881; 'The Ceres Vegetarian Restaurant', 12 May 1888; 'The Spread Eagle', 2 February 1889; 'The Lombard Restaurant', 1 February 1892, all in Restaurant Files, boxes C–F, G–L, M–P, Q–S, London Cuttings, Bishopsgate. Regarding the West End, see 'The Hotel Metropole', *Caterer*, 15 June 1885, p. 155; 'The New Piccadilly Restaurant', *Caterer*, 15 February 1886, p. 32.

that would fuse medical and culinary expertise, targeted at the chronic dyspeptic. On arriving, the diner would be examined by a doctor, who would then 'prescribe' a menu at a moderate cost. The resulting meal would be tailored to the particular needs of the diner, who might be offered 'the particular mineral water suitable to the state of his liver, with, more probably, an extra course, or rather one substituted for the dessert, comprising a pill or two it may be, a pepsine sandwich, or a wedge of lactopeptine toast'. Improved digestion, and thereby good health, would then be secured, even if at the cost of an unappetizing meal. Some diners, the article asserted, might have preferred 'indigestion, with all its terrors, to the prescribed fare of the "Sanitary Restaurant"'.[97]

If such a project seemed far-fetched, there were particular types of restaurants in late Victorian and Edwardian London that promoted their fare in terms of improving the physical, and even the moral, well-being of their patrons. Prominent in this regard were those establishments that self-consciously advertised themselves as either temperance or vegetarian restaurants. The former was part of a broader national temperance movement that aimed to improve the morals of the working classes by enticing them away from the public house. Working men, it was thought, had few places to resort to, 'but public houses where they could get their own bit of meat, a chop or a steak, cooked for them, or already cooked viands served up; and when they go to the public house they are expected, of course, to drink alcoholic liquors whether they wish to or not', as an 1880 report by the Society for the Diffusion of Useful Knowledge argued.[98] Once frequenting the public house became a habit, the worker then developed a taste for drink, which led to his inability to do without it.[99] Because he met other men like himself there, the public house became his club, which, given the amount of time he spent there, inevitably meant that his home life suffered. The need for temperance refreshment houses, therefore, was fuelled by such concerns about the degradation of the working classes. By providing cheap and wholesome meals (where tea, coffee, and cocoa were staple drinks), convenient locations, and a cheery atmosphere (with not only dining rooms, but in some cases libraries and smoking rooms), temperance restaurants were meant to offer an attractive alternative to the pubic house.[100]

In London, this reform movement gave rise to a variety of limited companies, such as the Coffee Tavern Company, which created refreshment

---

[97] 'Sanitary Restaurant', *Anti-Adulteration Review* (December 1882), 365.
[98] 'The Temperance Refreshment House Movement', in *Companion to the British Almanac of the Society for the Diffusion of Useful Knowledge* (London, 1880), 39–40.
[99] *Ibid.* 40.   [100] *Ibid.* 42.

houses for working men. This company set up twenty such establishments by 1880.[101] One of the more successful ventures was the People's Café Company, a project associated with the Earl of Shaftesbury and Samuel Morley, which opened a number of 'attractive and cheerful places of public refreshment and recreation, in suitable situations in the more densely-peopled parts of London... to serve as a counterattraction to the public-house and gin-palace'.[102] It should not be assumed that these establishments were merely fanciful outlets for high-minded reformers to enact their fantasies of a rational, ordered, and moralized urban population. A branch of the People's Café Company in St Paul's Churchyard, on a Thursday in 1883, apparently served a sixpenny fish dinner to 400 persons.[103] Opening the first branch in Whitecross Street in 1875, Shaftesbury was at pains to urge his associates that, while prioritizing the philanthropic aspects of the scheme, they should be 'taking care to make it pay'.[104] In fact, temperance restaurants proved an attractive commercial proposition for restaurateurs. This was particularly true with the expansion of the clerical sector within the City, where lower-middle-class clerks were eager to take lunch in establishments that underlined their commitment to sobriety and respectability.[105]

Chain restaurants certainly found their association with temperance something they were eager to promote. The Spread Eagle boasted having a 'higher class' of temperance restaurants that were 'luxuriously appointed'. Among its five City branches, their Leadenhall Street establishment was said to attract nearly 5,000 persons daily in 1890.[106] Its Lombard Street refreshment room was evidently popular with 'gentlemen in the banking houses adjoining' it.[107] The company opened an additional two establishments in the City a year later.[108] Its management understood that 'men of commerce' enjoyed 'a quiet smoke' and a cup of coffee after lunch, and, to that end, it offered smoking and luncheon rooms in each branch. Lockhart's, another chain, had a branch in Fetter Lane that attracted employees

[101] *Ibid.* 48–9.

[102] 'People's Café Company', 17 April 1875, Restaurant Files, box M–P, London Cuttings, Bishopsgate.

[103] 'Six Penny Fish Dinners', 29 September 1883, Restaurant Files, box M–P, London Cuttings, Bishopsgate.

[104] 'People's Café Company', 17 April 1875, Restaurant Files, box M–P, London Cuttings, Bishopsgate.

[105] 'Opening of a People's Café in Gracechurch-Street', 13 November 1878, Restaurant Files, box M–P, London Cuttings, Bishopsgate.

[106] 'The Spread Eagles', 7 June 1890, Restaurant Files, box Q–S, London Cuttings, Bishopsgate.

[107] 'The Spread Eagle Bread Company', 4 December 1889, Restaurant Files, box Q–S, London Cuttings, Bishopsgate.

[108] 'Luxury for City Men', 18 November 1891, Restaurant Files, box Q–S, London Cuttings, Bishopsgate.

from the printing and machine works in the vicinity.[109] There were other large temperance concerns, namely Pearce's refreshment rooms, which by the mid-1890s numbered forty-six, fourteen of which had hotels attached to them. While originally founded in order to satisfy the needs of the working classes in search of coffee and a hearty meal at low cost, Pearce's British Tea Table restaurants catered for young City clerks requiring 'something superior'. Pearce capitalized on the popular taste for coffee, tea, and, increasingly, cocoa. As an assurance of quality control within his establishments, the owner told one reporter in 1896 'you will notice that we only use Fry's Concentrated Cocoa'.[110]

As with temperance, the vegetarian restaurant showed a similar alignment of prescriptive moralizing and commercial opportunity. Inevitably, much of the momentum for vegetarian restaurants came from those who argued for the improving effects of renouncing meat.[111] London was home to a number of vegetarian advocacy groups, including the Natural Living Society and the London Vegetarian Society, but also hosted overseas visitors who drew on their own dietary customs and conventions in order to help Britons tackle 'the flesh-eating problem'. The prospectus for the *Vegetarian*, a self-declared forum 'for the promotion of humanity, purity, temperance, health, wealth, and happiness', first published in 1888, characterized itself as a 'radical, yet rational, reformer, cutting at the roots of our nation's vices and sorrows'.[112] It linked dietary reform to a cluster of other causes dear to the radical conscience, including temperance, the land question, and the Nonconformist religious revival. Some vegetarian advocates were even active in the social purity rescue movement, the twenty-two women and girls rescued from the streets in Camberwell in 1888 being offered, not merely housing and weekly sewing classes, but also free vegetarian breakfasts and dinners.[113] In 1890, the *Vegetarian* reviewed the progress of the meatless movement over the previous two decades and concluded that results had been mixed. However, where education and advocacy had not always been effective, vegetarian restaurants, 'in the metropolis and elsewhere', had been quite successful, 'and the number of their customers proves that the test of practical experience has convinced where arguments might perhaps have

---

[109] 'New Coffee Palace in the City', 11 February 1885, Restaurant Files, box G–L, London Cuttings, Bishopsgate.

[110] W. J. Wintle, 'Round the London Restaurants', *Windsor Magazine* (1896), 448.

[111] See James Gregory, *Of Victorians and Vegetarians: The Vegetarian Movement in Nineteenth-Century Britain* (London: I. B. Tauris, 2007), 134–41.

[112] 'Prospectus', *Vegetarian*, 7 January 1888, p. 1.

[113] 'Occasional Notes', *Vegetarian*, 7 January 1888, p. 3.

failed'.[114] That there was an apparent vogue for vegetarian restaurants in London in the late 1880s and early 1890s would seem to be borne out by the considerable interest in meatless establishments in mainstream catering papers, even if they remained unconvinced that this was anything other than a passing fashion.[115] Nevertheless, the *Weekly Star and Vegetarian Restaurant Gazette* calculated in 1889 that there were between thirty and forty vegetarian restaurants in London, the *British Journal of Catering* (possibly a more objective observer) putting the figure at thirty, the *Caterer*, two years later, estimating the number at thirty-two.[116]

Significantly, the subtitle of the *Weekly Star* made explicit the vegetarian restaurant's role in promoting a broader project of moral improvement: it declared itself to be 'the Anti-Alcohol, Anti-Tobacco, Anti-Vaccination, Anti-Vivisection, Anti-Physic, and Anti-Gambling Journal'.[117] For reformers, the association between vegetarianism and a broader spectrum of improving causes was not entirely unproblematic. This was particularly true in regard to its relationship to temperance. With less to drink, workers were possibly likely to require more to eat, and they would also have potentially more disposable income to buy meat.[118] Moreover, giving up drink did not necessarily guarantee the broader embrace of 'simplicity' that both vegetarian and temperance advocates sought. A correspondent to the *Vegetarian* pointed out that temperance coffee houses, for all their good work in freeing working men from the tyranny of the bottle, often provided food that was far from wholesome. Indeed, their regular recourse to ham, pastries, and white bread was 'surely sapping the foundations of the manhood' of the British working classes as much as beer was.[119] Some authorities insisted that, without a vegetarian diet, teetotalism was unlikely to be effective. H. S. Salt, a prominent figure in the vegetarian movement, asserted that a craving for alcohol was lessened by the repudiation of 'flesh-food'.[120] If 'Food Reform' was a critical precondition of 'Drink Reform', as Salt argued, then the vegetarian restaurant was a vital instrument in the broader programme of reform and improvement.

As had been the case with temperance restaurants, the association with reform did not preclude the pursuit of profit. When a dissatisfied

[114] 'Is Flesh Eating on the Decrease?', *Vegetarian*, 4 January 1890, p. 4.

[115] See, e.g., 'Vegetarianism', *Caterer*, 15 June 1887, p. 199.

[116] 'The Vegetarian Diet', *Weekly Star and Vegetarian Restaurant Gazette*, 10 August 1889, p. 106; 'Editorial', *British Journal of Catering*, 1 December 1889, p. 9; 'The Caterer's Notebook', *Caterer*, 15 April 1891, p. 123.

[117] *Weekly Star and Vegetarian Restaurant Gazette*, 7 September 1889, p. 1.

[118] 'Is Flesh Eating on the Decrease?', *Vegetarian*, 4 January 1890, p. 4.

[119] 'Eating Houses for Working Men', *Vegetarian*, 22 March 1890, p. 188.

[120] H. S. Salt, *A Plea for Vegetarianism and Other Essays* (Manchester: Vegetarian Society, 1886), 26.

correspondent in the *Vegetarian* asserted in 1888 that most vegetarian restaurants had been 'created with a view to gain' (and therefore provided poor-quality offerings), the proprietor of the Alpha angrily retorted that such establishments were, of course, 'run as commercial speculations'.[121] The debate was joined by an editorial, which also defended existing establishments, and pointed out that any expressions of dissatisfaction were actually a healthy development, suggesting rising expectations associated with the increased presence and permanence of the vegetarian restaurant. It concluded that 'the commercial enterprise manifested in connection with the [vegetarian] movement during the past few years has been beyond all praise'.[122] How regularly commercial ends aligned with reformist and philanthropic expectations is not easy to establish with any certainty. The *Caterer* pointed out that it did not follow that those who enjoyed a vegetarian luncheon in the City might not have a more conventional meal when they returned home in the evening. The journal celebrated 'variety of diet', but more in terms of its novelty value than as a force for social improvement.[123] True, it would appear that the proprietors of many vegetarian restaurants shared the reformers' belief that those who preferred meatless meals also had no need for alcoholic beverages. The surviving menus of vegetarian restaurants usually identified their drink provisions as non-alcoholic beverages—for example, lemonade. However, that commercial and reform imperatives might easily diverge is apparent in one suggestive source: an 1885 menu from the Charing Cross Vegetarian Hotel and Restaurant. Whereas H. S. Salt confidently declared that 'another habit which is rendered almost impossible by a fleshless diet is that of smoking', this vegetarian dining room on the Strand incorporated a 'well appointed smoking and coffee room'.[124]

The disconnect between grounded realities of functioning vegetarian restaurants, on the one hand, and the strictures of reformers, on the other, is perhaps most striking in relation to issues of hygiene. Those who promoted the vegetarian diet attempted to supplement their case by claiming that most meat consumed in London was of questionable provenance and quality. An investigation by one Dr Carpenter found

[121] 'Correspondence: to the Editor of the Vegetarian', *Vegetarian*, 6 October 1888, p. 427; 13 October 1888, p. 443.
[122] 'Correspondence', *Vegetarian*, 20 October 1888, p. 458.
[123] 'The Caterer's Notebook', *Caterer*, 15 April 1891, p. 123. The notion that those enjoying vegetarian lunches were City clerks who were not committed vegetarians is confirmed by 'Vegetarianism in the Metropolis', *Temperance Caterer*, 13 August 1887, p. 154.
[124] Salt, *A Plea*, 42; Menu, The Charing Cross Vegetarian Hotel and Restaurant (*c*.1885), Evanion Collection 6671, British Library.

that about 70 per cent of the meat brought to the metropolitan market 'is absolutely diseased, and entirely unfit for food'.[125] The Vegetarian Café Company, created, not to add to the existing number of vegetarian restaurants, but to promote 'the scientific demonstration of vegetarian cookery', intended its establishments to set a benchmark of cleanliness and quality. It was, therefore, ironic that a correspondent in the *Vegetarian*, whom we encountered at the beginning of this chapter, complained in 1899 that, on entering one of the branches of the Vegetarian Café Restaurant, he encountered dirty table linen, damaged tableware and glasses, and spilt fruit juice.[126] While subsequent letters contested the accuracy of this report, the *Caterer* sequestered this complaint in order to make a broader criticism of the 'extreme slovenliness with which many vegetarian restaurants are conducted'.[127] In March 1888, a diner at the Vegetarian Restaurant in St Bride-street lauded this establishment for the whiteness of its table cloths and brightness of its gas lighting. However, in a letter to the *Vegetarian*, he expressed his concern that not a single window was open, and so the diners were denied the fresh air that was so important to 'man's well-being'.[128] The correspondent, 'A Lover of Fresh Air', frustratingly concluded: 'in the headquarters of the Vegetarian cult, surely one ought not to find one of the leading principles of the sanitarium movement so outfacedly contravened'.[129] In the following month, a letter to the same paper, this time from 'Aeolus', made a similar complaint.[130]

Apologists for the vegetarian restaurant inevitably repudiated such negative observations. The *Temperance Caterer* relayed the impressions of a correspondent who had dined at five vegetarian restaurants in the City[131] and found in all of them that 'the most scrupulous cleanliness prevails'.[132] Significantly, in line with broader debates about hygiene in the restaurant, all of these establishments were praised for situating their dining rooms on the second or third floor. Nevertheless, vegetarian restaurants were not immune from the scrutiny of official regulators and inspectors. Indeed, vegetarian restaurants feature regularly among the list of establishments that were responsible for smoke nuisances.[133]

[125] 'The Vegetarian Diet', *Weekly Star and Vegetarian Restaurant Gazette*, 10 August 1889, p. 106.
[126] 'Correspondence: To the Editor', *Vegetarian*, 26 August 1899, p. 408.
[127] 'Odds and Ends', *Caterer*, 15 September 1899, p. 427.
[128] 'Correspondence: To the Editor', *Vegetarian*, 31 March 1888, p. 8.   [129] *Ibid.*
[130] 'Correspondence: To the Editor', *Vegetarian*, 14 April 1888, p. 8.
[131] They were the Apple Tree, the Arcadian, the Porridge Bowl, Queen Victoria, and the Bouverie.
[132] 'Vegetarianism in the Metropolis', *Temperance Caterer*, 13 August 1887, p. 154.
[133] See, e.g., Report of the Medical Officer of Health, 14 July 1885, p. 194, CLA/006/AD/05/28; Report of the Medical Officer of Health, 14 September 1886, p. 200, COL/

The problem for many vegetarian restaurants was that maintaining high standards of appropriate wholesomeness required raising tariffs to levels that excluded the poorer workers that the reformers hoped to reach. The general expectation at the time was that a vegetarian meal should cost less than a non-vegetarian one, but critics dredged up plenty of examples of two-course vegetarian meals costing the same as a plate of meat at a coffee house.[134] It was a particular grievance that non-dinner items, such as porridge, bread and butter, fruit, and eggs, were much better value when obtained at a coffee tavern. Such criticisms were not mere niggling, given that vegetarian reformers had emphasized financial continence (and the possibility of working-class saving) as one of the rewards of the meatless meal. The Garden vegetarian restaurant in the City, for instance, advertised itself as 'Economical, Healthful and Humane'.[135]

It was not merely an issue of cost. Vegetarian restaurants had difficulty in presenting themselves as good value for money. A Scottish missionary, the Revd James Gilmour, who had adopted vegetarianism during his time in China and Mongolia, complained that even the three-course dinners for sixpence offered by some London vegetarian restaurants could not be considered cheap. Moreover, possibly alluding to the robust requirements of muscular Christianity that his calling demanded, Gilmour argued that his meals had been 'insufficient...and deficient in staying power'. On one occasion, he found the middle course of his meal little more than an apology 'for the absence of something real to eat' and concluded that, unless vegetarian restaurants did more to fill the stomachs of their diners, 'vegetarianism will only be looked upon as a modified kind of fasting and asceticism'.[136] Another potential failing of the vegetarian restaurant was the difficulty conventional diners, wedded to the explicit lexicon of 'meat and two veg', had in assembling the elements on the menu into a coherent meal. A correspondent to the *Vegetarian* confessed that 'I have a rough idea that peas to follow beans would be as bad taste as salmon followed by roast pork, but have no knowledge beyond that crude ideal and I find large numbers of people in the same condition'.[137]

PHD/AD/03/05; Report of the Medical Officer of Health, 12 May 1896, p. 171, CLA/006/AD/05/40, LMA; Report of the Medical Officer of Health, 19 February 1897, p. 93, CLA/006/AD/05/41; Report of the Medical Officer of Health, 2 March 1897, p. 119, CLA/006/AD/05/41; Report of the Medical Officer of Health, 27 July 1897, p. 341, CLA/006/AD/05/41; Report of the Medical Officer of Health, 21 September 1897, p. 364, CLA/006/AD/05/41, LMA.

[134] 'Vegetarian Restaurants', *Temperance Caterer*, 10 December 1887, p. 327.
[135] 'The Garden', *Vegetarian*, 7 January 1888, p. 10.
[136] 'China and the Mongols', *Vegetarian*, 9 November 1889, p. 713.
[137] 'Correspondence: To the Editor', *Vegetarian*, 28 April 1888, p. 59.

Even those wishing to risk such travails in the pursuit of dietary experimentation might have actually found it quite difficult to find a conveniently located vegetarian restaurant. Most of these establishments were to be found in the City, and vegetarian advocates often complained about their relative absence from other parts of the metropolis. It also appears that, after a period of relatively high visibility in the late 1880s and early 1890s, the vegetarian restaurant in London went into something of a decline. In January 1900, the Vegetarian Federal Union conference estimated that, while there had been thirty-three vegetarian restaurants in London 'a few years back', there were now little more than half a dozen.[138] Similarly, C. W. Forward, speaking at the National Vegetarian Congress the previous year, while he argued that the vegetarian movement was as popular as ever, was forced to concede that 'ten years ago he had a list of between thirty and forty Vegetarian restaurants in London, while at the present time there were less than a quarter of the number'.[139] He consoled himself that the increased demand for light refreshments as a midday meal created new opportunities for the promotion of vegetarian cuisine, but this was countered by increased availability of affordable tinned meat. He was also concerned that the fastidious standards of the organized vegetarian movement were being compromised within the vegetarian restaurant. He claimed to have evidence that many purported vegetarian restaurants were nothing of the sort, since they were run by non-vegetarians and served meat to their diners.[140]

The highly visible presence of restaurants in the records of official regulatory bodies and the literature produced by social reformers is a testimony to the increased centrality of public eating to the metropolitan experience in late Victorian and Edwardian London. The restaurant was simply too ubiquitous, and too significant, for it not to be a site of interest for those engaged in the promotion of public health, whether they be LCC bureaucrats and inspectors, or the moralizers of the temperance and vegetarian movements. As smoke replaced sewage as the major concern of London's official health inspectors, the restaurant's association with the production of noxious air ensured that it was rarely absent from the agenda of those who hoped to produce a more regulated urban environment. London's rapidly growing population meant that an increasing number of workers took at least one meal a day away from home, which, in turn, required advocates of both good health and moral improvement to pay increased attention to what was on offer in the restaurant dining room.

---

[138] 'A Vegetarian Banquet', *Caterer*, 15 January 1900, p. 15.
[139] 'National Vegetarian Congress', *Vegetarian*, 23 September 1899, p. 454.
[140] *Ibid.*

However, while official regulators and moral improvers helped frame the development of London's restaurant culture, they were not ultimately foundational to it. The extent of contamination and adulteration of food served in restaurants was more likely to be determined by profit margins than by official intervention. Tensions between official inspectors and restaurateurs were not unheard of, but they were far from universal, largely because the latter could usually be relied upon to satisfy the most pressing demands of the former. The major factor shaping the prevalence of temperance and vegetarian restaurants was not the degree of earnestness of their philanthropic advocates, who sometimes seemed frustrated by the difficulty of practical implementation of their, often unwieldy, ideals. As a consequence, the fortunes of temperance and vegetarian restaurants inevitably relied on the simple issue of whether removing drink or meat from the menus was more, or less, likely to bring in customers. Ultimately, as in many other aspects of late-nineteenth-century London urban culture, it was the commercial domain that was the final arbiter in shaping the metropolitan environment. These commercial forces were also deeply imbricated within a late-nineteenth-century economy that was genuinely global, and ensured that the restaurant would have a definite transnational inflection. It is to this cosmopolitan dimension to public eating that we now turn.

5

Gastro-Cosmopolitanism and the Restaurant

'The cosmopolitan character of London is generally known, but perhaps indifferently realised', *Chambers's Journal* observed in an essay fittingly entitled 'Our City of Nations' in 1891.[1] This survey of London's immigrant populations, and their respective subcultures, paid particular attention to shops, stalls, and social clubs, but also included a brief, exoticized, description of an Italian restaurant, with its 'strange oozing cake'.[2] The tantalizing reference to public eating in 'Our City of Nations', and its explicit linkage to the notion of London as a cosmopolitan city, is a useful reminder of the importance of the international and global dimension to the London restaurant in the Victorian and Edwardian eras. Indeed, the restaurant serves as a critical, yet undervalued, site on which to explore the relationship between British metropolitan culture and the wider world.

Historians have become increasingly aware of how integral food cultures are to a globalized understanding of history,[3] not least in their relationship to other transnational forces, such as trade, slavery, diaspora, and immigration.[4] More pertinently, recognition of the global dimension to public eating in London in this period allows the restaurant to take its place in a more broadly conceived history of modern Britain, which

---

[1] 'Our City of Nations', *Chambers's Journal*, 8/394 (July 1891), 453.

[2] *Ibid.* 454.

[3] For an encyclopedic, transnational typology, see Kenneth F. Kiple and Kriemhild Coneè Ornelas (eds), *The Cambridge World History of Food* (2 vols; Cambridge: Cambridge University Press, 2000).

[4] On trade and the international movement of food commodities, see, e.g., Paul Freedman, *Out of the East: Spices and the Medieval Imagination* (New Haven: Yale University Press, 2008), and Marcy Norton, *Sacred Gifts, Profane Pleasures: A History of Tobacco and Chocolate in the Atlantic World* (Ithaca, NY, and London: Cornell University Press, 2010). On slavery, diaspora, and food migrations, see, e.g., Judith A. Carney, *Black Rice: The African Origins of Rice Cultivation in the Americas* (Cambridge, MA: Harvard University Press, 2001); On immigration and ethnic food, see, e.g., Hasia R. Diner, *Hungering for America: Italian, Irish, and Jewish Foodways in the Age of Migration* (Cambridge, MA: Harvard University Press, 2001).

emphasizes the need to think beyond the nation.[5] While many of the works that would seem to embody this post-foundational agenda have dealt with (largely if not exclusively) imperial stories, there has also been a growing emphasis on placing British history in an international framework that is not restricted to the parameters of formal empire.[6] The London restaurant offers a particularly compelling example of the rewards of going, not merely beyond the nation, but beyond the imperial turn. This chapter deploys the notion of what will be termed gastro-cosmopolitanism to reveal the complex ways in which the global and the local interrelated in the late-nineteenth- and early-twentieth-century metropolis. Critically, this term encompasses not merely the food on the diner's plate, but also the broader context of the dining experience, featuring an international cast of caterers and diners.

Acknowledgement of the existence of the restaurant's importance as a site of transnational and global cultural exchange complicates, and qualifies, how cosmopolitanism in *fin-de-siècle* London has been understood by scholars. First, the cosmopolitan culture surrounding public eating reveals that cultural difference not merely existed at a discursive level in the metropolitan imaginary, but was also materially grounded. Second, London's cosmopolitan food culture reveals that encountering the cultural 'other' was as likely to be associated with positive, as with negative, connotations. It therefore highlights another aspect of the restaurant that indicates that historians may do well to move beyond tropes of danger and anxiety and do more to acknowledge countervailing forces of attraction and pleasure that were no less significant to the metropolitan experience.

It cannot be denied that there were numerous restaurants that served fare that probably had limited foreign influence in either derivation or execution, and some actively promoted a nativist public image. As discussed

---

[5] See Antoinette Burton, 'Who Needs the Nation? Interrogating "British" History', *Journal of Historical Sociology*, 10 (1997), 227–48; Paul Gilroy, *The Black Atlantic: Modernity and Double Consciousness* (Cambridge, MA: Harvard University Press, 1993).

[6] Examples would be Mrinalini Sinha, *Specters of Mother India: The Global Restructuring of an Empire* (Durham, NC: Duke University Press, 2006); Susan D. Pennybacker, *From Scottsboro to Munich: Race and Political Culture in 1930s Britain* (Princeton and Oxford: Princeton University Press, 2009); Antoinette Burton, *The Postcolonial Careers of Santha Rama Rau* (Durham, NC: Duke University Press, 2007). For concerns that the imperial turn in British scholarship may have entrenched 'a new form of boundary-drawing that risks disembedding imperial relations from larger transnational relations which move across and beyond the British Empire', see the introduction and contributions in Kevin Grant, Philippa Levine, and Frank Trentmann (eds), *Beyond Sovereignty: Britain, Empire and Transnationalism, c. 1880–1950* (Basingstoke: Palgrave Macmillan, 2007), esp. 7. For a review of the interdisciplinary contributions to this field, see Brenda Assael, 'Beyond Empire: Globalizing the Victorians', *Victorian Literature and Culture*, 43 (2015), 643–50.

in Chapter 1, the venerable chophouse was inevitably associated with a self-consciously 'English' character and cuisine, although such forms of identification were to become increasingly articulated in terms of loss and nostalgia as the century progressed. One writer, recalling the Bay Tree in St Swithin's Lane during its heyday in the 1840s, extolled the virtues of its 'remarkable and cheap lunch' composed of 'huge joints of cold roast and boiled meat, bread and half a pint of porter or mild ale in a pewter tankard'.[7] However, the moribund status of the chophouse by the end of the century suggested that appeals to a robust and authentic 'Englishness' were no longer a guarantee of popularity or success. As one observer asserted in 1891, 'comfortable and cosy taverns which only a few years since flourished and prospered in our midst' had been 'sent to the wall' by competitors who, significantly, were characterized 'by their gaudy adornments and French dishes'.[8] Of course, some restaurants retained their 'Englishness' as a source of pride and, if anything, sought out diners who were uncomfortable with the growing heterogeneity of public eating. For example, at Galt's in Cheapside, one reviewer was pleased to report that 'everything about the place is English. No foreign meat enters its portals...The manager, Mr Arthur Lane, is an Englishman, the chef-de-cuisine is also an Englishman, and the young ladies who wait upon customers with such civility and attention are all of English birth.'[9] In fact, the emphasis on policing the boundaries of the culinary nation was not entirely effective here, since the specialism of the restaurant was turtle soup, prepared from live creatures imported by the proprietor from the West Indies. It is also true that unimpeachably 'English' dishes such as scrambled eggs on toast, steak and kidney pudding, and gooseberry tart were also prominent in the menus of the Lyons' restaurants that played such an important role in servicing London's burgeoning white-collar workforce from the 1890s onwards. However, the quintessential Englishness of Lyons' establishments obscured the fact that the company had been founded by an extended family of émigré German Jews.[10]

---

[7] Clipping, *City Press*, 9 January 1897, Norman Collection, London Guildhall Library [hereafter LGL].

[8] 'Baker's Chop House', *City Press* (1891), Norman Collection, LGL.

[9] Clipping, 'Turtle Soup for the Million: A New Cheapside Enterprise', *City Press* (November 1903), Norman Collection, LGL.

[10] Of the founders of the company in 1887, Isidore and Montague Gluckstein were the sons of Samuel Gluckstein, a German Jew who arrived in England in 1841, while Barnett Salmon and Joseph Lyons were London Jews. See Peter Bird, *The First Food Empire: A History of J. Lyons & Co.* (Chichester: Phillimore & Co., Ltd, 2000). There were obviously Jewish-owned restaurants with a more pronounced Jewish cultural inflection, notably those serving Kosher food. However, this did not preclude them from attracting a clientele that was less exclusive. For example, Nathaniel Newnham-Davis dined at the Kosher restaurant

Indeed, among London's burgeoning population was a rising number of continental immigrants who brought with them new food customs and foods, a type of 'portable property'.[11] In the era of German and Italian unification, immigrants from these two countries became a more visible presence in London. Census records indicate that London's German population, which was already 9,566 strong in 1851, rose to a peak of 27,290 by 1911.[12] The Italian presence in London increased from 1,604 to 11,668 over the same period of time.[13] If Germans and Italians constituted the largest groups of continental Europeans in London, there was also a not inconsiderable number of French, Czech, Swiss, Russians, and Poles. Political émigrés and those seeking employment opportunities in London were joined in the closing decades of the nineteenth century by large numbers of Jews fleeing persecution under the Russian Empire.[14] The appearance and customs of these immigrants were the subject of widespread interest. For some contemporaries, the distinctiveness of these newly arrived immigrants was apparent not merely to the eye and ear, but also to the nose. Soho's Italian community was singled out for specific attention by journalist and epicurean George Augustus Sala, who observed in 1859 that the smell of cookery from its various boarding houses, cookshops, and eating houses was 'very marked'.[15]

Some observers insisted that these places were just for foreigners: 'The London foreign population has its own restaurants', asserted the *Hotel*'s 'Looker On' in 1895.[16] The 'Looker On' added that there was an exclusivity around both these foreign restaurants and the more established

in the City, Goldstein's, and there are also references to Kosher restaurants that served German dishes with a view to attracting both Jewish and non-Jewish diners. See Nathaniel Newnham-Davis, *Dinners and Diners: Where and how to Dine in London* (London: Grant Richards, 1899); 'Hotel News', *Caterer*, 15 February 1895, p. 53.

[11] John Plotz, *Portable Property: Victorian Culture on the Move* (Princeton: Princeton University Press, 2008), pp. xiv–xv, 5–7.

[12] Panikos Panayi, *German Immigrants in Britain during the Nineteenth Century, 1815–1914* (Oxford: Berg, 1995), 92–3. Particularly prominent among these German immigrants were clerical workers. See Gregory Anderson, 'German Clerks in England, 1870–1914: Another Aspect of the Great Depression Debate', in Kenneth Lunn (ed.), *Hosts, Immigrants and Minorities: Historical Responses to Newcomers in British Society, 1870–1914* (Folkestone: Dawson, 1980), 201–21.

[13] Lucio Sponza, *Italian Immigrants in Nineteenth Century Britain: Realities and Images* (Leicester: Leicester University Press, 1988), 13; Robin Palmer, 'The Italians: Patterns of Migration to London', in James L. Watson (ed.), *Between Two Cultures: Migrants and Minorities in Britain* (Oxford: Blackwell, 1977), 245.

[14] For an overview, see Colin Holmes, *John Bull's Island: Immigration and British Society, 1871–1971* (Basingstoke: Macmillan, 1988), 19–85.

[15] George Augustus Sala, *Gaslight and Daylight* (London: Chapman and Hall, 1859), 181.

[16] 'The Looker On', *Hotel*, 16 October 1895, p. 17.

ones. 'It is a common remark that the restaurants of London are in the hands of foreigners, but strangely enough foreigners resident in London do not patronize to any great extent those restaurants which the average Londoner regards with the most favour.'[17] Instead, he added, the foreign diner went to those 'unpretentious' restaurants where they 'hide themselves away' and where 'the cooking is just as good and everything is just as nice and clean, but the charges are only about a fourth of those the poor deluded native has to pay'.[18] But even this testimony to ethnic exclusivity and segregation was unsustainable. The 'Looker On' himself allowed for the possibility that these dining experiences were available to a broader swathe of London's population when he tantalizingly insisted that 'the very names and whereabouts [of these smaller places] are known only to very few Londoners. Should you desire to make the acquaintance of the interior of one of these warm, cosy, cheerful, animated little café restaurants you will need a guide.' He added coyly, 'on another occasion I may tell you more about them'.[19] Even without him naming names, the restaurants to which he referred served as a demonstration of the panoply of urban life and occupied an important place in the metropolitan imaginary at a discursive level, enticing readers to find their own 'foreign' London by letting their taste buds lead the way.

Gastro-cosmopolitanism existed as an element within patterns of consumption, whether directly, or in the domain of the imaginative or vicarious, but it can be equally applied to the restaurant when considered as a unit of production or a key element in London's service sector. Certainly some contemporaries testified to the apparent dominance of foreign restaurants. In 1889, the *British Journal of Catering* asserted: 'strip the United Kingdom of all its foreigners, and our kitchens and bakers' shops would be next to empty', while a few years later the *Hotel* insisted 'if we rule out these foreign houses then London catering is a wilderness indeed'.[20] While none of these observers offered quantitative support for their claims, qualitative evidence from the trade press and census materials reveals, not merely the extensive presence of foreign food in London's dining rooms, but also the prevalence of foreign-born individuals in the restaurant trade.

Several notable restaurants in London were owned and managed by entrepreneurs born overseas. Establishments whose proprietors were foreign born included Carlo Gatti's Café-restaurant near Charing Cross

[17] *Ibid.*   [18] *Ibid.*   [19] *Ibid.*
[20] 'Cookery and Food Exhibitions', *British Journal of Catering*, 1 March 1889, p. 17; 'Sunday Refreshments', *Hotel*, 21 August 1895, p. 13.

(Gatti was Italian–Swiss), Kettner's in Soho (founded by Frenchman Auguste Kettner, formerly chef to Napoleon III), and the Café Royal in Regent Street (established by Frenchman Daniel Nicols).[21] In addition, there were more obscure establishments, such as the Florence Restaurant near Shaftesbury Avenue owned by the Italian L. Azario, the King's Cross Restaurant founded by the Italian–Swiss brothers Louis and Peter Reggiori, and the German-owned Wenzel's in Tottenham Court Road.[22] While Italians, Italian–Swiss, French, and Germans were most prominent, there were owners who arrived from more distant ports, notably Australian caterers Felix Spiers and Christopher Pond, whose empire encompassed both chain restaurants and ultimately the stately Criterion in Piccadilly.[23] There were also countless restaurants where the owners' surnames suggest they may have been foreign born, but, in the absence of additional evidence, such identifications can only be speculative.[24]

Those who worked in kitchens and dining rooms were similarly poly-glot. In 1885, for instance, the *Caterer* estimated that there were 7,000 German waiters in London, as well as 4,500 'others of various foreign nationalities', of whom the Swiss were considered to be the largest single subgroup.[25] In 1891, the same publication calculated that there were approximately 2,000 Italian cooks and waiters earning 'respectable incomes' in London.[26] Considering that, according to the census of that year, the number of Italians in the capital was approximately 5,138 and the number of Germans, 26,920, it seems obvious that a high proportion (possibly as high as 40 per cent of Italians and 25 per cent of Germans) of

[21] Peter Barber and Peter Jacomelli, *Continental Taste: Ticinese Emigrants and their Café-Restaurants in Britain, 1847–1987* (London: Camden Historical Society, 1997); Felicity Kinross, *Coffee and Ices: The Story of Carlo Gatti in London* (Sudbury: Lavenham Press, 1991); 'A Dinner at Kettner's', *Caterer*, 15 February 1898, pp. 64–6; 'The Café Royal and its Creator', *Caterer*, 15 June 1896, p. 253; 'The Café Royal and its Founder', *Caterer*, 15 February 1898, p. 74.

[22] *The Florence Restaurant* (London, c.1900), D 93.2 London Collection Pamphlets, Box 323/18, Bishopsgate. 'The Development of the Swiss Café in London: A Visit to Reggiori's Restaurants', *Caterer*, 16 August 1897, p. 434; 'The King's Cross Restaur-ant', *Caterer*, 16 February 1891, p. 69; 'A Dinner at Wenzel's', *Caterer*, 15 June 1892, p. 225.

[23] 'Spiers and Pond's Silver Grill at Ludgate Station', 6 January 1866, Restaurant Files, box C–F, London Cuttings, Bishopsgate; 'The Genesis of Spiers and Pond', 15 April 1898, *Caterer*, p. 188.

[24] For example, the proprietors of the Walbrook Grand Café Restaurant were identified as F. Giordano and A. Casiraghi. Handbill, Walbrook Café, c.1880, LGL.

[25] 'On the Wing', *Caterer*, 15 May 1885, p. 119. Some other estimates suggest that the total number of foreign waiters in the capital was even higher, one authority offering a figure of 17,000. See 'Notes and Notions', *Hotel Review and Catering & Food Trades' Gazette* (November 1886), 132.

[26] *Caterer*, 15 April 1891, p. 153.

both national groups were engaged in the trade in some form.[27] Over the next two decades, the number of foreign waiters who found their 'calling' in London's 'many new restaurants' swelled to approximately 30,000, according to a 1911 inquiry conducted by the Apprenticeship and Skilled Employment Association of London.[28]

There were certainly a sufficient number of foreign waiters in London to justify the establishment of a number of collective organizations that sought to maintain and enhance their welfare. A contributor to *Good Words* in 1892 observed that there were 'some half-dozen clubs or unions with employment registries attached, and these clubs have established relations with employers, to whom they guarantee the character of the servants they supply'.[29] For instance, the large community of German waiters in London led to the creation of a branch of the German Waiters' Union (Deutscher Kellner-Bund), an organization with headquarters in Leipzig, and with fifty chapters in various European towns and cities. The London branch, which sought to promote 'the moral and material elevation of its members', provided not merely a relief fund and employment office, but also a property at 84 Charlotte Street in Fitzroy Square, that in 1885 had a clubhouse and twenty-two beds for lodgers.[30] Twenty-five years later, on this very site, resided the International Chefs and Waiters Society, an amalgamation of the Austrian Hotel Employees' Society and the late Chefs' Society.[31]

In addition to those international workers fortunate enough to be represented by voluntary, philanthropic, and union organizations, there were undoubtedly large numbers of foreign restaurant workers (particularly women, and those employed in institutions not specializing in food from their ancestral home) whose existence is betrayed only by anecdotal evidence or fleeting, not to say obscure, references in the print media. For example, in 1886, a Mr Thomas Frederick Marshall, a self-described 'countryman' from Headley in Hampshire, on returning home from business in London, shared with the readers of the short-lived, but wonderfully named, *Coffee Tavern Gazette and Journal of Food Thrift* his recommendations for dining in the West End. He singled out for particular praise the Star, a 'coffee-tavern' in Wigmore Street, where he not

---

[27] Sponza, *Italian Immigrants*, 13; Panayi, *German Immigrants*, 97.

[28] Miss K. I. M. Medley and Ernest Lesser, *An Inquiry into the Waiter's Calling* (London: Apprenticeship and Skilled Employment Association, 1911), 4.

[29] C. H. d' E. Leppington, 'Work and Wages in Hotels and Restaurants', *Good Words*, 33 (1892), 756.

[30] *Hotel Review and Catering & Food Trades' Gazette* (June 1886), 52; 'Hotel Notes and Trade News', *Tourist and Traveller, and Hotel Review* (December 1885), 304.

[31] 'The International Chefs and Waiters Society', *Restaurant* (May 1910), 225.

merely commended the attentiveness and hospitality of the owner but also praised, in passing, his host's 'Greek cook; her pastry is delicious'.[32]

In a few rare cases, it is possible to gain a more detailed account of the lives of foreign-born restaurant staff in London. In his memoirs published in 1960, Mario Gallati (by this point celebrity proprietor of the Caprice) described how, having worked as a child waiter in restaurants in Milan and Nice, he went to London in 1905 as a waiter at the Savoy Restaurant. Interestingly (in a further testimony to the international nature of the restaurant labour market), Gallati had intended a brief stay in London to learn English and 'to study the methods in British restaurants and hotels', before continuing on to the United States, at that point considered 'the land of opportunity for would-be restaurateurs'.[33] However, Gallati changed his plans after falling in love with a 'vivacious... amber-eyed girl named Josephine', who lived adjacent to his boarding house on Charlotte Street, which catered specifically for Italians who had just arrived in London.[34] After holding positions at the Hotel Cecil, Russell Hotel, and the Queen's Restaurant, Gallati returned to Italy in 1909 to satisfy the requirements of military service, at the end of which he went to work as a waiter in Paris, 'the very fountain-head of the art of the *cuisine*'.[35] In a letter written to Josephine in 1911, which has survived among his unpublished papers, he described his plans to leave Paris for Monte Carlo, where he intended to work as a chef, but his fear that she might marry another suitor motivated his speedy return to London, where he became *chef de rang* (or head waiter) at the fashionable Monico, in Shaftesbury Avenue.[36] He then moved to Romano's on the Strand, where he worked under fellow countryman Luigi Naintre, whom Gallati dubbed 'the Toscanini of restaurateurs'.[37] As Gallati hopscotched across Europe in pursuit of new job opportunities, he accumulated experience and know-ledge in one place that might serve the advancement of his career in another. Gallati initially hoped that success in London might further his ambitions in the United States, while, later on, he was convinced that familiarity with Paris and French cuisine would serve him well as an aspiring head waiter, and eventually proprietor, in London. Gallati's story reminds us that London was merely one node in a broader interconnecting

---

[32] 'Correspondence', *Coffee Tavern Gazette and Journal of Food Thrift*, 24 April 1886, p. 28.

[33] Mario Gallati, *Mario of the Caprice: The Autobiography of a Restaurateur* (London: Hutchinson and Co., 1960), 36.

[34] *Ibid.* 35.   [35] *Ibid.* 44.

[36] Letter from Mario Gallati to Giuseppina Frasca, 24 October 1911, WBA, 896/24, City of Westminster Archives Centre, London.

[37] Gallati, *Mario of the Caprice*, 45.

network of culinary entrepôts, one that relied on both an international labour market and a culture of peer recognition between London's restaurants and hotels and their equivalents, both on the Continent and in the United States.[38]

Foreign-born proprietors and staff were noticeable enough in the catering trade that their presence sometimes provoked a nativist backlash. In April 1900, a Charing Cross Road Italian restaurant keeper and two of his waiting staff were convicted of conducting their premises 'in a disorderly manner'. The presiding magistrate took the opportunity to launch an extended tirade against 'low Italians and other foreigners' who used the restaurant business as a cover for 'illegitimate and despicable' activities. Moreover, he claimed that 'case after case of exactly the same sort, carried on in the same way, by the same sort of people, came before him' on a regular basis, and, while fining the defendant in this particular case, made clear that his preference would be to use more punitive sanctions in future.[39]

However, what provoked the greatest anxieties was the apparent threat posed to British workers concerned with protecting their place in the labour market. These pressures led to the creation of specific workers' unions, particularly for waiters, such as the Central Waiters Union in 1886, the English Hotel, Restaurant, Club and Tavern Servants Union in 1889, and the more overtly politicized Amalgamated Waiters' Society, organized in 1896 by an individual with the ironically German-sounding name of Paul Vogel.[40] The latter's aim was not only to standardize pay and work hours, which foreign workers were seen to undermine and adversely to distort, but also 'to combat the powerful German Waiters' Union, and thus allow Britishers to hold their own'.[41] The Amalgamated Waiters' Society extended its autarkic protestations beyond the restaurant kitchen and dining room, to indict foreign-born proprietors and managers as an integral part of a broader conspiracy against the English waiter. It claimed it was 'quite a common practice' for foreign owners and managers to employ exclusively their own countrymen, indignantly referencing the case of a German manager who discharged all his British waiting staff from

[38] For one example of the internationalism of the labour market in the trade, see Patricia Van den Eeckhout, 'Cooks and Waiters on the Move: The World and International Exhibition in Ghent, 1913, as a Destination for Hospitality Workers', *Food and History* 11/2 (2013), 287–316.

[39] 'Disreputable Restaurant Keepers', *Daily News*, 11 April 1900, p. 9.

[40] 'Gastronomic Items', *Caterer*, 15 July 1886, p. 198; *British Journal of Catering*, 1 December 1889, p. 10; *Caterer*, 15 May 1894, p. 206; 'The Waiters' Column', *Caterer*, 16 November 1896, p. 555. The Amalgamated Waiters' Society's mouthpiece was *The Waiters' Record*, founded in 1900.

[41] 'The Waiters' Column', *Caterer*, 15 June 1896, p. 304.

a City restaurant and replaced them with Germans.[42] Whether such exclusionary practices existed in reality, as opposed to in the fevered imagination of English nativists, is difficult to establish, although other testimony suggests that the German and Austrian restaurants 'in the little colony off Tottenham-court Road' served as informal employment agencies for their countrymen.[43] It is also possible that national–ethnic conflicts were further sharpened by the issue of skill. The 1911 Apprentice-ship and Skilled Employment Association of London report on the 'waiter's calling' asserted that, while domestic waiters appeared satisfied with the status of casual labourers, foreign-born ones saw their work as skilled, not surpris-ingly given their commitment to achieving a facility with foreign languages, and the undertaking of apprenticeships that might last over two years and take place in many different countries, as Mario Gallati's story shows.[44]

While campaigns to restrict foreign waiters were tainted by a distinct xenophobia, they also—conversely—provide testimony to not merely their notable presence, but also their indispensability, in London. Accord-ing to the trade press, the 'English Robert' (slang for English waiters) failed to compete with the foreign waiter because, in this 'age of travel', the latter 'are linguists... and generally converse in four or five languages, whereas English waiters... can seldom speak any language but their own'.[45] Crowded out by the 'constantly increasing influx of Germans, Poles and other foreigners', many English waiters, as noted by one correspondent for the *Caterer*, sought refuge in New York restaurants, where they were highly rated, thus revealing that, in the trade's international labour mar-ket, London acted as a site of departure as well as a site of arrival and settlement.[46] The anti-alien sentiment directed at foreign-born propri-etors, managers, and waiters inevitably manifested itself at times when national and ethnic differences were being sharpened more generally—for example, in the build-up to the 1905 Aliens Act and at the outbreak of the First World War. However, while the emerging unionization of restaurant workers was undoubtedly entangled in the discourses of nativism, the dominant opinion expressed in the trade press was that the presence of foreign waiters and proprietors in London's restaurant scene was an

[42] As reported in 'Caterer's Notebook', *Caterer*, 15 April 1899, p. 148. For more extensive statements made by the Amalgamated Waiters' Society, see *Waiters' Record* (February 1900–September 1914).
[43] 'Foreign London at Dinner: The Resorts of our Permanent Visitors', 1897, Norman Collection, LGL.
[44] Medley and Lesser, *An Inquiry*, 4–6.
[45] 'Notes and Notions', *Hotel Review and Catering & Food Trades' Gazette* (November 1886), 132.
[46] 'Catering Notes', *Caterer*, 15 March 1893, p. 111.

inevitable and understandable manifestation of a transnational labour market, which, in turn, reflected a continued (if increasingly strained) commitment to the internationalist principles of free trade.[47]

Londoners' exposure to new culinary cultures was not confined to continental Europe, nor to groups with a numerically significant diasporic population. Nathaniel Newnham-Davis, reviewing the menu offerings at Romano's, an Italian-owned and managed restaurant with a generally continental menu, made intriguing reference to both 'a ground nut soup, the one delicacy that Nigeria has added to the cookery book' and 'a Malay curry cooked as it is cooked in Malaya and served in the Malay fashion, with sambals and with shining Malayan shell spoons for the rice'.[48] Chinese food was also undoubtedly present in the capital, although it remained relatively insignificant prior to the emergence of Chinatown in the 1950s.[49] In 1913, *The Times* claimed there were thirty Chinese shops and restaurants adjacent to opium dens in the East End, but the particularly transient nature of London's Chinese population (linked as it was to the shipping industry) makes this estimate speculative.[50] The *Restaurant* reported in the same period the existence of a Chinese restaurant close to Piccadilly Circus patronized by 'students sent over by the Chinese Government to learn our ways', who, in a possible acknowledgement of the cultural diversity of London's diners that will be discussed at more length later in this chapter, offered recommendations from the menu to those unfamiliar with Chinese dishes, not merely in English, but also in German and French.[51] However, Londoners were more likely to have been exposed to Chinese food through temporary exhibitions, such as the Health Exhibition of 1884, which featured pastiche eating houses supposedly from China (and Japan), than through the restaurant dining room.[52]

---

[47] See, e.g., *Hotel Review and Catering & Food Trades' Gazette* (November 1886), 132; *Restaurant* (August 1909), 6; and the following references in the *Caterer*: 16 November 1885, p. 307; 15 August 1893, p. 354; and 15 June 1896, p. 304—all of which admitted to the superiority of the continental training of waiters, especially in Germany and Switzerland.

[48] Nathaniel Newnham-Davis, *Gourmet's Guide to London* (London: Grant Richards, 1914), 109.

[49] This is not to say that Chinese restaurants did not appear in the popular imaginary. Brilliant Chang, who featured in the notorious 1922 case of Freda Kempton, a night club *habitué* who died from cocaine poisoning, owned a Chinese restaurant on Regent Street, while the 1929 film *Piccadilly* included several images of Chinese restaurants. See, e.g., 'Freda Kempton's Death, Suicide from Cocaine Poisoning, Chinese Restaurateur's Evidence', *The Times*, 25 April 1922, p. 9; Marek Kohn, *Dope Girls: The Birth of the British Drug Underground* (London: Lawrence & Wishart, 1992).

[50] 'Chinatown in London', *The Times*, 25 November 1913, p. 6.

[51] 'China in London', *Restaurant* (September 1911), 343.

[52] Even this exposure to 'Chinese' food was possibly somewhat limited, given that one contemporary observer asserted that the food served at the exhibition's Chinese restaurant

It was Indian food that was to be, in the late nineteenth century as indeed it is in the twenty-first, one of the most significant non-indigenous cuisines in the metropolis. In part, the popularity of Indian food can be accounted for by the presence of Indian students, the majority of whom (especially those reading for the Bar) resided in London.[53] However, there was also a market for Indian meals among Indian businessmen and, most critically, Britons engaged (either currently or formerly) in imperial administration in the subcontinent. As the *Caterer* explained in 1891, 'the civil service of our great Eastern dependencies is ever expanding, and it must ever be that a perpetually growing population of persons having Indian tastes in matters gastronomic must be located in London'.[54] The Bombay Parsi journalist and social reformer Behramji M. Malabari also observed this growing taste for Indian food, noting a couple of years later that 'Indian dishes, rice and curry ... with chutneys and condiments, are struggling into favour', largely because diplomats, former administrators, Indian visitors, students, and anyone curious about all things Eastern— and there were many—craved Indian dishes.[55] Newnham-Davis, who, prior to becoming a journalist and gourmand, had been an army intelligence officer in Simla, was inevitably alert to the presence of both people and dishes originating from the subcontinent. Recollecting a meal taken at the Hotel Cecil in the Strand, he introduced 'the Nabob', an uncle who had also served in 'the gorgeous East'. When the Nabob asserted that 'there is no good curry to be had outside the portals of his club, the East India', Newnham-Davis retorted by insisting that he himself had 'eaten good curry at the Criterion, where a sable gentleman is charged with its preparation'.[56] Newnham-Davis and his uncle, having summoned the curry cook 'clothed in white samite, and with his turban neatly rolled' to their table, where he was put through an examination about his art (conducted in Hindustani), then proceeded to dine on 'a genuine Indian curry' and 'chutnees galore'.[57]

There are references in the pages of the *Caterer* in this period to at least twenty individual establishments that offered Indian fare. For instance, in 1885, it was reported that a former chef on one of the P and O steamers,

---

(the work of a French chef who had formerly been resident in Beijing) was more reminiscent of that served in Paris than that found in China. See J. A. G. Roberts, *China to Chinatown: Chinese Food in the West* (London: Reaktion, 2002), 142–4.

[53] Estimates of the number of Indians in Britain at the turn of the century put their numbers at between 1,000 and 2,000. See K. Chowdray, 'The Indian Students in England', *Student Movement*, 12 (1910), 86–8, and F. H. Brown, 'Indian Students in Great Britain', *Edinburgh Review*, 217 (1913), 150–1.

[54] 'Wanted, an Anglo-Indian Restaurant for London', *Caterer*, 15 June 1891, p. 211.

[55] Behramji M. Malabari, *The Indian Eye on English Life; or, Rambles of a Pilgrim Reformer* (London: Archibald Constable and Co., 1893), 45.

[56] Newnham-Davis, *Dinners and Diners*, 59.   [57] *Ibid.* 61, 63.

Mr Hewitt, who had founded the Falcon Restaurant in Fetter Lane, near the Strand, offered Indian and Malay curries that were considered sufficiently fiery to 'revive the dead'.[58] In the following year, readers were informed that 'Indian curries are now a standing dish' at the Crown Hotel in Leicester Square owned by Mr R. Banks.[59] Interestingly, a handbill relating to this institution has survived, which declared that its restaurant 'serves a real Indian curry', and that the chef was advised by Mr Friday, 'the G[rea]t. Madras authority on Curry', who was also scheduled to give lectures and practical demonstrations at the Cookery and Food Exhibition at the Royal Aquarium that winter.[60] Also in 1886, a correspondent who described himself as 'an Old Indian traveller' wrote to the *Caterer*, telling its readers that the best house in London for an Indian curry was Purssell's in Finch Lane in the City, 'where an Indian cook is kept to prepare them'.[61] A decade later, when the kitchens of the St James's Hall Restaurant were under the direction of chef M. C. Brezzo and his assistant Mr Pugh, there was a specialized section devoted to Indian cookery that was under the charge of M. Futymed of Calcutta.[62] A few years later, the *Caterer* reported that Mrs Turner's Indian restaurant in Hammersmith, 'much frequented by native Indian students in London', not merely served diners on site but was also willing to send 'a complete Indian dinner... kept warm in baskets' to any address that could be reached 'by means of the District Railway or the "Twopenny Tube"'.[63] Given that many of these establishments had non-Indian proprietors or Anglicized names, it is possible that the full extent of the presence of Indian food in London's restaurants may be even more considerable than suggested here. Even the unimpeachably English name of the Falstaff Restaurant, in Eastcheap, did not preclude the serving of 'excellent Indian curries', and even the provision of punkahs in the dining room.[64]

The preparation of such dishes obviously required both the provision of ingredients in the metropolitan vicinity and a broader global supply chain. This was facilitated by joint-stock companies, such as the London and India Docks Joint Committee, which responded to the rising demand for cheap food imports, particularly meat, by expanding its holding capacity.

[58] 'Chops and Changes', *Caterer*, 16 February 1885, p. 41.
[59] 'Chops and Changes', *Caterer*, 15 April 1886, p. 112.
[60] Handbill, 'Curry, Curry, Curry: R. Banks', 1886, Evanion Collection 6443, British Library; 'The Cookery Exhibitions', *Caterer*, 15 November 1886, p. 326.
[61] *Caterer*, 15 March 1886, p. 71. More speculatively, there is an intriguing reference to Indian curry being served in a metropolitan railway refreshment room. See 'The Curried Dishes of the Indian Empire', *Caterer*, 15 January 1887, p. 4.
[62] 'St James's Hall Restaurant', *Caterer*, 15 June 1897, p. 332.
[63] 'Indian Cookery in London', *Caterer*, 15 December 1900, p. 661.
[64] 'Chops and Changes', *Caterer*, 15 February 1892, p. 60.

In 1894, for instance, it was reported that, while the company had twenty-one large storage chambers at the Victoria Docks fitted with refrigerators for nearly a quarter of a million carcasses imported from Australia, New Zealand, and South America, more space was needed, and the company was to build more 'extensive chambers' in Smithfield market.[65] If Smithfield served as the main market for meat, restaurants were able to obtain fish from Billingsgate, and fruit and vegetables from Covent Garden, all of which opened at roughly five o'clock in the morning. It was the business of the restaurant chef to take detailed notes of his stock and 'calculate his next day's requirements' before sending out his buyer to these markets. 'The buying is most responsible work', observed the *Caterer* in 1891, adding that 'no doubt the ideal buyer is the proprietor or manager himself', who can be trusted to know the prices of things and the people with whom he trades, but 'he can hardly be in the market at 5 or 6 a.m., and looking after his waiters and cooks . . . till past midnight' the night before, so he usually sent a subordinate.[66]

In cases where goods were procured from other sources, they sometimes came from individual dealers like D. R. Evans and Co., in Farringdon Street, which, originally founded as a general grocers in the eighteenth century, by the late nineteenth century exclusively supplied the restaurant and hotel community, reflecting the rapid development of this sector. By importing directly from producers in France, Italy, and America, the firm claimed to 'offer large consumers many special advantages by avoiding intermediate profits, their long experience and extensive business connection giving them facilities for close buying in the best markets'.[67]

There were also specialized dealers that traded in one commodity only. For instance, the Adelphi Hotel Company Ltd sold West Indian turtle meat, a delicacy that gained popularity and attracted other importers like T. K. Bellis of Jeffrey Square, in the City, whose firm contracted the Mexican Gulf Fisheries to catch shipments of turtles that arrived in London every fourteen days by steamer.[68] Similarly, Indian food importer Messrs Veeraswamy and Co. (subsequently the official caterer for the Indian Pavilion at the 1924 British Empire Exhibition and proprietors of what became London's longest-running Indian restaurant) sold foodstuffs

---

[65] 'Cold Storage of Meat in London', *Caterer*, 15 September 1894, p. 384.
[66] 'Restaurant Marketing', *Caterer*, 15 April 1891, p. 150.
[67] 'Odds and Ends', *Caterer*, 15 July 1895, p. 328.
[68] 'Live Turtle!', *Hotel Review and Catering & Food Trades' Gazette* (February 1887), 22; 'Real Turtle', *Caterer*, 15 June 1898, p. xl.

to caterers from a depot at 234 Rye Lane in Peckham.[69] Its most popular item, 'Nizam Madras Curry Powder', was said to be 'piquant without being fiery'. As an added bonus for customers, the firm advertised in the trade journal the *Chef* in 1896 that it was 'willing to send a thoroughly experienced curry cook to any hotel, club or restaurant in order to show the best modes of preparing a real Indian curry'.[70] While Veeraswamy's curry may have been in high demand, its shop was not the only one to sell this spice mixture. Some years earlier, the *Caterer* noted that a shop on Brompton Road in Knightsbridge owned by Mr Friday (whom we encountered previously) sold tinned curries, curry powders, pastes, chutneys, and Indian condiments of all descriptions, with the express purpose of 'initiating novices into the art of curry-making', while Mr Edmund's shop in Stonefield Terrace in Islington displayed a special gold medal 'Empress' curry powder, which conjured up 'visions of old East Indians at table, and of millionaire nabobs regaling on delicacies of which the West only knows little or nothing'.[71] Where the ingredients needed for exotic dishes were unobtainable, chefs often worked imaginatively to find or devise convincing substitutes. Returning to the Malay curry at Romano's, Newnham-Davis, who clearly regarded himself as an expert (with some possible justification, given his former military service in the Straits), commended the restaurant's renowned chef for an act of effective culinary improvisation: 'What substitute M. Ferrario has found for the fresh cocoa-nut pulp which is the foundation of all Malay curries, I do not know.'[72]

The international element in food culture in this period is also evident from contemporary cookbooks. Some of these were authored by well-known chefs and may have informed the dishes served to restaurant diners. Most though were likely to have been used in a predominantly domestic context, although one could speculate that some of them found their way into hotel and restaurant kitchens, or that, for diners, exposure to international cuisine at home might have bolstered the enthusiasm for more exotic dishes while eating out. Whatever their intended constituency, the titles of books such as *Cosmopolitan Cookery* (which included recipes for Russian bear paws and 'Chicken Curry, Indian fashion'), or, more specifically, *Anglo-Indian and Oriental Cookery* and *Wyvern's Indian*

[69] Lizzie Collingham, *Curry: A Biography* (London: Chatto and Windus, 2005), 153–4; 'A Good Indian Curry', *Chef*, 18 July 1896, p. 10. Veeraswamy's restaurant first opened in 1926.

[70] 'A Good Indian Curry', *Chef*, 18 July 1896, p. 10.

[71] 'Chops and Changes', *Caterer*, 15 April 1887, p. 123; 'Curries, Sauces, &c.', *Caterer*, 15 December 1890, p. 487.

[72] Newnham-Davis, *Gourmet's Guide*, 109.

Cookery Book, suggest that the gastro-cosmopolitanism of the restaurant meal was supported and sustained by a broader culinary infrastructure.[73] It is true that many cookbooks featuring Indian recipes were intended for the Anglo-Indian rather than the British market. However, a review in the *Caterer* of a collection of Wyvern's recipes, while it noted that the book was written 'for the special benefit of Anglo-Indians' and published in London and Madras, also insisted that many of its menus might, 'with certain alterations and modifications, be adapted for home use' by 'caterers and chefs'.[74] Even books with more generic titles, such as Anne Bowman's *The New Cookery Book* or Eliza Acton's *Modern Cookery*, contain extensive discussion of, not merely English, but 'foreign cookery'.[75] Bowman, in particular, was keen to promote Indian dishes that were as 'authentic' as possible, berating English cooks who persisted in adding minced bacon to chicken curry, thereby destroying 'the Oriental character of the dish'.[76] Mrs Beeton's legendary *Household Management*, while extolling the virtues of classic English dishes, still found space for more internationally oriented recipes, including one for mango chutney that she claimed had been given 'by a native to an English lady, who had long been a resident in India'.[77]

To return to the restaurant, it is in examining the contents of diners' plates that we are granted the most effective demonstration of how food was able to transcend the binary between Britain and the world beyond. Menus reveal not merely the presence of individual foreign dishes, but also the way the foods of different nations or cultures might be mixed in the course of a meal, on a single plate, or even in a single recipe. A menu from the Grand Hotel in Trafalgar Square in 1897 appeared eager to promote its exotic and cosmopolitan attractions by including in the menu 'huîtres a l'Américaine', 'condé a la West Indienne', and 'bisque a la Norvégienne'.[78] In other restaurants, otherwise conventional menus usually included at least one exotic (not to say obscure) dish—to take two examples also dating from 1897, the 'chaud-froid Algerienne' offered at the Monico or

[73] Urbain Dubois, *Cosmopolitan Cookery* (1870; London: Longmans, Green & Co., 1886); Grace Johnson, *Anglo-Indian and Oriental Cookery* (London: W. H. Allen & Co., 1893); Arthur Robert Kenney-Herbert, *Wyvern's Indian Cookery Book* (1878; London and Madras: Higginbotham & Co., 1904).
[74] 'Book notices: *Culinary Jottings* by "Wyvern"', *Caterer*, 16 August 1886, p. 242.
[75] Anne Bowman, *The New Cookery Book: A Complete Manual of English and Foreign Cookery on Sound Principles of Taste and Science* (1867; London: Routledge, 1890); Eliza Acton, *Modern Cookery* (1845; London: Longmans, Green & Co., 1887).
[76] Bowman, *New Cookery Book*, 345.
[77] Isabella Beeton, *Mrs Beeton's Book of Household Management* (1861), ed. Nicola Humble (Oxford: Oxford University Press, 2000), 124.
[78] Menu, Grand Hotel, Trafalgar Square, 3 November 1897, item no. 1897–296, Buttolph Collection of Menus, New York Public Library [hereafter NYPL].

'timbales de bonnard Américaine, riz Pilau' served at the Savoy.[79] What added to this cultural messiness was that, even when the food was genuinely multinational, French still served as the predominant *lingua franca* for many eating houses. The menu that was written *en français* served to complicate the story by inserting into the dining experience an additional cultural formation that reconfigured an already delicate cultural negotiation. In his recollections of his life as a bohemian in the 1880s, journalist George R. Sims wrote of a dinner at Krehl's in Coleman Street where 'the menu was in French but some of the dishes had the flavour of the Fatherland about them', which was not surprising, given that Krehl's was a German restaurant.[80] While Austria ultimately remained outside the boundaries of the unified German state that emerged in 1871, a more fluid relationship between the two nations' food cultures characterized public eating in London for the remainder of the century. For example, an Austrian husband and wife team opened what was described as 'a German and Austrian delicatessen' in Leicester Square that later expanded into a fully fledged restaurant called the Vienna Café in 1895.[81]

These developments were nothing new if the experience of the Peninsulaire Restaurant in Glasshouse Street, off Regent Street, was typical. An 1880 handbill advertised that the house served English, French, and Italian cuisine;[82] but a menu from the same year revealed an even more complicated story. Its Parisian dinner (for 3s. 6d.) included a soup of lobster bisque (with its intimation of East Coast American cuisine), whitebait à la diable, and pomme nouvelle au beurre (two dishes that incorporated staples of English cuisine, but that were accorded French-language labels). These were followed by poulet au cresson (despite the French appellation, a traditional English dish of roast chicken with watercress), Bavarois au Maraschino (a Bavarian dessert), and, to conclude the dinner, a cheese dish of Camembert along with Turkish coffee. A cheaper dinner (for 2s.) at the restaurant included a Ris à l'Andalouse (which was an Andalusian refashioning of an Italian risotto with clams), followed by cod in Hollandaise sauce (which would have been familiar to most British diners), an entrée of a round of veal à la Duchesse (the provenance and preparation of which is unclear), and a two-stage dessert consisting of French meal fritters or doughnuts followed by a quintessentially English

[79] Menu, Monico, 22 July 1897, item no. 1897–237, NYPL; Menu, Savoy Restaurant, 22 April 1897, item no. 1897–128, NYPL.

[80] George R. Sims, *My Life: Sixty Years' Recollections of Bohemian London* (London: Eveleigh Nash, 1917), 95–6.

[81] 'The Looker On', *Hotel*, 27 November 1895, p. 17.

[82] Handbill, Peninsular [*sic*] Restaurant (November 1880), Evanion Collection 6639, British Library.

plate of Cheshire cheese.[83] Clearly, dinner at the Peninsulaire in 1880 consisted of integrating the flavours of many nations, rendering cultural hybridity a part and parcel of the meal itself.

Nor was the Peninsulaire unique. At the Holborn Restaurant in 1882, diners had a choice of how they comprehended the menu linguistically (in either French or English), and within the menu they could choose from French-sounding dishes or cultural hybrids like cauliflower in béchamel sauce, which was then followed by a Mediterranean or Levantine dessert menu consisting of olives, raisins, and almonds, pistachio jelly, or Italian meringue.[84] This cultural mixing occurred at less rarefied eating houses as well, such as an unidentified 'cheap Italian restaurant' where a côtelette Milanese (or veal cutlet dipped in egg and covered with breadcrumbs), normally served with a wedge of lemon, was instead served with curry sauce, which, according to one writer for the *Caterer*, 'gives it a distinctive excellence'. 'Its crisp breadcrumbs will become slightly moistened by the sauce, but the eggs will hold good against curry and gravy.'[85] Here and elsewhere the restaurateur and the chef showcased the range of culinary possibilities that the diner might encounter at their restaurant.[86] This might simply have been a case of attracting attention by the range of exotic products on offer. It could also have been that the culinary traditions being referenced might have been familiar to diners, either because they had experience of travelling abroad through business or leisure, or because the diners themselves were foreign nationals.

Certainly, patrons were drawn to London's dining rooms from a variety of different countries. Some of them went to restaurants where the food was familiar, but others went to prestigious restaurants with experimental menus that featured regularly in tourist guidebooks. American visitors became a not insignificant presence in London's dining rooms in this period. If American readers in 1865 might have been dissuaded from travelling to London by a claim in the New York periodical the *Nation*

[83] Menu, Hotel and Restaurant Peninsulaire, 15 May 1880, Evanion Collection 6672, British Library.

[84] Menu, Holborn Restaurant, 1 April 1882, 134.127/1, A3 Box Food and Drink, Ephemera Collection, Museum of London [hereafter ML].

[85] 'Catering Notes and Comments', *Caterer*, 16 March 1885, p. 59.

[86] For other examples of menus (excluding banquets and other private occasions) that advertised hybrid dishes, see 24 April 1901, Hotel Metropole, FF 942–1371, Hotel Metropole Album, City of Westminster Archive; 18 July 1914, Prince's, A3 Box Food and Drink, ML; 20 July 1892, (Gatti's) Adelphi Theatre Restaurant, item no, 1892–095, NYPL; 22 April 1897, Savoy Restaurant, item no. 1897–128, NYPL; 22 July 1897, Monico, item no. 1897–237, NYPL; 11 November 1898, Epitaux's Restaurant, item no. 1898–305, NYPL; 18 July 1896, Frascati's, item no.1896–149, NYPL; *c.*1889, (L. Azario's) Florence Restaurant, Evanion Collection 6798, British Library; Horse Shoe Hotel and Restaurant, 1882, Evanion Collection 4234, British Library.

that 'there are one or two eating-houses in London which have the air of restaurants, until a fair trial shows the hollowness of their pretensions', in the decades that followed travel guides to the metropolis intended for American travellers regularly recommended visiting specific restaurants.[87] Charles Eyre Pascoe's *A London Directory for American Travellers*, published in 1874, aimed 'to furnish a concise, reliable, handy, and cheap "directory"' for Americans arriving for the first time. Pascoe's publication was followed a decade later by his *London of Today*, which had a chapter devoted to dining for those visitors 'without the trusted friend at hand to offer advice'.[88] On arrival in London, American visitors would have encountered advertising materials intended to direct them to a particular eating house. For example, a handbill insisted that 'American travellers sojourning in London' 'should not fail to pay a visit to Overton's splendid Oyster Saloon, opposite Victoria Station', while a pamphlet promoting the Hotel Cecil insisted that in its lounge bar and restaurant 'will be found all the comfort and peculiarities dear to the American traveller'.[89] In 1902, an American journalist resident in London, Elizabeth Banks, asserted that 'there are few special American dishes which one cannot find at various eating-places in London if one will but inquire for them'. She even supplied an example, a restaurant in Charing Cross where 'pork and beans, Boston style, and salted cod-fish' were served to a party of Americans 'as the merest matter of course when asked for'.[90] Significantly, the *Caterer* frequently featured articles appraising the latest developments in restaurant culture in New York, thereby corroborating an ongoing dialogue between Britain and America on the subject of dining.[91]

Less specifically, trade papers like the *International Travellers' Journal* alerted overseas visitors to London to the fact that certain restaurants subscribed to foreign-language newspapers.[92] The proprietor of the

---

[87] 'Restaurants and their Function', *Nation*, 1 (1865), 562.

[88] Charles Eyre Pascoe, *A London Directory for American Travellers* (Boston: Lee and Shepard and Dillingham, 1874), 5; Charles Eyre Pascoe *London of Today: An Illustrated Handbook for the Season* (London: Sampson Low & Co., 1885), 43.

[89] Handbill, Overton's Oyster Saloon (November 1887), Evanion Collection 7068, British Library; *The Hotel Cecil* (London: Hotel Cecil, 1896), D 93.1 London Collection Pamphlets, Box 323/35, Bishopsgate.

[90] Elizabeth L. Banks, 'American London', in George R. Sims (ed.), *Living London* (3 vols; London: Cassell and Co., 1901–3), vol. ii, sect. 1, p. 107. For a discussion of Banks as witness to, and critic of, British society, see Seth Koven, *Slumming: Sexual and Social Politics in Victorian London* (Princeton: Princeton University Press, 2004), ch. 3.

[91] See, e.g., Howard Paul, 'How They Eat in New York', *Caterer*, 15 December 1888, pp. 470–1; Howard Paul, 'At "Delmonico's," New York', *Caterer*, 15 November 1889, pp. 417–18.

[92] See, e.g., various establishments listed in 'Noted Restaurants and Cafes', *International Travellers' Journal* (January 1873), 3.

Gambrinus in the City advertised that, by offering these journals (and continental food), he hoped to make 'his restaurant a place where foreigners in London will feel entirely at home'.[93] Besides advertising, some newspapers like the *Caterer* reported on a 'foreign' presence in the restaurant by publishing reports of elaborate dinners like the one in 1889 including members of the Chinese Embassy who occupied a private room at the St James's Hall Restaurant, whose cooks were said to be French, Italian, English, and Indian, as we have seen. There, they feasted on 'salmon and whitebait with occasional stewed eels', 'pur et simple', without 'the ordinary sauces and regulation condiments' that 'we English are wont to do'.[94] For this reviewer, Howard Paul, whose dining column appeared in the *Caterer* regularly between 1889 and 1890, and then intermittently until 1898, there needed to be an understanding of cuisine, not just food—and this project was internationally grounded. If press reviews, brochures, handbills, and guidebooks aimed to steer foreigners, whether resident or visiting, to London's dining rooms, there is evidence that they were successful. Author Frederick Leal was moved to write about the restaurant Frascati that 'every spoken tongue may be heard here as you thread your way through the labyrinth of little tables in the Grand Salon'.[95]

The appearance of transnational diners in London's restaurants should not be represented only in terms of incoming traffic. Britain's global and imperial ties inevitably created a restaurant clientele that travelled backwards and forwards between Britain and other parts of the world, notably those, like Newnham-Davis, engaged in military service or colonial administration. An article in the *Caterer* in 1897 insisted that Indian dishes served in West End establishments had a delicacy and refinement that might lead 'winter tourists in India' to find the curries served there less appetizing than they had done previously.[96] Interestingly, the author of the article located the difference between the taste of curries offered in metropole and colony in an abandonment by the London-based Indian cook of the 'time-honoured simplicity of his condiments and ghee' in favour of an attempted fusion with 'the cultured mysteries' of French cuisine, thereby highlighting the interconnectedness of the transnationalisms that characterized both dinners and diners.[97]

[93] 9 April 1890, Restaurant Files, box G–L, London Cuttings, Bishopsgate Library.

[94] Howard Paul, 'Dining Here and There', *Caterer*, 15 February 1889, p. 49.

[95] [Frederick Leal], *The Restaurant Frascati*, with illustrations by Horace Morehen (London: Spottiswoode and Co., *c.*1894), D 93.2, London Collection Pamphlets, Box 322/6, Bishopsgate. The same comment was made in 'The Restaurant Frascati', *Era*, 31 August 1895, p. 16.

[96] 'Caterer's Notebook', *Caterer*, 15 January 1897, p. 15.   [97] *Ibid.*

The presence of the foreign waiter in the dining room obviously added an additional constituent to the already extensive cultural heterogeneity of the restaurant. Here cultural mixing could just as easily promote cultural confusion. Referring to a dinner at the Gaiety where the menu was in French, one reviewer for the *Caterer* pondered: 'it is all very well for me, but how is a plain John Bull to make it out, especially if the waiters, chiefly of foreign nationality, are unable to expound the items satisfactorily?'[98] However, beyond the isolated diner confronted with a French menu, there were still other possible pitfalls. The potential for cultural confusion was even greater when diners were drawn from the non-European world, even in those establishments that deliberately sought to create a successful matching of diner and meal. For example, the Japanese painter Yoshio Markino was bewildered when a group of English actors took him to what they termed a 'Samurai dinner' at various London restaurants.[99] Whether the diner left the table satisfied or not, it cannot be denied that his or her experience of public eating was one that could be inscribed with international elements, derived from the meal itself, the staff, and fellow diners. Such encounters encapsulate the complex matrix of cultural formations and identities that lay beneath the apparently simple term, gastro-cosmopolitanism.

Viewing the London restaurant through the prism of gastro-cosmopolitanism highlights a number of aspects of the way that transnational and global cultural forces operated in late-nineteenth-century and early-twentieth-century Britain. At a basic level, it suggests the need for a more extensive synthesis of the studies of the urban metropolis, on the one hand, and immigrant and diasporic populations, on the other. Many of the seminal works that have obliged us to take British history beyond the nation have been, in one sense or the other, studies of diasporic populations.[100] More specifically, a study of the restaurant in London demonstrates the necessity of considering not merely the dispersal of cultures, communities, and individuals but also the points of convergence where multiple diasporas meet, overlap, and interrelate.[101] It is also obvious that

[98] 'Paris Catering Notes', *Caterer*, 15 January 1886, p. 10.

[99] Yoshio Markino, *A Japanese Artist in London* (London: Chatto and Windus, 1910), 100.

[100] Burton, *Postcolonial Careers*; Gilroy, *Black Atlantic*.

[101] Studies of immigrant populations in this period have tended to focus on discrete ethnic or racial groups, and their relationship with the host population, conceived in binary terms, rather than within a more complex trans-diasporic matrix. See, e.g., Roger Swift and Sheridan Gilley (eds), *The Irish in the Victorian City* (London: Croom Helm, 1985); Sponza, *Italian Immigrants*; Jeffrey Green, *Black Edwardians: Black People in Britain, 1901–1914* (London: Frank Cass, 1998); Shompa Lahiri, *Indians in Britain: Anglo-Indian Encounters, Race and Identity, 1880–1930* (London: Frank Cass, 2000); By contrast, see the

an undue preoccupation with transnational precursors of the modern 'celebrity chef' has obscured the way that culinary cosmopolitanism functioned at all levels of society, not least in the more modest eating houses that feature regularly within this book. The simultaneous presence in the restaurant scene in London of French menus, Italian cooks, German waiters, and Chinese and American diners reveals the complexity of the relationship between populations and places. The fact that a Greek pastry chef could be found in a coffee tavern (which in this case was an attempt to produce a reimagining of the traditional English pub, minus alcohol) or that an Italian chef in a continental restaurant sought to create a Malaysian curry (and without one of the key ingredients) testify to the multidimensional ways in which cultural exchange operated, creating formations that transcend unfeasible distinctions between 'authentic' and 'ersatz' aspects of restaurant culture. At the very least, the presence of these workers and diners highlights the necessity of adopting a transnational rubric that is not confined to the boundaries of Britain's formal empire.

In particular, the emphasis on empire in transnational histories has risked undervaluing the extent to which continental Europe mattered to contemporaries, in myriad ways. Literary scholars have paid attention to the exchange between British and continental writers in the nineteenth century.[102] Historians, by contrast, have been less inclined to investigate the interrelationship between continental culture and nineteenth-century metropolitan Britain, despite the existence of a number of intriguing sites that would suggest the value of more sustained and synthetic exploration, and to which a study of public dining would be a useful addition.[103] The restaurant also reveals that Britain's relationship to the culture of globalization incorporated not merely the empire and continental Europe, but also other parts of the world, notably the United States, Latin America, the Middle East, China, and Japan.[104]

---

more sophisticated treatment, David R. Roediger, *The Wages of Whiteness: Race and the Making of the American Working Class* (New York: Verso, 2007).

[102] e.g. Margaret Cohen and Carolyn Dever (eds), *The Literary Channel: the International Invention of the Novel* (Princeton: Princeton University Press, 2002).

[103] For an example of the rewards to be accrued from this approach, see Emma L. Winter, 'German Fresco Painting and the New Houses of Parliament at Westminster, 1834–51', *Historical Journal*, 47/2 (2004), 291–329.

[104] There has been extensive attention to the 'Americanization' of British culture, but most of this literature has focused on the decades after 1918. See the contributions to the special issue of *Cultural & Social History*, 4 (2007). Exceptions would be Judith R. Walkowitz, 'The "Vision of Salome": Cosmopolitanism and Erotic Dancing in Central London, 1908–1918', *American Historical Review*, 108/2 (2003), 337–76; Koven, *Slumming*, ch. 3. For Latin America, see Robert D. Aguirre, *Informal Empire: Mexico and Central*

Gastro-cosmopolitanism in London's restaurants in this period does more than merely highlight the importance of considering globalization in the broadest geographical sense. It also accords with an increasing emphasis on plurality in the study of cosmopolitan culture more broadly in a number of academic disciplines. Sociologists and political theorists concerned with contemporary transnational social, political, and cultural forces have demonstrated an increased preference for the term 'cosmo-politanisms' to describe the range of global interdependencies that they associate with the postcolonial and postmodern condition.[105] Literary scholars have reminded us that, in nineteenth-century Britain, the term cosmopolitanism had connotations that embraced both the progressive and the pejorative and that the term possessed a 'constitutive ambivalence'.[106] Similarly, historian Judith Walkowitz's study of late-nineteenth- and early-twentieth-century Soho reveals a double-edged cosmopolitanism, an urban space that was 'simultaneously safe and dangerous', characterized by ambivalence and cultural inconsistency.[107] In the section of her study dedicated to the Italian restaurant, Walkowitz emphasizes the association of Soho's catering industry with what she terms 'dangerous cosmopolitan-ism', citing media exposés 'of adulterated food, prepared in unhygienic settings and served by deracinated foreigners' that constituted an 'alimen-tary threat to the British body politic'. In fact, press and industry responses to London's restaurants suggest that most contemporary references to public eating tend to be either neutral or clustered around progressive, rather than negative, associations and connotations of cosmopolitanism.[108]

There is no doubt that negotiating a dining culture characterized by internationalism and hybridity could at times be a trying experience. One cannot but sympathize with the diner whose difficulty in comprehending a French menu was aggravated when he enlisted the assistance of his German waiter, whose grasp of both English and French proved to be

America in Victorian Culture (Minneapolis: University of Minnesota Press, 2005). For the Middle East, see Eitan Bar-Yosef, *The Holy Land in English Culture, 1799–1917: Palestine and the Question of Orientalism* (Oxford: Oxford University Press, 2005). For Britain's relationship to China, see Sascha Auerbach, *Race, Law, and 'the Chinese Puzzle' in Imperial Britain* (New York: Palgrave Macmillan, 2009); Ross G. Forman, *China and the Victorian Imagination: Empires Entwined* (Cambridge: Cambridge University Press, 2013).

[105] Pheng Cheah and Bruce Robbins (eds), *Cosmopolitics: Thinking and Feeling beyond the Nation* (Minneapolis: University of Minnesota Press, 1998).

[106] Tanya Agathocleous and Jason R. Rudy, 'Victorian Cosmopolitanisms: Introduc-tion', *Victorian Literature and Culture*, 38 (2010), 389.

[107] Walkowitz, *Nights Out*, 5–7.

[108] *Ibid.* 102. Support for Walkowitz's claim that journalists, politicians, and fiction writers 'returned again and again' to this motif of 'dangerous cosmopolitanism' is confined to a single article in the *Caterer* from 16 October 1905 and a brief reference to H. G. Wells's 1909 novel, *Tono-Bungay*.

inadequate to the task.[109] However, such encounters suggest that the negative connotations of gastro-cosmopolitanism remained largely confined to frustration or irritation rather than fear or pathologization. For those hoping to use the dining experience as an index of anxiety and deracination, an obvious intersection between urban danger and hybrid food culture would be food poisoning. As was seen in the previous chapter, adulteration and contamination were certainly widespread problems in restaurants in London and featured not merely in local government sanitation reports, but also in court cases that were widely reported in the press. However, restaurants offering non-British foods of varying degrees of hybridity (and those employing non-British staff) were rarely singled out for attention and censure in regard to this issue. If the reports of London's official health inspectors and press coverage are accurate indicators, diners appeared to be more at risk in the traditional English chophouse, vegetarian restaurant, or fried fish shop, all of which were regarded as particularly prone to adulterated food and filthy surroundings.[110] By contrast, some observers specifically singled out foreign restaurants for maintaining the highest standards of hygiene.[111]

Indeed, the largely positive connotations of gastro-cosmopolitanism in late-nineteenth- and early-twentieth-century London suggest that a study of London's dining culture might be aligned with recent interventions in the history of nation and sexuality that emphasize cultural mixing and indeterminacy, rather than distance and 'otherness'.[112] Food, like sex, was experienced at the level of the intimate and the material, not merely in the domain of discourse. The cosmopolitanism of public eating was experienced directly and immediately, and, if anything, it may have permeated the city's culture to such an extent that it became almost commonplace, or

[109] 'Dining Experiences in London', *Tourist and Traveller, and Hotel Review*, 1 January 1885, p. 11.

[110] See, e.g., the numerous sanitation inspectors' reports collected in the records of the Commissioner of Sewers of the City of London, CLA/006/AD/05, and the London County Council Public Health Department, LCC/Ph/Reg/5, London Metropolitan Archives. For press coverage of specific complaints about the chophouse, see *Hotel*, 24 July 1895, pp. 15–16; *Nineteenth Century*, 23:133 (March 1888), p. 466. On unhygienic vegetarian restaurants, see *Caterer*, 15 September 1899, p. 427; *Vegetarian*, 31 March 1888, p. 8 and 14 April 1888, p. 8; *Food and Sanitation*, 30 December 1893, p. 410, and 23 March 1893, p. 91. On fried fish shops and sanitary infractions, see *Food and Sanitation*, 27 March 1897, p. 154; 6 November 1897, p. 533; 12 February 1898, p. 702; *Anti-Adulteration Review and Food Journal* (July 1882), 284, and (April 1893), 450.

[111] For general comments, see 'The Looker On', *Hotel*, 16 October 1895, p. 17; and, more specifically, see 'The Café Monico Restaurant', *Anti-Adulteration Review and Food Journal* (May 1883), 479; 'Where to Dine in London', *Food and Sanitation*, 3 March 1895, p. 72; and 'Chinatown in London', *The Times*, 25 November 1913, p. 6.

[112] See, e.g., Mica Nava, *Visceral Cosmopolitanism: Gender, Culture and the Normalisation of Difference* (Oxford and New York: Berg, 2007), 3–15.

'indifferently realised' in the words of the writer for *Chambers's Journal* with which this chapter opened.

While gastro-cosmopolitanism might have been woven into the fabric of the metropolis, it should not be assumed that London was unique. Given that gastro-cosmopolitanism was a phenomenon that emphasized transnational cultural exchange and the movement of people and commodities, it is very likely that it featured in the cultural fabric of other metropolitan centres. It was certainly true of New York, where a diverse food culture was rooted in the city's history of immigration and diasporically derived identities.[113] Moreover, London's extensive international culinary culture was contingent and vulnerable. The outbreak of the First World War dealt a not insignificant blow to two of the most important minority groupings associated with foreign-owned and staffed restaurants. As was seen in previous chapters, German waiters, subject to either internment or deportation, effectively disappeared from London's dining rooms in the autumn of 1914, while large numbers of Italians engaged in the restaurant business returned to their homeland and offered their services to Italy's war effort after 1915.[114] The dislocation of world trade and widespread food shortages during the First World War also adversely affected the range of food choices available in the capital.

Of course, this diminution of London's international culinary culture ultimately proved not to be fatal. Some scholars have argued that the century since the First World War (and particularly the decades following post-1945 Commonwealth immigration) has seen a culinary revolution in Britain, in which food has served as an index of a broader shift towards multiculturalism.[115] An unfortunate corollary of such narratives has been to downplay, or even entirely to disregard, the international character of public eating in late-Victorian and Edwardian London, an absence that is all the more striking at a time when the scholarly literature on the *fin-de-siècle* metropolis (and modern Britain, more generally) has become increasingly attentive to transnational and global forces. The London restaurant can be best understood as a cultural formation that registers both broad transnational movements and the more intimate, and embedded, domains of the dining experience and the individual diner, to whom we now turn.

---

[113] See, e.g., William Grimes, *Appetite City: A Culinary History of New York* (New York: Farrar, Straus and Giroux, 2009), and Annie Hauck-Lawson and Jonathan Deutsch (eds), *Gastropolis: Food and New York City* (New York: Columbia University Press, 2009).

[114] 'Foreign Waiters and their Position', *Restaurant and Hotel Review* (September 1914), 460. See also Gallati, *Mario of the Caprice*.

[115] See, e.g., Panikos Panayi, *Spicing up Britain: The Multicultural History of British Food* (London: Reaktion, 2008).

6

Dining in the Restaurant

The heterogeneity of the London restaurant, illustrated most dramatically in terms of gastro-cosmopolitanism, was no less evident in the extraordinary range of people who participated in the culture of public eating in the metropolis. By the last decade of the nineteenth century, the restaurant had become such an important feature of the urban landscape that its patrons encompassed labourers feeding at penny restaurants, male and female clerks taking lunch in the City, and theatregoers having a meal in the theatre restaurant before the play. In this chapter, a sketch of London's diners will be offered, emphasizing their diversity, not merely in terms of social class, but also, critically, in terms of gender. More significantly, these different types of diner will be related to broader patterns of social development in the metropolis, notably the changing world of both work (such as the impact of suburbanization and the expansion of the service sector) and leisure. In particular, studying the restaurant diner can further our understanding of new forms of heterosociability and the interrelationship between domestic and public spaces. Inserting the restaurant diner into our understanding of Victorian and Edwardian metropolitan culture requires us to qualify, and even repudiate, some of the more influential interpretations of how identities were fashioned and performed at this time. It is very possible that public eating had a role to play in new forms of selfhood, or at least in the subjectivities of London's diners. However, there is little evidence of the emotional context to public dining, so this is not predominantly the focus here.

To the question who was the quintessential Victorian and Edwardian diner, the answer is everybody. It has already been pointed out that restaurants were ubiquitous, and not confined to areas of elite consumption. Perhaps the best way of accessing the social and cultural make-up of the diner is to focus on the question why they were dining. Some people required food as fuel in order to negotiate the working day. Others experienced eating out within the context of broader patterns of leisure and sociability. Of course, these different imperatives were not necessarily mutually exclusive. At the most obvious level, the expansion of London in the second half of the nineteenth century dramatically lengthened the distances between residences and places of employment for many of London's workers. In particular, the various phases of suburbanization meant that workers in London's central districts requiring a hot meal during their lunch break were obliged to find a caterer appropriate to both their tastes and their budget.

It is important not only to establish *who* ate out, but also to achieve some clarity about *when* people ate out. In the 1901 edition of *Food and Feeding*, surgeon and polymath Sir Henry Thompson asserted that, in the English provinces, breakfast was 'at 8 or 9, a dinner at one or two, a light tea about five, and a supper at nine or ten'. However, he insisted that the prevailing system in London was of three meals daily: breakfast between eight and ten, lunch at about two, and dinner from half past seven, eight, or even later.[1] Thompson's phraseology might imply there was also a differentiation in regard to the labels applied to each of the main daily meals in London as compared to the provinces, but other sources suggest there was inconsistency among restaurateurs, diners, and the press about what exactly they were talking about when they used the term 'dinner' or, to a lesser extent, 'tea'. In regard to the times at which meals were taken, while he was not specific on the matter, Thompson was most likely referring to the times of meals at home. Two o'clock certainly seems too late for lunch eaten by office workers. An article from 1898 on 'the City Dinner Hour', published in the *Quiver*, described City workers having their lunch break at midday, although it observed that (in contrast to Paris) meals were consumed with 'businesslike dispatch', taking no more than half an hour, leaving workers either to browse a popular periodical or sensational novel in one of the reading rooms around Ludgate Circus or (less prepossessingly) to engage in gambling, or to wander aimlessly looking into shop windows.[2] Much to the obvious disappointment of this evangelical and improving publication, very few of the City workers appeared to rush their lunch in order to attend the midday services hosted by the numerous churches in the Square Mile. Other observers in the same decade also spoke of the convention of a one-hour lunch break, especially in the City, but placed this (confusingly termed 'great dinner hour') between one and two o'clock.[3] More senior figures in the financial sector may well have forgone lunch entirely, choosing to leave the City

---

[1] Sir Henry Thompson, *Food and Feeding* (London: Frederick Warne & Co., 1901), 215–16.

[2] 'The City Dinner Hour', *Quiver* (1898), 724–8.

[3] 'The Dinner Hour', *All the Year Round*, 9/229 (1893), 473; N. L. Doss, *Reminiscences, English and Australasian; Being an Account of a Visit to England, Australia, &c.* (Calcutta: M. C. Bhowmick, 1893), 43.

relatively early to spend their afternoons in their West End clubs before returning home.[4]

In theory, evening dining could take place at any time after working hours. A French chef in 1910 bemoaned what he regarded as the peculiar attachment of the English to the five o'clock dinner.[5] Conversely, some restaurant handbills promised suppers between eight o'clock in the evening and two o'clock in the morning.[6] Most restaurant evening dining probably took place between six o'clock and eight o'clock, as is evidenced by regular complaints about the fact that dining hours coincided with curtain calls at West End theatres.[7] From the 1880s, there seemed to be something of a consensus that the fashionable hour for dining was as late as 8.30 or 9.00.[8] During the First World War, commentators explicitly referred to a shift back from 8.30 to 6.30.[9] In more fashionable restaurants, the reservation of tables became more common by the turn of the century, facilitated by technological innovations such as the telegraph or telephone. However, it was clearly not yet standard. Gentleman-soldier turned restaurant critic Lieut.-Col. Nathaniel Newnham-Davis found it expedient to make a reservation at the Ship in Greenwich by telegram and also to use the telephone to secure a table at very short notice for Sunday dinner at the Savoy.[10] However, he was just as likely to walk over to establishments nearer to his home to make a reservation for later in the day, and, in many cases, simply turned up at a particular restaurant when the mood took him.[11] The trade paper the *Restaurant* stated in 1910 that it was in vogue for larger restaurants to offer reservations, but they were 'apt to be loose and untrustworthy in the working'. The newspaper recommended restaurants should systematize reservations on the lines of theatre box offices.[12] Even someone as well connected as Newnham-Davis had difficulty in securing a table at the time and place that he preferred

---

[4] To take one example, stockbroker Arthur Philip Cazenove, as related in David Kynaston, *The City of London*, ii. *The Golden Years, 1890–1914* (London: Chatto and Windus, 1995), 327.

[5] 'Correspondence: The Decadence of Dining', *Restaurant* (May 1910), 229.

[6] See, e.g., menu, 'Cash's Oxford and Cambridge Restaurant Hotel, 290 Strand, WC', *c.*1885, Evanion Collection 6644, British Library.

[7] See the discussion later in this chapter on the clash between the dinner hour and curtain call.

[8] 'Dinner', *Caterer*, 4 December 1880, p. 215; 'The Dinner Hour', *Caterer*, 15 March 1883, p. 54; 'Caterer's Notebook', *Caterer*, 15 June 1895, p. 243; 'Late for Dinner', *Caterer*, 16 March 1896, p. 119.

[9] 'The Vagrant's Jottings', *Restaurant and Hotel Review* (July 1916), 329.

[10] Nathaniel Newnham-Davis, *Dinners and Diners: Where and how to Dine in London* (London: Grant Richards, 1899), 177, 73.

[11] *Ibid*. 22–3, 9–10.   [12] 'Reserved Tables', *Restaurant* (May 1910), 246.

(on one visit to Gatti's he was obliged to sit with the owner).[13] There was continuous discussion in the trade press about restaurant closing times, particularly among licensed restaurants.[14] This meant that both proprietors and diners could often be frustrated, but it also created an opportunity for humble catering enterprises—the coffee stall and fried fish shop—to exploit demand.[15]

Arguments about the appropriate time for meals were obviously most acute among the metropolitan elite. For London's working population (particularly those engaged in manual occupations) access to public eating was determined by the regimes of employment and the availability of affordable food. It is important that we do not confine the term 'diner' to those partaking of the pleasures of fashionable West End restaurants. At the very bottom of the social scale, even the non-working poor and those close to subsistence levels of existence were touched by the culture and economy of public eating in the capital. Arthur Harding, whom we encountered earlier, often recalled his *fin-de-siècle* East End boyhood by referencing food (or its absence). Hunger was sometimes relieved by recourse to missions, where the poor fed on scraps donated from local restaurants. Harding remembered helping his brother collect the 'leavings' for a local mission, though, as he said, 'I would sooner have pinched it', since the food amounted to more than just 'scraps' but might be half a leg of lamb or a ham bone, which was 'good to look at and good food for a hungry family'.[16] Given their commitment to moral and social improvement, it is not surprising that vegetarian and temperance restaurants proved to be particularly keen to reach beyond their usual clientele to the needy in the wider community. In 1889, the Ceres vegetarian restaurant in Aldgate Street provided Christmas dinner (consisting of green pea soup, Irish stew, and plum pudding) for 150 poor parish children who were selected by the local vicar.[17] In 1887, a temperance publication endorsed mitigating the sufferings of the unemployed by

---

[13] Newnham-Davis, *Dinners and Diners*, 70–1.

[14] See, e.g., 'Correspondence: Early Closing of Restaurants', *Caterer*, 16 March 1896, p. 122; *Referee*, 26 May 1895, p. 7; 'Caterer's Notebook', *Caterer*, 15 June 1895, p. 243.

[15] 'Gutter Hotel', *Caterer*, 15 December 1899, p. 595; 'How the Million Feed', *Caterer*, 15 September 1898, p. 427.

[16] Raphael Samuel (ed.), *East End Underworld: Chapters in the Life of Arthur Harding* (London: Routledge and Kegan Paul, 1981), 29. During the Hungry Forties, renowned chef Alexis Soyer set up his own soup kitchen. See Helen Morris, *Portrait of a Chef: The Life of Alexis Soyer, Sometime Chef to the Reform Club* (Cambridge: Cambridge University Press, 1938), 78–9.

[17] 'Occasional Notes', *Vegetarian*, 12 January 1889, p. 22. Not surprisingly, Christmas was a popular time for the provision of free meals to the poor. See, e.g., 'Correspondence', *Temperance Caterer*, 24 December 1887, p. 24; 31 December 1887, p. 355.

issuing tickets to be exchanged at coffee taverns for food, this being preferable to the distribution of money, which 'in idle hands' would be squandered in public houses. Apparently, this initiative had been carried out in the previous year in an arrangement between a certain Canon Barker and the Ossington Coffee Tavern in Marylebone.[18] The moralizing aspect to schemes such as these was even more overt in the penny dinners provided for the poor by the Black Bess coffee tavern in Finchley, where the dispersal of tickets was placed in the hands of the Charity Organization Society, which contributed a farthing towards each dinner. However, there was clearly some convergence between philanthropic instincts and commercial opportunities, one commentator arguing that such schemes would allow access to food for the poor, who, when their circumstances subsequently improved, would return to these establishments 'to spend more of their own money'.[19]

More direct than this provision of food tickets that could be redeemed for meals at restaurants was the scheme devised by Henry Roberts, described by one of his boosters as 'one of the greatest restaurateurs in London', to incorporate 'food debris' (food waste derived either from kitchens or from dining rooms) into soup, which would be offered to the undernourished poor.[20] Significantly, a contemporary review implied that Roberts's scheme was relatively rare and that too many restaurants were guilty of passing on surplus food to pig keepers, when it could have gone to the hungry masses.[21] Indeed, for the most unfortunate in society, the presence of the restaurant was an upsetting reminder of their lack of access to regular meals. On a visit to London, the Indian journalist and social reformer Behramji M. Malabari, possibly in the process of critiquing notions of Western superiority, claimed to observe in the City 'boys and girls thrusting their heads into kitchens under the houses and restaurants, or gazing hungrily at shop windows', adding that they seemed to 'feed themselves on the smells and sights of the food, smacking the lips every few minutes'.[22]

The boundary between the working and non-working poor was always highly unstable, particularly in occupations like those connected to the

---

[18] 'The Unemployed and Coffee Taverns', *Temperance Caterer*, 22 October 1887, p. 257.

[19] 'Food for the Foodless', *Temperance Caterer*, 10 December 1887, p. 337. Presumably, the intention was that they would return to the coffee tavern, rather than to a licensed establishment.

[20] 'A Necessary Reform', *Anti-Adulteration Review* (November 1885), 1065.

[21] *Ibid.*

[22] Behramji M. Malabari, *The Indian Eye on English Life; or, Rambles of a Pilgrim Reformer* (London: Archibald Constable and Co., 1893), 84.

docks, where short-term and seasonal patterns of employment were extremely common. An East End restaurant founded by nuns from the Order of St Katharine's in the 1880s sought to address the specific needs of workers. Inside their establishment, men currently in work were able to obtain a sixpence dinner in an attractively furnished hall, adorned with pictures, homilies, and plants. However, around eleven o'clock every day, five hand trucks were dispatched from the restaurant, carrying huge cans of soup and cylinders of pudding, which were sold to unemployed dock labourers at below market prices.[23]

Elsewhere, the relationship between working men and the commercial domain of public eating was dictated much more by the prerogatives of supply and demand than it was by those of sentiment or improvement. Testimony to the range and diversity of these establishments was provided by a report for the *Morning Leader* in 1898, which traversed 'the busy industrial spots about London', in search of businesses offering what it termed 'humble catering'. The reporter was up and about at midnight at Waterloo Bridge, where he encountered a 'coffee caravan-man' who dispensed coffee and tea, bread and butter, and cake and eggs to policemen, cabmen, and miscellaneous workmen. In Covent Garden, at four o'clock in the morning, he found breakfast had already been served at Lockhart's, Pearce and Plenty's, and many smaller coffee houses and dining rooms that catered to 'the horny handed market porter' and carriers from the market gardens in the farther suburbs. By six o'clock in the morning, he was in Commercial Road, where he witnessed stevedores in a large coffee house enjoying bread, eggs, ham, kippers, bloaters, and haddocks, prior to assembling at the dock gates. The report also sampled some lunchtime venues for working-class Londoners, but here its survey was confined to larger establishments such as the Globe, a coffee and dining room in Bloomsbury, and a branch of Pearce and Plenty's in Farringdon Street. At establishments such as these, meals averaged anywhere between four and eight pence (see Figure 6.1).[24] As was discussed earlier, branches of Pearce and Plenty proved an increasingly popular choice at the turn of the century for men taking their meals during the working day. One observer claimed the Farringdon Street branch seemed to be 'the dining saloon of every kind of labourer in London'.[25]

However, these large-scale, well-publicized establishments were supplemented by myriad smaller-scale operations, whose presence in the historical record is more obscure, but nevertheless important. Even in the docks,

[23] 'An East-end Restaurant', *Caterer*, 16 February 1885, p. 37.
[24] Cited in 'How the Million Feed', *Caterer*, 15 September 1898, p. 427.
[25] 'How London Feeds', *New Penny Magazine*, 7/90 (1900), 597.

a British Tea Table Co.'s establishment at one p.m. will lunch quite sumptuously for a shilling; how the commercial man fares at dinner; and how the well-to-do, going to the Opera or the theatre, first dine in a palatial hotel, such as the Savoy or the Hotel Cecil, and although spending probably some £3 on a *recherché* little dinner (including wine and cigars), will not eat, as

provided with a half-pint mug of cocoa for a halfpenny, two slices of bread and butter, each quite an inch thick, which cost a penny, two hard-boiled eggs for twopence; and, as a bystander remarked, "I dashed it" by ordering as a slight "fill-up," a slice of currant cake, three inches by four inches, and quite an inch thick, costing a halfpenny, and mulcting me altogether in the exorbitant outlay of ½d.

WHAT YOU GET FOR SEVENPENCE AT "PEARCE AND PLENTY'S."
(Photo: Cassell & Co., Ltd.)

Figure 6.1. 'What You Get for Sevenpence at "Pearce and Plenty's"', *New Penny Magazine* (1900). (Reproduced with permission of the Bishopsgate Institute)

an area in which provision of public eating had been extremely limited prior to the 1890s, there was an expansion of affordable restaurants to cater to the needs of what had been once described as the 'worst fed men in England'.[26] In this case, dock workers were the beneficiaries of collaboration between the Dock Company and various philanthropic bodies, concerned about the exploitation of workers by 'low-class restaurant keepers' (who were able to demand relatively high prices from men who worked at some distance from their homes) and by the lure of the public house.[27] For example, the North Side Coffee Tavern in the Victoria Dock, opened in 1891, was in a building paid for by the Dock Company, but with utensils provided by the Coffee Tavern Company.[28] One celebratory essay by advocate of the 'People's Kitchen' Edith Sellers declared that these dockside coffee houses had transformed 'rough hard men, the veriest Ishmaels, who looked as if they had passed their whole lives on the tramp, or in prison' into good-natured, even decorous, men who were finally 'at peace with mankind'.[29] In the context of the conclusion to the famous strike of only five years before, the possibility that these workers would get a meal at full value for money had important implications for social order

---

[26] Edith Sellers, 'The Dockers' Restaurants', *Good Words*, 35/327 (1894), 327.
[27] *Ibid.*   [28] *Ibid.* 328.   [29] *Ibid.* 332.

in the metropolis.[30] As Sellers reminded her readers: 'Hungry men lose their heads at very slight provocation.'[31]

Affordability became an important motif in the provision of food for London's working class. However, it should not be assumed that the need to keep down prices produced meals that were limited or low quality. Some entrepreneurs focused on their strengths and kept prices low by seriously reducing the infrastructure of dining. For example, one Mr Harris, a pork-sausage manufacturer of Smithfield, had four eating establishments where tables and chairs were entirely absent. His patrons were required to take their meal standing up against a narrow ledge, and had sufficient room only to swallow their food and then depart, in order to make room for another 'who generally fills his place immediately'. In addition to his signature sausages, Harris sold sixpence meals offering a choice of pork chops, beef steaks, potatoes, bread, and fried onions, but, unfortunately for the thirsty diner, not 'a drop of water or anything else'.[32] It is important to acknowledge that restaurants were catering not merely to a working class that appreciated value for money, but also to one whose expectations as consumers were definitely increasing.[33] Highly suggestive in this regard is an establishment that featured in the *Caterer* in 1896. Although called the 'Penny Restaurant', it offered a range of dishes for a farthing each, which included pickled cabbage, sausages, bread, and either butter or cheese, or, for those better off, a halfpenny worth of tinned lobster or salmon.[34] The proprietor of the establishment claimed that his

---

[30] In this new climate, an hourly wage of sixpence covered the cost of a cheap, but wholesome, meal at a dockers' restaurant.

[31] Edith Sellers, 'The Dockers' Restaurants', *Good Words*, 35/327 (1894), 327. Sellers's statement suggests that we might need to incorporate eating outside the home into studies concerned with how far working-class diets were sufficient to provide energy for physically demanding work. A study by Ian Gazeley and Andrew Newell concludes that, by 1900, Britain was close to having a working population where very nearly all households had a diet that provided sufficient energy for sustained labour, but this appraisal excludes consideration of food consumed outside the home. See Ian Gazeley and Andrew Newell, 'Urban Working-Class Food Consumption and Nutrition in Britain in 1904', *Economic History Review*, 68/1 (2015), 101–22.

[32] 'Cheap City Coffee-Bars and Restaurants', *Caterer*, 15 October 1884, p. 231.

[33] Increased expectations were obviously linked to rising living standards and a relative decline in the proportion of household budgets devoted to basic necessities. See, e.g., Paul Johnson, 'Conspicuous Consumption and Working-Class Culture in Late Victorian and Edwardian Britain', *Transactions of the Royal Historical Society*, 38 (1988), 27–42. While there is no longer any debate about the overall improvement of working-class life in the late-Victorian period, some scholars have emphasized that this pattern was uneven and far from universal. See, e.g., Ian Gazeley, 'The Cost of Living for Urban Workers in Late-Victorian and Edwardian Britain', *Economic History Review*, 42/2 (1989), 207–21; C. H. Feinstein, 'What Really Happened to Real Wages? Trends in Wages, Prices, and Productivity in the United Kingdom, 1880–1913', *Economic History Review*, 43/3 (1990), 329–55.

[34] 'Caterer's Notebook', *Caterer*, 15 August 1896, p. 377.

customers were mostly factory people in the East End whose chief meal of the day came from his shop.[35]

The notion of the City diner as a distinct archetype was already in existence in the early nineteenth century, if not earlier.[36] However, it was obviously the establishment of London as a major financial centre in the second half of the nineteenth century that created a dramatic increase in the number of clerks and other white-collar employees seeking refreshment in the Square Mile. The total working population of the City increased from 261,000 in 1881 to 332,000 two decades later.[37] An article on 'The Dinner Hour' in 1893 declared that, at one o'clock, in the City 'the intentness [*sic*] of business or pleasure seems to give way to an equal intentness of hunger'. The article argued that the streets of the City had always been busy, but they were now almost impassable at lunchtime. Cheapside, in particular, became at one o'clock 'a mighty stream of people with circling eddies about each eating-house or popular coffee-room'.[38] The possibility that these workers might find it difficult to negotiate these crowds, secure a meal, and return to their office within an hour may account for the initiative in the late 1890s by some larger commercial City firms to provide their clerks with free meals on the premises.[39]

For the vast majority who did venture out to eat, one might assume that there was limited opportunity to linger over their meals. The four branches of Slaters' restaurant in the City provided 2,000 lunches daily, by having six sittings between one and three o'clock.[40] However, an article by 'Wanderer' in 1883, in the process of defending City restaurants against complaints that they were overpriced, reported the testimony of a restaurateur who claimed that he could provide better and cheaper meals were it not for diners who loitered over their food (he had only a limited number of tables). The proprietor made clear his contempt for the convention of giving clerks an hour, or sometimes longer, for dinner. In his opinion, half an hour was more than enough, but he found clerks 'chat

---

[35] Ibid.

[36] 'London Eating Houses', *Chambers's Edinburgh Journal*, 282 (June 1837), 173–4; 'Public Refreshments', *Penny Magazine*, 12/697 (1843), 56.

[37] Kynaston, *City of London*, ii. 242. For late-Victorian and Edwardian clerks, see David Lockwood, *The Blackcoated Worker: A Study in Class Consciousness* (London: Allen & Unwin, 1958), and Gregory Anderson, 'The Social Economy of Late-Victorian Clerks', in Geoffrey Crossick (ed.), *The Lower Middle Class in Britain, 1870–1914* (London: Croom Helm, 1977).

[38] 'The Dinner Hour', *All the Year Round*, 9/229 (1893), 473.

[39] 'Caterer's Notebook', *Caterer*, 15 October 1896, p. 477. Some City workers may well have had less time to find a meal and return to the office. Herbert de Fraine, who began work at the Bank of England in 1886, recalled that only thirty-five minutes were allowed for lunch. See Kynaston, *City of London*, ii. 28–9.

[40] W. J. Winkle, 'Round the London Restaurants', *Windsor Magazine*, 4 (1896), 450.

or linger over a pennyworth of cheese . . . or cracking their jokes with a waitress in a way that makes one out of all patience to look at them'.[41] However, larger establishments were probably able to rectify the problem of tardy diners by providing divans or smoking rooms, where patrons could retire after lunch, to enjoy a slightly less rushed coffee and cigarette.[42] What particularly vexed the restaurateur interviewed by 'Wanderer' was his belief that, given the enormous number of eating houses in the City, a diner should be able to secure a meal 'within a stone's throw' of his office.[43] It was certainly true that, by the turn of the century, workers seeking lunch and lacking the will to negotiate crowded thoroughfares benefited from the replacement of traditional merchants' homes and workshops by the modern office block, in which business headquarters were interspersed with a variety of retail outlets, including not merely barbers, tobacconists, and clothiers, but restaurants.[44]

This new category of salaried workers certainly had more money to spend on meals than their working-class peers. Even cheap dinners for clerks were predicated on customers spending around 1s. 0d. or 1s. 2d.[45] This is not to say that white-collar workers were not highly receptive to the strictures of economy. An article on 'Life on a Guinea a Week' in 1888 suggested that single male clerks, having spent around one-third of their income on rent, had about 7s. 8d. a week to spend on meals.[46] Many of these meals may have been provided by their landladies. This was definitely true of Sundays, although the rather unappealing fare described in this article ('dollops of fatty beef, greasy pork, or underdone mutton') may have discouraged the unfortunate clerk from returning home for an

[41] 'City Clerks and their Dinners', 10 October 1883, Restaurant Files, box A–B, London Cuttings, Bishopsgate.

[42] This was the case at the Spread Eagle in New Broad Street, for example. See 'Luxury for City Men', 18 November 1891, Restaurant Files, box Q–S, London Cuttings, Bishopsgate.

[43] 'Clerks and their Dinners', 10 October 1883, Restaurant Files, box A–B, London Cuttings, Bishopsgate.

[44] Charles C. Turner, 'The City at High Noon', in George R. Sims (ed.), *Living London* (3 vols; London: Cassell and Co., 1901–3), vol. 2, sect. 1, p. 125. This juxtaposition is particularly evident in photographic images of City thoroughfares and trade directories. This integration of the production of financial wealth and its consumption in a single site has been discussed in relation to retail men's wear by Christopher Breward, 'Fashion and the Man: From Suburb to City Street. The Spaces of Masculine Consumption, 1870–1914', *New Formations*, 37 (Spring 1999), 47–70. Of course, the demolition of old City buildings did in some cases imply the disappearance of existing, often venerable, eating houses—for example, the demolition of Crosby Hall, a medieval palace that had become a restaurant. Kynaston, *City of London*, ii. 246.

[45] 'Cheap Dinners', *British Journal of Catering*, 1 February 1889, p. 33.

[46] 'Life on a Guinea a Week', *Nineteenth Century*, 23/133 (1888), 465.

evening meal during the week.[47] A sketch of City dining houses in 1874 pointed out that bachelor City clerks who lived in suburbs such as Hackney, Dalston, Camberwell, and Camden Town were obliged to dine in the City.[48] Whether this meant relying largely on a meal taken at lunchtime, or whether it meant supplementing this with a further meal taken in a restaurant close to their place of work, prior to returning home, is less easy to establish. It is also possible that, by 1900, improved transportation links made it easier for City workers to return home in time for an evening meal. It is likely that this was the preferred option for married clerks. One anonymous observer in 1904 declared that 'the average City man goes home to a substantial dinner in the evening and consequently does not require a heavy lunch in town'.[49] This is not to say that there were not also restaurants in suburban areas catering to lower-middle-class residents. In Holloway, the neighbourhood of Mr Pooter, the fictional City worker who famously delighted in mundane evenings spent at home, was to be found Beale's, a six-storey establishment comprising 'a handsome café-restaurant' along with 'dining, grill, smoking, and billiard rooms'.[50]

We should not assume that lunchtime meals in the City were entirely about economy or convenience. While historians have been at pains to suggest the diversity and complexity of late Victorian and Edwardian lower-middle-class lives, some contemporary observers nevertheless bemoaned the apparent drabness and uniformity of office life in the City.[51] It was possible, for many, that their midday meal provided a welcome respite from the drudgery of clerical work. P. G. Wodehouse, who had been a clerk at the Hong Kong and Shanghai Bank before becoming a novelist, was presumably speaking from experience when he declared that

few workers in the City do regard lunch as a trivial affair. It is the keynote of their day. It is an oasis in a desert of ink and ledgers. Conversation in a city

---

[47] *Ibid.* 466.

[48] 'City Scraps: London Dining Houses', 1874, Restaurant Files, box A–B, London Cuttings, Bishopsgate.

[49] 'A New Quick Lunch Restaurant', 12 March 1904, Restaurant Files, box Q–S, London Cuttings, Bishopsgate.

[50] George Grossmith and Weedon Grossmith, *The Diary of a Nobody* (Bristol: J. W. Arrowsmith, 1892); 'Beale's Restaurant and Electrical Station, Holloway', 15 March 1890, Restaurant Files, box A–B, London Cuttings, Bishopsgate.

[51] See the special issue on masculinity and the lower middle class in the *Journal of British Studies*, 38/3 (July 1999), especially Peter Bailey, 'White Collars, Gray Lives? The Lower Middle Class Revisited', 273–90; for a more recent revision, see Michael Heller, 'Work, Income and Stability: The Late Victorian and Edwardian London Male Clerk Revisited', *Business History*, 50/3 (2008), 253–71.

office deals, in the morning, with what one is going to have for lunch, and in the afternoon with what one has had for lunch.[52]

Of course, the City was also a place of employment not just for clerks, but also for the more rarefied stockbrokers, bankers, and merchant princes. Whereas, in the 1870s, these men might have arrived late to their offices and left early, dining in their own mansions and country houses, by the end of the century, with the consolidation of the City as the hub of finance capital, the pattern had changed.[53] By this point, there were those for whom lunch was something of a novelty because their working day was so hectic.[54] Still others undoubtedly saw meals as an opportunity for networking and deal-making (and possibly also for professional gossip). Certainly there were 'high-class' luncheon rooms such as the Woolpack in Gracechurch Street (formerly a chophouse) that were said to attract the 'Nitrate King' of Chile, 'Colonel' John Thomas North, and other tycoons. However, many other leading businessmen tended to dine outside the City, either in fashionable West End restaurants and clubs, hotel dining rooms, or at the townhouses of their social peers.[55] For instance, the bachelor–stockbroker Edward Wagg would often dine at the Savoy and then go to the Garrick for a game of bridge. Charles Addis, who was manager at the Hong Kong and Shanghai Bank in London, recorded in his diary of 1906 a dinner at the Carlton Hotel with other businessmen to discuss investment opportunities in the Chinese railways. Two years later, he noted a private dinner at a townhouse in Belgrave Square, where six men served twelve guests, adding that it was 'less boring than usual'.[56]

The reference to dinners at townhouses and clubs is a reminder that, for the wealthier sections of London society, eating outside the home was not restricted to the restaurant. Nevertheless, there is plentiful evidence that, by the Edwardian period, the restaurant was eclipsing these two venues as a site of elite sociability and display. The well-publicized (if often exaggerated) decline of aristocratic fortunes from the 1870s onwards certainly impacted on the ability of patricians to entertain in their London residences.[57] Moreover, the enlargement and diversification of high society,

[52] P. G. Wodehouse, *Psmith in the City* (1910; repr. London: Adam and Charles Black, 1923), 39; See also Kynaston, *City of London*, ii. 245.

[53] 'London Dining Houses', *Caterer*, 1 June 1878, p. 43.

[54] For instance, H. Osborne O'Hagan, as cited in Jonathan Schneer, *London 1900: The Imperial Metropolis* (New Haven: Yale University Press, 1999), 69.

[55] Clipping, City Press, 9 January 1897, Norman Collection, London Guildhall Library [hereafter LGL].

[56] Kynaston, *City of London*, ii. 327, 330–1.

[57] See David Cannadine, *The Decline and Fall of the British Aristocracy* (New Haven and London: Yale University Press, 1990).

particularly its increased association with what became 'celebrity culture', may have been more compatible with the public forum of the restaurant than it was with the more private and intimate spaces of the home, associated as they were with a circumscribed, tightly managed set of ties based on kinship. West End clubland continued to thrive, and indeed expand, after the 1870s, with the creation of new institutions and the opening-up of clubs previously dominated by aristocrats, military figures, and diplomats to men of business and finance.[58] Clubs were increasingly run on business lines and introduced higher standards of comfort and convenience, not merely in regard to technological innovations such as electricity and the telephone, but also in regard to the quality of meals provided. The continued success of the West End club may lie more with such modern improvements than with a more generic flight of middle-class men from the obligations of domesticity.[59]

However, the continued vitality of clubland between the 1870s and 1890s did little to slow the expansion of the restaurant sector, and, in the opening decade of the twentieth century, the latter had eclipsed the former as the primary venue for wealthy Londoners eating outside the home. Writing from the perspective of 1911, one observer claimed that old-fashioned clubmen of the mid-nineteenth century consistently 'declined to dine out, because they said they got a better dinner at the club for some ten or twelve shillings than at the best houses in town'.[60] By contrast, their turn-of-the-century counterpart appears to have been much less misanthropic, and presumably was not averse to crossing the threshold of his club in search of a meal.[61] Even the most committed clubmen might have found dining at a restaurant preferable on those occasions when some of the petty restrictions (particularly involving dress) that applied at the club seemed especially irksome. After being detained in Fleet Street one Saturday until dinner time, Newnham-Davis came across this problem. 'I was in the

---

[58] Ralph Henry Nevill, *London Clubs: Their History and Treasures* (London: Chatto & Windus, 1911), 139.

[59] See John Tosh, *A Man's Place: Masculinity and the Middle Class Home in Victorian England* (New Haven: Yale University Press, 1999). For a critique of this, see Martin Francis, 'The Domestication of the Male? Recent Research on Nineteenth- and Twentieth-Century British Masculinity', *Historical Journal*, 45/3 (2002), 637–52. Tosh admits that he may have overstated his case. See John Tosh, 'Home and Away: The Flight from Domesticity in Late-Nineteenth Century England Re-Visited', *Gender & History*, 27/3 (2015), 561–75. For an account of clubland that argues that it was simultaneously homosocial and domestic, see Amy Milne-Smith, 'A Flight to Domesticity? Making a Home in the Gentleman's Clubs of London, 1880–1914', *Journal of British Studies*, 45/4 (2006), 796–818.

[60] Nevill, *London Clubs*, 140.   [61] *Ibid.* 142, 149.

clothes I had worn all day ... I could not well dine at a club without evening clothes.'[62] In the decade immediately before the First World War, commentators increasingly reported an apparent 'slump' in clubland. In 1908, the *Observer* reported that, while some clubs continued to have long waiting lists for membership, these were not as long as they had been in the past. Moreover, kitchen accounts reveal that there had been a decrease in the numbers of meals taken in clubs.[63] Six years later, *The Times* addressed this apparent decline, asserting 'if a single reason must be given to account for this, that reason must be found in the restaurant'. This article insisted that lunches were still popular at clubs, but, in the evening, men 'prefer the animation and diet of a restaurant'. 'For the married man', it continued, 'this has a charm beyond its deserts; for the bachelor it has a charm irresistible.'[64] Here was laid bare one of the most obvious limitations of dining at one's club—namely, the exclusion of women. The answer to Newnham-Davis's 1906 article 'Is Club-Life Doomed?' lay very much in the affirmative. 'The restaurants', he averred, 'have done more towards killing the clubs than any other enemies of the species.' Not merely was dinner at a restaurant 'more lively, more amusing, and in nine cases out of ten better cooked', but, most critically of all, ladies could now dine at restaurants, while the doors of most of the older clubs were 'shut against them'. For 'the man of gallantry gives his dinners where ladies can be of the party'.[65] Thus, while the advocates of clubland presented its exclusive homosociability as one of its attractions, the restaurant was much better positioned to engage in a new culture that incorporated, and even encouraged, the increased mixing of the sexes in public spaces.

Middle-class married women were probably major beneficiaries of this new urban climate, although their increased presence in the public spaces of the West End appears to have been deemed (at least by the end of the century) as sufficiently quotidian and innocuous as not to require sustained interest or controversy.[66] The attractions of restaurants to

[62] Newnham-Davis, *Dinners and Diners*, 9. Newnham-Davis often went to the Service Club, of which he was a member, in the early evening to seek out a companion who might accompany him to have a meal in a restaurant. In this, he was often met with mixed results; he failed to persuade an old comrade who 'would have followed me ... into any danger of battle without the tremble of an eyelid' to join him on an excursion to a vegetarian restaurant. *Ibid*. 91.

[63] Clipping, 'The Slump in Clubland', *Observer*, 10 May 1908, 42b, Norman Collection, LGL.

[64] Clipping, 'London Clubs: Their Decline and its Causes—The Restaurant Habit', *The Times*, 25 April 1914, 40a, Norman Collection, LGL.

[65] Nathaniel Newnham-Davis, 'Is Club-Life Doomed?', *Daily Mail*, 3 December 1906, p. 5.

[66] This should not be taken to imply that women were entirely absent from the culture of public eating in the early years of the century. There are tantalizing, but unfortunately

middle-class families were possibly enhanced by the somewhat fraught business of preparing meals at home. An article in the *Restaurant* in 1912 argued for increased provision of restaurants for families in the suburbs, in part as a means of overcoming what it intriguingly referred to as the increasing servant difficulty.[67] While it did not specify what it had in mind here, complaints about the burdens of recruiting and retaining domestic staff, and the increasing costs of doing so, were a regular feature in the press at this time. One report, only slightly tongue-in-cheek, declared that 'a revolution among his retainer and servitors, more especially those of the kitchen and scullery', had placed a heavy burden on the Englishman's 'pleasures and privileges of domesticity'. Expedients such as 'sending their wives and daughters to schools of cookery' had proved to no avail, since it was beyond their gastronomic abilities to serve a dinner, given the limited appliances within their home. As a consequence, a vastly increased number of people 'have adopted the Continental fashion of taking their meals in public'. The cry of every aggrieved paterfamilias was 'let us to a restaurant'.[68] Even those who were able to continue to afford an extensive kitchen staff may well have been encouraged to dine out by the inability of their cooks to match the quality of the food on offer in restaurants. In 1896, the *Caterer* insisted that a wife who had dined with her husband at the Trocadero or 'at one of these palatial homes of the gastronomic art' might have subsequently felt compelled to give more attention and care to the domestic menu.[69] The *Caterer* was, of course, unlikely to be impartial on this matter, but it regularly bemoaned the low standards of domestic cooks.[70]

Not surprisingly, it was to be the presence of single women, or women dining alone, or in the company of other women, that was to attract more attention from contemporaries. 'Should Women Dine in Restaurants?' was the arresting headline of an article in the *Lady* in July 1899. The premise of this article was that 'a surprising change' had taken place in the manners and customs of fashionable women. Thirty years previously, women had never dined in public except with their husbands on very

unelaborated, references to the presence of women in post-theatre eating houses in the 1850s. See, e.g., Edmund Yates, *Fifty Years of London Life: Memoirs of a Man of the World* (New York: Harper & Bros, 1885), 105.

[67] 'Trade Topics: Suburban Restaurants', *Restaurant* (March 1912), 120.

[68] Clipping, 'Dining Out in 1905', Norman Collection, LGL.

[69] 'Caterer's Notebook', *Caterer*, 15 October 1896, p. 469.

[70] For example, 'Are We to be Cookless?', *Caterer*, 15 December 1898, p. 606. Some earlier examples from the *Caterer* include: 'The Art of Dining', 4 September 1880, pp. 155–6; 'English Popular Cookery', 16 January 1882, p. 16; 'Lady Cooks', 15 August 1892, p. 307; 'Dinners and Diners', 15 March 1893, p. 128; 'Catering for Householders', 15 October 1894, p. 428.

rare occasions and, even then, in only one or two select establishments, it argued. Now, however, 'it has become the fashion for women of all classes to dine and lunch habitually at many of the well-known restaurants of London, with large or small parties, with or without their husbands'.[71] Offering a condemnatory gloss on the latter phenomenon, the article warned of the possible damaging effects on the home. Husbands retreated to their clubs and the children suffered neglect, only catching 'an occasional glimpse of [their mother] as she rushes in with not a moment to spare: a hasty kiss and she is off again for a luncheon party at the Berkeley...'.[72] The children were then 'given over into the hands of hirelings' in the form of nurses and governesses, 'with the worst results'. Moreover, the article cautioned, family fortunes could easily lead to ruin, not merely because of the 'appalling expense' of the meals consumed, but also because of the demand by these women for new jewels and dresses to wear while they were out dining.[73] While making the case that fashionable restaurants contributed to the moral and material debasement of the family, the *Lady* exposed anxieties about unchaperoned women eating in public.

The single woman suffered even more scrutiny in the press in this regard. In fiction, she was embodied famously by the eponymous heroine in H. G. Wells's *Ann Veronica* (1909), who leaves her suburban family home for a life as a bohemian student at Imperial College. On a number of occasions in the novel, Wells uses the restaurant to illustrate the paradox of the increased visibility of women in the public sphere. On the one hand, women were increasingly able to move freely through spaces formally dominated by men, but, conversely, their novel presence in these spaces permitted men to presume their sexual availability. Early in her 'flight to London', Ann Veronica finds herself the object of the predatory gaze of a man who has followed her into the British Tea Table near Oxford Circus, where she takes tea alone. Like an animal stalking its prey, the man takes up a position across from her and looks at her with the aid of a mirror, which makes her feel vulnerable and angry. She therefore leaves, and he trails behind her, before vanishing into the night.[74] This encounter compares innocuously, however, with a later, far more savage, one in a *cabinet particulier* (or small, private dining room in a restaurant), where Ann Veronica and a trusted family friend, Ramage, go initially to talk about a romantic misunderstanding they had had the night before at an opera. However, Ann Veronica's naivety as to the purpose of their meeting is exposed when, having served the wine and dinner, the waiter leaves, and

[71] 'Should Women Dine in Restaurants?', *Lady*, 27 July 1899, p. 132.   [72] *Ibid.*
[73] *Ibid.*   [74] H. G. Wells, *Ann Veronica* (1909; London: J. M. Dent, 1993), 73–4.

Ramage then locks them both inside the room.[75] What happened next—a sexual assault that she narrowly thwarts—propelled her from a state of innocence to 'shabby knowledge'.[76] That this outrage occurs in a private dining room links the restaurant to a seedy world of male privilege and female debasement. Ramage's statement to her, 'Look here... I brought you here to make love to you', makes clear the idea of the restaurant (or at least the private room in the restaurant) as a place of disreputability and base pleasures. That his actions were repelled by her forces him to ask, 'why the devil... do you let me stand you dinners and the opera—and why do you come to a *cabinet particulier* with me?'[77] By allowing him to 'keep' her and by not reciprocating in kind, Ann Veronica spectacularly fails to play by the rules of Ramage's ungentlemanly game, albeit one set amid wine glasses and soup tureens.

The fictional experience of Ann Veronica in the *cabinet particulier* might suggest that the restaurant provided yet another example of the narratives of sexual danger that once dominated accounts of late-nineteenth-century women's growing participation in public life. In this characterization, the restaurant functioned as yet another public space in the metropolis in which any woman roaming without the care of a chaperone was likely to be deemed little better than a street walker.[78] While such understandings of late-nineteenth-century London now appear both hyperbolic and hackneyed, it cannot be denied that, as Erika Rappaport makes clear in her account of female shoppers in the West End, 'the growth of commercial institutions and mass journalism spoke a good deal about the new woman in the city while also placing new constraints on female behaviors'.[79] It cannot be ignored that women's increased presence in London's restaurants was, on occasion, not achieved without friction. In 1895, the *Hotel* claimed that many restaurants were displaying placards indicating that 'no ladies can be served between the hours of twelve and three'. It made clear that women were much more welcome at vegetarian restaurants and aerated bread shops, but that 'few and far between are the restaurants where they can enjoy a steak or a cut off the joint'.[80] The attraction of the vegetarian restaurant to female diners was endorsed by the manager of such an establishment on Jewin Street in the

---

[75] *Ibid.* 144.   [76] *Ibid.* 145.   [77] *Ibid.* 147.

[78] Judith R. Walkowitz, *City of Dreadful Delight: Narratives of Sexual Danger in Late-Victorian London* (Chicago: University of Chicago Press, 1992); Deborah Epstein Nord, *Walking the Victorian Streets: Women, Representation, and the City* (Ithaca, NY: Cornell University Press, 1995).

[79] Erika D. Rappaport, *Shopping for Pleasure: Women in the Making of London's West End* (Princeton: Princeton University Press, 2000), 7.

[80] 'The Restaurants', *Hotel*, 16 October 1895, p. 18.

City, who condescendingly claimed that his customers included 'a thousand demure little factory maids' served 'plain and healthy' meals 'in a way to satisfy and please any feminine taste'.[81] It cannot be denied that the unwanted attention of men, dining or otherwise, was not a genuine concern for many. 'Koorblup', writing to the editor of *Temperance Caterer*, was troubled that there were very few City restaurants where female clerks could obtain lunch 'without being ogled by a lot of men'.[82] However, in yet another example of the need to give attention to commercial, as opposed to cultural, forces, the restaurant sector itself sought ways to lessen female discomfort in regard to this issue. Several established restaurants incorporated ladies' dining rooms, while there is evidence of women-only restaurants being set up by female entrepreneurs such as Miss I. Brayshay of the Bond Street Luncheon Rooms in the heart of the fashionable shopping district.[83]

More significantly, such references to sexual confrontation can be offset by registering the restaurant as an important domain for the emergence of a new heterosocial culture, particularly in the fashionable West End. Wells's *Ann Veronica* may be less representative than George Gissing's Polly Sparkes, the unlikeable protagonist in the *Town Traveller*, who is taken to dinner by a young man who frequents the theatre where she works, selling programmes.[84] The greater degree of informality between the sexes, and the pleasures of mixed company, were most clearly apparent in extensive writings about the restaurant composed by Nathaniel Newnham-Davis.[85] In 1897, the editor of the *Pall Mall Gazette*, Douglas Straight, commissioned a series of restaurant reviews for a readership whose tastes varied widely and for whom nothing short of 'a formidably long list of places' would suffice. In selecting an author for this series,

[81] 'How the Million Feed', *Caterer*, 15 September 1898, p. 427.

[82] 'Restaurants for Ladies: To the Editor of the *Temperance Caterer*', *Temperance Caterer*, 29 October 1887, p. 270.

[83] 'Chops and Changes', *Caterer*, 16 February 1891, p. 55. Most of these establishments have been relatively obscured in the historical record. The Dorothy, a women's only restaurant in Mortimer Street, received considerable contemporary, and subsequent scholarly, attention, however. See, e.g., 'Hotel and Restaurant News', *British Journal of Catering*, 15 June 1889, p. 3, and 15 July 1889, p. 3; 'Chops and Changes', *Caterer*, 16 May 1892, p. 196; 'Occasional Notes', *Vegetarian*, 31 August 1889, p. 505; see also Rappaport, *Shopping*, 102 and n. 146.

[84] George Gissing, *The Town Traveller* (London: Methuen, 1898), 31–3.

[85] For a more in-depth discussion of this, see Brenda Assael, 'On *Dinners and Diners* and Restaurant Culture in Late Nineteenth-Century London' (2012), in Dino Felluga (ed.), *BRANCH: Britain, Representation and Nineteenth-Century History*, extension of *Romanticism and Victorianism on the Net*, <http://www.branchcollective.org/?ps_articles=brenda-assael-on-dinners-and-diners-and-restaurant-culture-in-late-nineteenth-century-london> (accessed 11 October 2017).

Straight sought someone who would be 'a thoroughly experienced, trust-worthy, and capable commissioner, who would deal with the task enrusted to him in a pleasantly mixed anecdotal and critical spirit, while at the same time supplying useful guidance to persons wanting to know where to dine and what they would have to pay'.[86] His choice fell on Newnham-Davis, a retired army officer, who had served in the Zulu campaigns of 1877–9, as well as in the Straits Settlements, China, and India, but was now editor of *Man of the World*, a penny paper preoccupied with high society, the stage, and the racing world. Each of the articles written by Newnham-Davis for the *Pall Mall Gazette* involved a visit to a particular restaurant, a discussion of his fellow diner (presented as a real-life personage, although it is possible these were fictional or composite characters), the menu, and the cost of the bill. Extended versions of these articles were eventually collected, after 'very many requests from various quarters', in an anthology entitled *Dinners and Diners: Where and How to Dine in London*, published in 1899.[87] Newnham-Davis's reviews were sufficiently well known, at least in elite, metropolitan circles, that they were satirized in the pages of *Punch*, where the colonel was unflatteringly presented, in an uncannily accurate pastiche of his prose style, as a name-dropping freeloader.[88]

A total of forty-seven dining establishments feature in *Dinners and Diners* drawn from geographical locations across the metropolis. Most, to be sure, were in areas of the West End well known for dining out, such as Piccadilly, the Strand, and Soho, but Newnham-Davis and his fellow 'devoted soldiers of the fork' also paid visits to restaurants in Holborn, the City, the East End, Earl's Court, and Richmond.[89] Many of the restaurants were prestigious dining rooms such as Simpson's, the Café Royal, Kettner's, or the high-end dining rooms of up-market hotels, such as the Hotel Cecil and the Savoy. However, Newnham-Davis's culinary compass also extended to more modest establishments, including taverns such as the Ship in Greenwich and more idiosyncratic experiences such as visits to Goldstein's, a Kosher restaurant in Bloomfield Street in the City, and the dining room of the House of Commons.

Newnham-Davis, when conducting his reviews, rarely dined alone. Sometimes his choice of dining companion was dictated by availability or reluctant obligation, but he often enjoyed more convivial company.

---

[86] Editor of the *Pall Mall Gazette* [Douglas Straight], 'Preface', in Newnham-Davis, *Dinners and Diners*, p. viii.

[87] *Ibid.*

[88] Mr F. Richardson, 'Dinners and Diners: With Apologies to the *P-ll M-ll G-z-tte*', *Punch*, 10 July 1897, p. 4.

[89] Newnham-Davis, *Dinners and Diners*, 254.

In particular, he frequently shared his meals with women, and, while his descriptions of these female diners are often patronizing, or even infantilizing, their presence in his book is testimony to the dynamic and diverse forms of sociability that were emerging in the late-nineteenth-century metropolis. Newnham-Davis did dine with male acquaintances, and some of the venues he discusses clearly encouraged masculine homosociability, even if they did not explicitly exclude women. However, one often gets the sense that Newnham-Davis dined in these all-male environments by default, rather than through an act of preference. His account of dining with an 'American Comedian' at the Holborn specifically refers to the fact that the two men did not have 'a lady to take out' and they entertained themselves during their meal by viewing, and speculating on, the identities of a panoply of diners at other tables that included 'a merry little party of three ladies' and 'a pretty actress'.[90] Indeed, Newnham-Davis, a bachelor, delighted in female companionship. Mixed male/female dining in *Dinners and Diners* is often an extension of familial ties. Newnham-Davis took his sister-in-law to the Café Royal while his brother was out of town. On other occasions he observed 'a white-bearded gentleman' dining with his 'two pretty daughters in evening dresses' at the Cavour in Leicester Square prior to an evening at the theatre, while at the Star and Garter in Richmond he spied 'a bald-headed gentleman entertaining a family party'.[91]

However, most of Newnham-Davis's female dining companions were friends, either married or single, with whom he enjoyed sharing gossip, especially from the world of the London stage, but also from the high society of New York, Paris, and the Riviera. Likewise, his descriptions of other mixed dining parties encompassed two young men 'with orchids in their buttonholes' dining with two young women (possibly, Newnham-Davis speculates, the groomsmen and bridesmaids from a wedding party) at the Holborn, a theatre manager dining with 'one of the most beautiful of our actresses and her husband' at the Savoy, 'a cricketer of fame' dining with two ladies at the Hotel Continental, 'a fat gentleman', who Newnham-Davis speculates is a Jewish financier, 'giving dinner to a girl with many rows of pearls round her throat and a glint of diamonds on her dress' at Earl's Court, and 'a well-known amateur coachman' having 'time to give his wife something to eat before going off to catch another train' at the Cavour.[92]

What is particularly notable in *Dinners and Diners* is the absence of reference to anxieties, on the part of either Newnham-Davis or other

---

[90] *Ibid.* 15, 18, 20.   [91] *Ibid.* 208, 200.   [92] *Ibid.* 18–19, 76–7, 125, 192, 207–8.

diners, about the presence of female diners, even if they were unac-
companied. Newnham-Davis refers to the Berkeley in Piccadilly as
being 'a place where ladies can dine and lunch without an escort', but
his reference to the unchaperoned status of his fellow diners is made
without the apparent need for further comment.[93] Similarly, after dining
with an American actress, a certain Miss Belle, at Epitaux's in the Haymarket, Newnham-Davis seems to welcome, rather than disapprove of,
the ability of young women to enjoy London's restaurant world, with or
without male escorts.[94] The heterosociability celebrated in *Dinners and
Diners* not merely brought men and women together in public spaces (and
in congenial, rather than confrontational, ways). It also functioned as an
intermediate space between private and public domains, exposing the
diner to the gaze and scrutiny of strangers, but also allowing the extension
of domestic and familial sociability outside the home. The *fin-de-siècle*
London restaurant therefore confounds the bleak narratives of both 'the
flight from domesticity' and 'sexual danger' that, while not as influential as
they once were, have continued to serve as important reference points in
our understanding of British culture in this period. Certainly, there needs
to be more appreciation of the more congenial, not to say progressive, and
less fraught aspects of the urban experience. Indeed, the theatre critic
Clement Scott, who shared Newnham-Davis's passion for both food and
the stage, remarked that dining rooms 'have had a very great deal to do
with the social emancipation of women' and 'the new restaurant, by
bringing men and women together to dine and sup without offence,
made life in London far more decent than it ever was before'.[95]

In Erika Rappaport's seminal study of how late-Victorian and Edwardian female shoppers helped reshape the relationship between gender ideals
and the public domain, the focus is inevitably on bourgeois women within
the context of the West End. Female *diners*, by contrast, were to be found
in all social classes and across the metropolis. Moreover, the presence of
these women in public spaces was a consequence of their status as workers,
rather than consumers. The increasing feminization of the service sector
required lunch venues for women shop assistants and office workers. Some
employers offered facilities on their premises. Female operators working in
the telephone exchanges in the City and Holborn in 1902 could take
meals in a 'cheerful room' set apart for this purpose, either by paying for
food prepared in-house or by bringing in their own chop to be grilled.
This innovation satisfied both the needs of female workers and the

---

[93] *Ibid.* 164.   [94] *Ibid.* 333.
[95] Clement Scott, *How they Dined us in 1860 and how they Dine us now* (London, n.d.
[*c.*1900]), 12.

solicitations of the National Telephone Company, which appeared concerned that the women, after a rushed lunch in a crowded tea room, might 'then return, to faint later at the switchboard for lack of proper nourishment'.[96] Two decades earlier, female clerks in the City initially seemed to have had difficulty finding suitably respectable venues within walking distance of their places of work. The issue here appeared to be the unwillingness of lower-middle-class female clerks to eat in places largely frequented by working-class men, an expedient forced on the women by their relatively low rates of pay.[97] Some establishments, such as Lockhart's, offered these women the use of their 'first-class' dining rooms, where they supplemented food they brought with them with a cup of coffee or a side order of potatoes. The need to find lunch venues that were affordable, accessible, and respectable may explain the particular attraction of the Aerated Bread Company (A.B.C.) and Lyons tea shops to middle-class working women from the 1890s onwards. It is important to recognize that working-class women diners, while rarely discussed at length by contemporaries, certainly existed, as is testified to by the activities of organizations such as the Women's Cooperative Restaurant Society, and by the solicitous (but not necessarily entirely altruistic) concerns about suitable environments for female dining raised by temperance and other improvement societies.[98] If references to women diners outside the West End are relatively limited, this should not imply their absence. Rather, it more likely suggests that heterosocial dining experiences, in which both men and women were present, were as much the norm in the City and other less rarefied parts of London as they were in the fashionable establishments of the West End.

While the provision of lunches in the City was a response to the needs of London's working population, one category of diner was much more clearly linked to new metropolitan cultures of leisure. These were the men and women who either participated in, or patronized, the remarkable concentration of theatres in the West End. Restaurants and theatres had a long-standing close relationship. Recollections of London's artistic and literary scene in the mid-nineteenth century often contained references to taking meals in taverns or supper rooms, either prior to, or immediately after, visiting the theatre. Clement Scott, in the preface to the memoirs of

---

[96] Henry Thompson, 'Telephone London', in Sims (ed.), *Living London*, vol. 3, sect. 1, p. 116.

[97] 'Restaurants for Women', *Temperance Caterer*, 5 November 1887, p. 277.

[98] 'The Welcome', 4 January 1882, 'The Welcome', 5 November 1884, Restaurant Files, box T–Z, London Cuttings, Bishopsgate; 'Proposed Women's Co-Operative Restaurant Society', 'Rules of the Women's Co-Operative Restaurant Society, Ltd' (1916) 2 LSW/FL368/1 Correspondence file 'C', Women's Library, London.

his mentor, the playwright and theatre critic E. L. Blanchard, recalled how, in the 1850s, 'we used to meet at the Edinburgh Castle or Carr's in the Strand... for dinner, and repair afterwards to the play'.[99] George Augustus Sala reminisced about post-theatre dinners at Evans's supper room, while George R. Sims fondly remembered the oyster shops on the Strand he visited after the theatre.[100] Journalist and novelist Edmund Yates provided a vivid description of the Blue Posts, a tavern on the Haymarket, that was 'the regular place of adjournment on the closing of the theatre and the dancing halls'. This establishment was so popular that no one was able to squeeze past the crush of men and women inside, save the waiter, well known for his peculiar cry 'Mind the sauce, please! Mind the sauce and gravy!' Yates presented the clientele as lively and noisy, but not rowdy, largely because of the presence of the kindly and respectable 'old Scotch couple' who owned the establishment.[101]

By the end of the century, the association between food and entertainment in the West End had become much more formalized, and in some cases even integrated. Restaurants and theatres were sited in close proximity. The *Caterer* declared in 1889 that London's restaurants 'cling with affection to the streets and districts where the theatres are built'.[102] Two decades later, the *Restaurant* argued that the West End restaurant was a 'veritable boon' to the 'theatre-going class', especially given its proximity to the expanding Underground. This allowed the restaurant to act as a rendezvous, where men 'coming straight from the City' might meet their wives and friends before moving on to a local theatre or music hall. The article, testifying to the significance of the restaurant in patterns of increasing public heterosociability and the changing nature of domesticity, went on to state: 'the husband is spared the terrible rush home, and thence to the theatre, while the wife is relieved from any thought of catering or getting the dinner through in time for the inexorable hour at which the place of entertainment begins'.[103] An article in the *Daily*

[99] Clement Scott, 'Preface', in Clement Scott and Cecil Howard, *The Life and Reminiscences of E. L Blanchard, with Notes from the Diary of William Blanchard* (2 vols; London: Hutchinson & Co., 1891), i, p. viii.

[100] George Augustus Sala, *Twice Round the Clock, or the Hours of the Day and Night in London* (1858; Leicester: Leicester University Press; New York: Humanities Press, 1971), 338–42; George R. Sims, *My Life: Sixty Years' Recollections of Bohemian London* (London: Eveleigh Nash, 1917), 2–3.

[101] Edmund Yates, *Fifty Years of London Life: Memoirs of a Man of the World* (New York: Harper & Bros, 1885), 105. According to Yates, the landlord and landlady lived in Hampstead and commuted to the Haymarket every night to oversee their business.

[102] Howard Paul, 'Dining Here and There', *Caterer*, 15 August 1889, p. 322.

[103] 'The Rise of the Middle Class Restaurant', *Restaurant* (March 1911), 100.

Telegraph in the same period asserted 'from restaurant to theatre, or from theatre to restaurant, is a natural sequence'.[104]

This 'natural sequence' appealed as much to entrepreneurs and investors as it did to diners. The most celebrated, if not necessarily typical, example was the role taken by theatrical impresario Richard D'Oyly Carte in the creation of the luxury hotel and restaurant that opened, to much fanfare, on the site adjacent to the Savoy Theatre in 1889.[105] With its state-of-the-art facilities, and its explicit intention to equal such famous establishments as Bignon's in Paris and Delmonico's in New York, one might think that the Savoy Restaurant provided a sufficiently exciting, and financially exacting, destination in its own right.[106] However, artist Edward Linley Sambourne recorded in his diaries a visit to the Savoy Theatre in December 1893 to see Gilbert and Sullivan's *Utopia, Limited*, after which the ladies in his party went to supper at the Savoy Restaurant.[107] The most obvious manifestation of the close relationship between theatres and restaurants was the decision of several prominent theatres to incorporate a restaurant within their building. The pioneer in this regard was the Gaiety Theatre and Restaurant, which opened in 1868–9.[108] Here, three dining rooms were available, each one attentive to the needs of particular classes of patron: a grand dining room at the level of the dress circle, a dining room leading off the upper circle, and a basement dining room 'for the refreshment of the unostentatious'.[109] The Gaiety was followed in 1874 by the Criterion, where the theatre was under the management of Henry J. Byron and E. P. Hingston, but the proprietors of the restaurant were Spiers and Pond. One puff for the Criterion asserted that it was a place where 'one can go to dine, go to the play, and sup without having to pass into the street in order to do so'.[110] Spiers and Pond were clearly alert to the rewards of integrating food and

[104] Article reprinted in 'The Rise of the Cheap Restaurant', *Restaurant* (September 1910), 330.

[105] See 'The Savoy Hotel', *Observer*, 4 August 1889; *Sunday Times*, 2 August 1889; 'New Place on the Embankment', *Pall Mall Gazette*, 1 August 1889, p. 989; 'The New Savoy', *Evening News and Post*, 2 August 1889, all in Newspaper Cuttings, Savoy Hotel, *c*.1889–90, Savoy Archives, London.

[106] See 'Savoy Hotel', *Daily Chronicle*, 27 September 1890; 'Savoy Hotel, Limited', *Financial News*, 27 September 1890, in Newspaper Cuttings, Savoy Hotel, *c*.1889–90; Prospectus, The Savoy Hotel Limited, 1889, Savoy Archives, London.

[107] Entry for 7 December 1893, Edward Linley Sambourne, Diaries, Royal Borough of Kensington and Chelsea Library, Local Studies, London.

[108] The restaurant opening was in October 1869, a year after the theatre opened. See 'Gaiety Theatre', *The Times*, 18 October 1869, p. 9.

[109] *Ibid.*

[110] Austin Brereton, *A Memory of Old London* (London: Spiers and Pond, 1903), 29.

entertainment, and they later took over the Gaiety in 1878.[111] Not surprisingly, therefore, Lyons, Spiers and Pond's competitor, also ventured into the domain of theatre restaurants, notably the Trocadero, which opened in 1896.[112] The commercial rewards of such forms of integration may account for the decision of the *Caterer* to include a column dedicated to the theatre in 1894.[113]

Testimony to the symbiotic relationship between restaurants and theatres is to be found in references to nearby theatres in restaurant handbills and menus. For example, the Horseshoe restaurant on Tottenham Court Road advertised itself as being 'within a few minutes walk of the principal theatres and concert halls' while the Palsgrave restaurant on the Strand was 'within easy distance of all the principal theatres and places of amusement'.[114] Alexander's, a 'celebrated' *à la mode* beef house on the Haymarket, more specifically boasted its location opposite the Prince's Theatre.[115] Conversely, theatre programmes included advertisements for places to eat after the performance. A 1907 programme from the London Hippodrome promoted Kettner's restaurant, while one from the Playhouse Theatre a year later advertised the grill rooms of the Grand Hotel, situated only 'two minutes' walk' of this theatre.[116] A 1904 programme from the Tivoli included an advertisement for the Ship restaurant in Charing Cross, but also a rather more arresting invitation headed 'Say now what's for supper?' This proved to be an advertisement for 52 Strand ('a few doors west of this hall'), where theatregoers could find 'Oysters! Fish! Entrees! Grill! Quick Service'.[117]

The affinity between restaurants and theatres might seem to be compromised by the fact that the two types of establishment were also potentially in competition, given that curtain call coincided with the dinner hour. The fact that the most popular hour of dining was eight o'clock, the very hour that most performances commenced, meant that theatregoers were obliged to rush their meals, resulting in half-eaten

[111] 'Gaiety Restaurant', *Caterer*, 7 December 1878, pp. 133–4.

[112] 'Trocadero Restaurant', *Caterer*, 15 October 1896, p. 491.

[113] 'Theatrical Caterer', *Caterer*, 15 February 1894, p. 84.

[114] Handbill, Horsehoe Hotel and Restaurant, 1886, Evanion Collection 4234; Handbill, The Palsgrave Restaurant, 1885, Evanion Collection 5854, British Library.

[115] Advertisement, Alexander's, *c.*1885, Evanion Collection 6807, British Library.

[116] Programme, London Hippodrome, 22 June 1907, and Programme, The Playhouse, 11 March 1908, in William Edmonds Collection, cup. 1247, ccc. 5, British Library.

[117] Programme, Tivoli, 22 July 1904, William Edmonds Collection, cup. 1247, ccc. 5, British Library. The exclamatory idiom raises intriguing questions about the Americanization of advertising in Britain in this period.

dinners and the possibility of dyspepsia.[118] George Augustus Sala's contribution to resolving this dilemma was to pressure theatre managers into providing trays of food during intervals, piled high with 'fortifying delicacies' like Bayonne ham or chicken sandwiches, 'Bologne sausage and *fois gras* with oysters'.[119] This rather drastic solution proved unnecessary, since numerous establishments offered pre- or post-theatre meals. For example, patrons at the Adelphi Theatre could take advantage of the three shilling supper, served from eleven o'clock until closing time at the eponymous restaurant next door owned by A. and S. Gatti.[120] Those leaving the dress circles and stalls of Shaftesbury Avenue and Leicester Square could take a short walk to Dean Street, where post-theatre meals were offered by the whimsically titled Klondyke restaurant at four shillings a head.[121] The writer Arthur St John Adcock claimed that the majority of theatre- and opera-goers went home for supper immediately after the play, but that 'a large minority prefer to sup in town'.[122] This is not to say that post-theatre dining was not at times somewhat fraught. Adcock noted that late-night diners, 'impatient with fears of missing last trains', all wanted serving at once, requiring waiters 'running their legs off with attentive zeal'.[123] Moreover, restaurateurs were forced to close at midnight, rather than 12.30, on Saturday nights, an inconvenience that was a subject of a parliamentary question in the House of Commons in 1896.[124]

The close association between the restaurant and the theatre was not merely a question of the physical and temporal proximity of theatregoing and dining. It also operated discursively, in the environment and experience of dining. Theatricality was as much a feature of the dining room as it was the stage. Scholars of Victorian London have demonstrated an ongoing interest in the commonalities between theatricality on the stage

---

[118] This was hardly a new complaint. See Louis Simond, *Journal of a Tour and Residence in Great Britain during the Years 1810 and 1811* (2 vols; Edinburgh: James Ballantyne & Co., 1817), i.p. 120. But the inconvenience continued, as observed in, e.g., 'Late Dinners and the Theatre', *Travellers' Journal and Hotel Gazette*, 27 November 1880, p. 3; 'Caterer's Notebook', *Caterer*, 15 December 1891, p. 445; 'Correspondence: Early Closing of Restaurants', *Caterer*, 15 March 1896, p. 122.

[119] 'Caterer's Notebook', *Caterer*, 15 December 1891, p. 445.

[120] *Caterer*, 16 January 1899, p. 7; menu, The Adelphi Theatre Restaurant, 20 July 1892, item 1892–095, box 14, Buttolph Collection of Menus, New York Public Library.

[121] 'Chops and Changes', *Caterer*, 15 December 1898, p. 626.

[122] Arthur St. John Adcock, 'Leaving the London Theatres', in Sims (ed.), *Living London*, vol. 2, sect. 1, p. 10.

[123] *Ibid.* 12.

[124] 'Correspondence: Early Closing of Restaurants', *Caterer*, 16 March 1896, p. 122; PP, *Hansard Parliamentary Debates*, 4th series, vol. 37 (1896), col. 676; *ibid.*, cols 1431–2; among the complaints in the press before the debate, see 'Caterer's Notebook', *Caterer*, 15 June 1895, p. 243; *Referee*, 26 May 1895, p. 7.

and in social life.[125] In particular, the increased provision of gas lighting turned 'the London streets into a stage... Gas created enchantment and illusion; it made the lives that it illuminated seem "staged" and unreal.'[126] Popular theatrical performances—notably that of the 'swell'—corresponded to new forms of selfhood and performativity in the metropolis more broadly.[127] In order to insert the restaurant into such historical understandings, it might be useful to return to Nathaniel Newnham-Davis. The career soldier turned theatre critic was also a devotee of amateur theatricals and would later author a number of plays and ballets.[128] Not merely were actresses prominent among the women who accompanied Newnham-Davis to dinner, but the presence of stage stars lent an air of exoticism to the dining experience of his non-theatrical companions. For instance, dining with a party of five male companions at the Cavour in Leicester Square, Newnham-Davis noted 'first to the feast comes a sprinkling of actors and actresses, making an early meal before going to the theatre. Then comes an incursion of white-shirt-fronted gentlemen and ladies in evening dress, dining before going to the play.'[129] Diners at the Savoy, Romano's, Kettner's, and Pagani's undoubtedly had their experience enhanced by the possibility of catching a glimpse of Sarah Bernhardt or Marie Tempest at an adjacent table. The restaurant, therefore, was a not insignificant site in an emergent celebrity culture at the turn of the century.[130]

Architecture and decor added to the sense of commonality between the restaurant and the theatre. Newnham-Davis's descriptions of many West End dining rooms call to mind the lavish interiors of opera houses and theatres, which often stood literally next door. For example, the grill room

[125] See, e.g., Nina Auerbach, *Private Theatricals: The Lives of the Victorians* (Cambridge, MA: Harvard University Press, 1990); Elizabeth Burns, *Theatricality: A Study of Convention in the Theatre and in Social Life* (London: Longman, 1972); and David Marshall, *The Figure of Theater: Shaftesbury, Defoe, Adam Smith, and George Eliot* (New York: Columbia University Press, 1986).

[126] Lynda Nead, *Victorian Babylon: People, Streets and Images in Nineteenth-Century London* (New Haven and London: Yale University Press, 2000), 98.

[127] See Peter Bailey, *Popular Culture and Performance in the Victorian City* (Cambridge: Cambridge University Press, 2003), ch. 5.

[128] Most notably, *Lady Madcap*, produced at the Prince of Wales Theatre in 1904. See 'A Versatile Soldier: Death of Lieut.-Col. Newnham-Davis', *The Times*, 30 May 1917, p. 3.

[129] Newnham-Davis, *Dinners and Diners*, 207.

[130] See Stephen Gundle, *Glamour: A History* (Oxford: Oxford University Press, 2008), ch. 4; Simon Morgan, 'Celebrity: Academic "Pseudo Event" or a Useful Concept for Historians?', *Cultural and Social History*, 8/1 (2011), 95–114. For the broader context, see Charles L. Ponce de Leon, *Self-Exposure: Human-Interest Journalism and the Emergence of Celebrity Culture in America, 1890–1940* (Chapel Hill, NC: University of North Carolina Press, 2002).

at Frascati's was 'a gorgeous hall of white marble, veined with black, with a golden frieze and a golden ceiling... as gorgeous as a pantomime transformation-scene'.[131] Having made one theatrical analogy, he then makes another. Noting that there was 'gold and silver everywhere', he details 'gilt rails to the balcony, which runs, as in a circus, round the great octagonal building'.[132] At Gatti's Strand restaurant, Newnham-Davis was more distracted by 'a party of girls in much-flowered hats who unmistakably belonged to some theatre' than he was by the decor that surrounded him, possibly because he was a regular visitor.[133] However, when the restaurant had opened just over a decade earlier, it had been lauded for its sumptuous use of mosaics, chandeliers, and a 'handsome staircase of white marble', which, taken together, presented 'a truly grand spectacle'.[134] Both theatre and restaurant in the West End traded on the world of fantasy, the décor of Romano's on the Strand comprising an extraordinary confection of Moorish, Ottoman, Italian, and Flemish styles.[135]

Spectatorship, fundamental to the theatre, was not entirely absent from the experience of dining. This was evident, not just in regard to the setlike decor of some dining rooms, but also, as already intimated, with respect to one's fellow diners. In the company of his sister-in-law at the Café Royal, Newnham-Davis was given a table that 'commanded a fine view of the room we were in'.[136] This arrangement was not unique to the Café Royal. An illustrated brochure for the Holborn Restaurant in 1894 shows diners on a balcony overlooking their fellow diners in the Grand Salon (see Figure 6.2). Just as in the music hall, mirrors allowed the individual diner to match his or her own self-presentation against that of the other people present in the room. This was not always a congenial experience. A 'Remonstrance by a Lady', which appeared in the *Caterer* in 1884, bemoaned the ubiquity of 'monstrous mirrors' in dining rooms, which made it impossible to escape being reminded of one's personal imperfections (especially for those women who after a day's shopping were 'probably haggard, possibly frowsy').[137] The *Caterer*'s columnist Howard Paul raged against the overabundance of mirrors in some restaurants: 'when one dines one does not care to glance around and find half a dozen reproductions of one-self more or less blurred going through the reflected process of conveying a fork to one's mouth'. He commended the restaurant Frascati

[131] Newnham-Davis, *Dinners and Diners*, 220.   [132] *Ibid.*   [133] *Ibid.* 70.
[134] 'New Catering Resorts', *Caterer*, 15 June 1888, p. 234.
[135] 'Chops and Changes', *Caterer*, 16 April 1895, p. 154.
[136] Newnham-Davis, *Dinners and Diners*, 212.
[137] 'The Mirrored Dining-Salon', *Caterer*, 15 December 1884, p. 266.

of Eve, I wanted to penetrate this mysterious chamber. I ascertained from the lady attendant

Figure 6.2. 'The Grand Salon', in Frederick Leal, *Holborn Restaurant Illustrated* (1894). (Reproduced with permission of the Bishopsgate Institute)

for its minimalist approach to these particular embellishments. However, even he suggested the necessity of a small mirror here and there, 'deftly placed so that Madame may peep at her hair or her bonnet'.[138] Taking the theatrical analogy further, clothes, like the lavish dresses and headgear worn by female diners, functioned as costume. Indeed, some diners coordinated dress with decor for maximum effect. Mrs Daffodil, on Newnham-Davis's advice, chose to wear a black, as opposed to a white, dress for her birthday dinner at the Princes' Hall in Piccadilly, since it was a better match for the white, gold, and red mouldings of the restaurant's grand salon.[139]

This element of performance in the dining experience was furthered by the accompaniment of music. Restaurants such as the Holborn had balconies that accommodated a small orchestra that played light classical music. A menu for the Holborn from 1882 also included a programme of

[138] Howard Paul, 'Dining Here and There', *Caterer*, 15 August 1889, p. 322.
[139] Newnham-Davis, *Dinners and Diners*, 2. On the shared vocabularies of the theatre and female fashion (although it does not include consideration of the restaurant), in the context of Gilded Age New York, see Marlis Schweitzer, *When Broadway was the Runway: Theater, Fashion, and American Culture* (Philadelphia: University of Pennsylvania Press, 2009).

music performed between six and nine o'clock at the *table d'hôte*.[140] At the Monico restaurant on Shaftesbury Avenue, diners ate to the accompaniment of the Bellini orchestra (from Naples), whose wide-ranging repertoire included popular marches, waltzes, overtures from operas by Mozart, Rossini, and Verdi, and an intriguingly titled Dervish Chorus. The fact that both lunch and dinner programmes concluded with a 'Gallop' might suggest that the management was keen to deploy the orchestra as a means to compel diners to expedite their meals before the kitchen closed.[141] The presence of music was not welcomed by everyone, as it was felt by some to interfere with conversation among the diners. A *Punch* cartoon in 1913, ironically titled 'The Joys of Restaurant Life', featured a group of diners at a table being obliged to shout over the clamour of the orchestra playing immediately behind them (see Figure 6.3).[142]

JOYS OF RESTAURANT LIFE.

WHY BE DULL AT HOME WHEN YOU CAN DINE BRIGHTLY TO MUSIC IN A PUBLIC ROOM?

Figure 6.3. 'Joys of Restaurant Life', *Punch*, 17 December 1913. (Reproduced with permission of Punch Ltd, www.punch.co.uk)

---

[140] Menu, the Holborn Restaurant, 1 April 1882, 134/127/1, A3 Food and Drink, Ephemera Collection, Museum of London.

[141] Menu, The Monico, 22 July 1897, item 1897–237, Buttolph Collection of Menus, New York Public Library.

[142] 'Joys of Restaurant Life', *Punch*, 17 December 1913, p. 511.

If theatrical conventions could be found in the dining room, then, conversely, restaurants featured on the stage. In 1900, audiences at the Alhambra Theatre in Leicester Square were treated to a sketch performed by the Rambler Troupe. The sketch opened with a well-dressed couple entering a dining room, where they were attended to by two waiters. However, once the two diners are seated, the routine is transformed into an elaborate series of juggling acts, involving rolled-up serviettes, silverware, plates, wine bottles, oranges, and even a tureen of real, steaming soup. The climax of the performance had the jugglers throwing and catching chairs, tables, lamps, and flower bouquets. Reviewing the sketch (by means of a series of sequential photographs that served as 'exact reproductions of the doings that take place on the stage'), the *Strand Magazine* offered a bill of fare to accompany 'this most extraordinary dinner'.[143] 'Sardines on the Wing' were to be followed by 'Flying salmon', 'Blanc mange all over the place', and 'Stilton à la Hurry'.[144]

While the Rambler Troupe used the restaurant as a setting for their dazzling tricks, entertainer Richard Corney Grain satirized the vanities of diners in a series of sketches entitled 'Dinners and Diners', performed at St George's Hall in 1891. The show contained acerbic commentary on *table d'hôte* dinners, where snobbish diners eyed each other competitively or where one risked being bored to death by a fellow diner 'who can talk of nothing but the delights of the lawn in his suburban garden'.[145] However, Grain also introduced a touch of pathos, in the form of 'two little half-starved boys' who watch an elegant society woman at a society dinner swallowing ices and champagne.[146] Three years later, the same venue produced another sketch by Grain entitled 'That Fatal Menu'.[147] In this comedy of marital manners, two women are able to expose the deceit of their husbands, Horatio and Theophilus. The two men's claim to have spent an evening at the Reform Club and the Hall of Science is blatantly contradicted by the emergence of a menu card from the Savoy, bearing their autographs and also those of Mr and Mrs Murry. Mrs Murry, it transpires, had, prior to both their marriages, been the object of Theophilus's affection. Maria, Theophilus's wife, accuses Mrs Murry of entrapping the two men into dining at the Savoy: 'they knew they'd get a good dinner—you can generally reach a man's heart from below'.[148]

---

[143] 'The Most Extraordinary Dinner on Earth', *Strand Magazine*, 19 (1900), 530.
[144] *Ibid.* 535.
[145] 'Mr Corney Grain on Dinners and Dining', *Caterer*, 15 June 1891, p. 215.
[146] *Ibid.*
[147] Richard Corney Grain, 'That Fatal Menu', 10 October 1894, LC, Add. MS 53558n, British Library.
[148] *Ibid.*, fo. 6.

These sketches may well have drawn on Corney Grain's own fondness for the restaurant, the *Caterer* identifying him as 'a great diner out'.[149] However, the sketches also suggest a broader familiarity of theatregoers with the restaurant and its significance in urban culture.

The close relationship between theatregoers and theatre-workers, on the one hand, and West End dining, on the other, was a testimony to the restaurant's significant role in broader patterns of leisure and consumption. The fact that some of these diners were families that assembled at a restaurant prior to going to the theatre is evidence of an increasingly complex relationship between gender roles and domesticity. More generally, the restaurant was a key site of new forms of heterosociability and the increasing attention given to women's presence in the public sphere. The needs of female clerks, and their male equivalents, seeking an affordable meal in the compressed lunch hour of the City, however, are a reminder that the restaurant was as much about fuelling London's working population as it was about dramatizing new forms of sociability.

Appreciating the sheer number, and diversity, of those eating out allows us to attain a holistic understanding of late-Victorian and Edwardian London. For, while narratives surrounding those social actors who have been privileged in much existing historiography are clearly significant to our understanding of the urban environment, their focus on the pronounced, the sensationalist, and the problematic underplays the quotidian and the congenial. Given that restaurants varied enormously in their fare and prices, it would be difficult to see them as an engine of equality in this period. Nevertheless, possessing as they did relatively limited and contingent forms of exclusion (beyond the ability to pay), restaurants can be seen to accord with the increasingly democratic ethos of the age. If this assertion might seem difficult to reconcile with the rarefied prices and decor of the Savoy or the Café Royal, we need to remember that eating out in London was an activity that ranged well beyond the elite West End restaurant, encompassing a myriad number of modest establishments throughout the metropolis. Likewise, we need to sustain an expansive definition of the diner, one that includes, among others, the market porter, the factory girl, the cabman, the female telephone operator, and the docklands stevedore.

---

[149] 'Mr Corney Grain on Dinners and Dining', *Caterer*, 15 June 1891, p. 215.

Epilogue

Remembering the Restaurant

Throughout this book, we have encountered the restaurant as a business, a workplace, and a site for mapping both social identities and cultural exchange. The restaurant also features in individual and collective memory, a field that has become an important part of historical scholarship in recent decades. For countless individuals in London, meals taken, dining room interiors, a familiar waiter, the smells emanating from the kitchen, or a pleasurable or tiresome companion at dinner, all these were to be found in personal recollection as well as everyday experience. If the recovery of these highly individualized memories is difficult, not to say impossible, it is the case that published memoirs and other life histories that appeared in the last decades of the nineteenth, and opening decades of the twentieth, centuries often referenced the restaurant. Scottish newspaper editor and writer David Masson, in an account, composed over fifty years later, of his life as a young man in London in the 1840s, detailed the venerable eating houses in which he enjoyed his evening meals. He testified to a particular fondness for the Cock near Temple Bar, which was already 'illustrious in dining-house legends' long before Masson encountered it, but which he lamented was 'extinct now, I believe'.[1] The passing of the tavern and the chophouse into history became a common marker of the distance between past and present, a testimony to a century characterized by rapid change. Donald Shaw, a self-proclaimed 'One of the Old Brigade', reminisced about 'the Guildhall Tavern, the Albion, and Simpson's', 'places where saddles and sirloins, marrow-bones and welsh rarebits were to be obtained in perfection'. Sadly, 'all have now disappeared, except in name, nor will the expenditure of fortunes in their resurrection ever bring back the indescribable air of solid comfort that characterized these hostelries of the [eighteen] sixties'.[2]

---

[1] David Masson, *Memories of London in the 'Forties'* (London: Blackwood and Sons, 1908), 120–1.

[2] One of the Old Brigade [Donald Shaw], *London in the Sixties* (London: Everett & Co., 1908), 169.

Implicit in these memories was regret for the eclipse of the more robust age of masculine homosociability, but also for the passing of a generation of literary lions who often frequented these establishments, notably Dickens and Tennyson.[3] Where some sought to elegize, others sought a more active response to the claims of nostalgia. In the perversely titled *A New Book about London* (1921), Leopold Wagner isolated for his readers a number of long-established eating venues that represented 'well preserved links with Bygone London'. Wagner was eager to reveal 'that Evans's, the Cyder Cellars, the Holborn Casino, Hanover Hall, the Argyll Rooms, and "Tom Cribb's Parlour" still stand intact, and have undergone but little change in a structural sense since the days of Pierce Egan, Thackeray and Albert Smith'.[4] As we have already seen, restaurants themselves were not averse to publicizing their longevity and heritage. In 1923, Simpson's produced a souvenir brochure, celebrating its bicentenary. However, while it declared that there was no other restaurant in London where there was 'so surprising a survival of the spirit of the past', it was no less insistent that, 'the old days were good old times, but the present days are better'.[5]

Indeed, it would be a serious mistake to identify memories of the restaurant exclusively with notions of dispossession, melancholy, and regret.[6] The distance between eating out in the middle of the nineteenth century and at the dawn of the twentieth century was often expressed through the sentiments of progress and improvement. In 1894, George Augustus Sala contrasted the luxurious decor and modern conveniences of a dining room in a major London hotel, in which one could enjoy a high-quality (but affordable) entrée, with the 'vile gravy', 'badly-roasted fowl', and inflated prices of its precursor forty years before.[7] The writer Edmund Yates, while recalling the pleasures derived from nocturnal excursions around London in the 1850s with a number of literary companions, was absolutely unequivocal in his view that

[3] Charles Harper, *London: Yesterday, To-day and To-morrow* (London: Cecil Palmer, 1925), 106.
[4] Leopold Wagner, *A New Book about London* (London: George Allen & Unwin, 1921), 6.
[5] John Wells Thatcher, *Two Hundred Years: Simpson's Restaurant [A Souvenir]* (London, n.d. [1923]), pp. xxi, xxiii.
[6] For a sophisticated discussion of the complex meanings of nostalgia, see Peter Fritzsche, 'Specters of History: On Nostalgia, Exile, and Modernity', *American Historical Review*, 106/5 (2001), 1587–1618.
[7] George Augustus Sala, *London up to Date* (London: Adam and Charles Black, 1894), 145–7. Referring to it as 'Hotel Brobdingnags', he clearly means it to be one of the grand railway hotel restaurants.

few places are more changed, and changed for the better, in the period of my memory, than the dining rooms and restaurants of London. In the days of my early youth, there was, I suppose, scarcely a capital city in Europe so badly provided with eating houses as ours; not numerically, for there were plenty of them, but the quality was all round bad.[8]

This narrative of improvement was explicitly articulated in Clement Scott's *How they Dined us in 1860 and how they Dine us now*, written at the close of Victoria's reign. Scott, a theatre critic and playwright, was gushing in his praise for the transformation of London's public eating effected by the impact of Spiers and Pond, and Lyons, both of which establishments he credited with raising standards and promoting respectability. Significantly, he associated these positive changes with the greater presence of women in the dining room: 'they dined us in 1860 clumsily and coarsely, and the women were left at home. They dine us now prettily, daintily, and luxuriously and lovely woman is at the side of attentive man [*sic*].'[9]

It is difficult not to characterize the status of the restaurant in the memory of individuals writing in the late-Victorian and Edwardian period as being one inflected by a certain degree of ambivalence. The restaurant emblematized change across the century, but it also suggested those changes could be regarded simultaneously as discomforting and congenial. This should come as no surprise to historians well attuned to the sophisticated paradoxes surrounding notions of progress in the Victorian period.[10] By contrast, as one moves from memory to history, these ambiguities fade from clear sight. In 1999, the Museum of London hosted an exhibition entitled 'London Eats Out: Five Hundred Years of Capital Dining'. The exhibition, while predominantly concerned with establishing London's contemporary status as 'the restaurant capital of the world', made a valiant effort to encourage visitors to recognize London's long and rich history of public eating. Indeed, the television *gourmand* Loyd Grossman's preface to the exhibition catalogue opens with an explicit proclamation that 'the current rather frenzied celebration of dining out ignores the centuries-old practice of eating in public'. Nevertheless, the specific content of the exhibition was less successful in countering one-dimensional and stereotyped understandings of public eating in the century before 1914.

[8] Edmund Yates, *Fifty Years of London Life: Memoirs of a Man of the World* (New York: Harper & Bros, 1885), 99.
[9] Clement Scott, *How they Dined us in 1860 and how they Dine us now* (London, n.d. [*c*.1900]), 19.
[10] The Victorians' willingness to demolish the past in the name of progress is discussed in Peter Mandler, 'The Creative Destruction of the Victorian City', unpublished MS.

Despite all the curators' best efforts, visitors to the exhibition might still have left with the erroneous impression that there was only a single restaurant serving Indian food in nineteenth-century London, that dining was gender-segregated until the early twentieth century, and that London's expanding population in the nineteenth century was afforded little more choice than the *haute cuisine* of the Savoy, the instrumental utilitarianism of the Lyons Corner House, or the indignities of the soup kitchen.[11]

More critical to my argument here, the exhibition explicitly attributed the contemporary dynamism and heterogeneity of London's restaurant culture to changes that had taken place only after 1945. In a telling passage in the exhibition catalogue, the notion that 'London's gastronomic network encompasses the globe' is explicitly presented as 'a far cry from the beginning of the century'. This assertion is justified by selective quotation from a decontextualized comment made by Clement Scott, whose apparent bemoaning of the limitations of late Victorian dining was actually intended to be satirical.[12] This reductionist approach to the history of public eating in London, especially the focus on the significance of post-Second World War social change, and the belated emergence of hybrid cuisines in Britain, has remained largely untested, not to say unchallenged.[13] The London restaurant therefore may be something of a scholarly anomaly, a peculiar survivor of the Whig view of history. It certainly sits oddly with the broader re-evaluation of the Victorian past that has taken place in the last four decades. Nineteenth-century attitudes to everything from sexuality to home furnishings have been increasingly accorded their full complexity, historians demonstrating the rewards of empathy as opposed to lofty condescension. No academic historian would today present the Victorian period as monolithically drab, homogeneous, and culturally repressive.[14] Inserting the London restaurant back into the history of Victorian and Edwardian Britain requires public eating to be aligned with that broader appreciation of heterogeneity and recovering the past in its own terms. For that to happen successfully, it has to be taken away from lazy, but sadly resilient, notions of historical periodization

---

[11] Edwina Ehrman, Hazel Forsyth, Lucy Peltz, and Cathy Ross, *London Eats Out: 500 Years of Capital Dining* (London: Philip Wilson, 1999), 7, 100. The exhibition catalogue did make some effort to suggest the wider fabric of public eating in the nineteenth century.

[12] *Ibid.* 88. The original passage is from Scott, *How they Dined us*, 16.

[13] Especially in Panikos Panayi, *Spicing up Britain: The Multicultural History of British Food* (London: Reaktion, 2008).

[14] For work that marked this transformation away from high-handedness, see Michael Mason, *The Making of Victorian Sexuality* (Oxford: Oxford University Press, 1994), and Miles Taylor and Michael Wolff (eds), *The Victorians since 1901: Histories, Representations and Revisions* (Manchester: Manchester University Press, 2004).

that imply that the extent of change to Britain's national culture in the post-Second World War decades has been demonstrably greater than that which took place in earlier periods.

An unfortunate consequence of the reduction of public eating in Victorian and Edwardian London to a rather dreary and uninspiring culinary dark age is that we may overlook the fact that there are definite affinities between the world of the pre-1914 restaurant and its modern counterpart. The restaurant sector remains a highly volatile element within the service economy, characterized by an often-breathless cycle of opening, expansion, contraction, and closure. The capital's current food hygiene rating system demonstrates that issues of contamination and adulteration emanating from the restaurant have not gone away. The widely publicized disclosure in 2017 that oil and food scraps were contributing to the creation of gigantic 'fatbergs' choking London's sewers would have come as little surprise to late-Victorian public-health inspectors.[15] While culinary hybridity has reached new levels of sophistication, gastro-cosmopolitanism, as we have seen, has a much longer lineage in the history of London. The much remarked upon dependency of London's restaurants today on workers born overseas would have been clearly recognizable to the Victorians and Edwardians.[16] Indeed, the restaurant provides yet another illustration, if one was needed, that Britain's economic and social development has long been set in a globalized context, even if the nation's responses have oscillated wildly between enthusiasm and anxiety. Concerns about pay and conditions among restaurant workers remain as pertinent in the early twenty-first century as they were a century and a quarter ago.[17] The need to satisfy the convenience of customers, while keeping labour costs down, is also as relevant today as it was before 1914. For example, the current fad for allowing diners to order their meal using an electronic tablet might be seen as little more than yet another stage of a practice that began with the widespread deployment

---

[15] See 'Fatbergs: 90% of London Restaurants are Contributing to Problem', *Guardian* (online version), 11 October 2017, <https://www.theguardian.com/environment/2017/oct/11/fatbergs-london-restaurants-oil-food-grease-traps> (accessed 11 October 2017).

[16] Recent press interest in this ongoing phenomenon has inevitably been inflected by considerations of the impact of Britain's departure from the European community. See, e.g., 'Restaurants Fear Brexit Will Turn Boom to Bust', *Guardian* (online version), 11 November 2017, <https://www.theguardian.com/business/2017/nov/11/restaurants-brexit-boom-to-bust-uk-hospitality-industry> (accessed 11 November 2017).

[17] In 2015, various high-street restaurant chains accused of creaming off a percentage of the tips that their staff earned led to a government initiative to stop the practice. See, e.g., 'Pay Staff their Tips, Business Secretary Tells Restaurant Chains', *Guardian* (online version), 21 August 2015, <https://www.theguardian.com/lifeandstyle/2015/aug/21/business-secretary-giraffe-restaurant-tips-directly-to-staff> (accessed 15 November 2016).

of the cash register. The pursuit of novelty also remains a constant, even if some of the more outlandish initiatives of recent years (dining in the nude, dining in the dark, on-site domestic animal petting) look unlikely to prove as enduring and popular as Victorian and Edwardian innovations such as the introduction of mirrors, palm trees, and musical accompaniment. Perhaps the most arresting example of the continuities in London restaurant culture has been the extraordinary popularity in recent years of the food truck. While these vendors regularly reference the contemporary street-food cultures of the Americas, Asia, and Africa, they might just as usefully be seen as the heirs to the pie-man, coffee stall, and Italian ice-cream seller of late-nineteenth-century London.

Nevertheless, recovering the lost history of the Victorian and Edwardian London restaurant does much more than satisfy the often fleeting imperatives of topicality. Returning the restaurant to a central role in our understanding of metropolitan history in this period requires us to think much more seriously about how the history of modern Britain is researched and written. Clearly, the cultural turn has made an important contribution, not merely to the methodological and conceptual approaches adopted by historians, but also to granting full recognition to a range of social identities that have been underrepresented in previous scholarship, particularly in the areas of race, gender, and sexuality. However, in a well-meaning effort to suggest how cultural practices may reveal the creation and performance of identities, there has been insufficient attention to the economic (particularly commercial) forces that were equally critical to shaping those practices. By contrast, this study insists that, while it served as an important site for the emergence and articulation of new forms of metropolitan experience and identity, the London restaurant has to be understood in the context of a vibrant and fiercely competitive marketplace. If we consider it as a business and as a workplace, the restaurant inevitably requires us to pay attention, not only to the more abstracted (if no less significant) motifs of representation, performance, and subjectivity that have been privileged in much of the existing scholarship in this field, but also, and even more, to the materially grounded aspects of the urban experience.

An unintended corollary to the predominant focus in much cultural history on a limited range of social actors has been to obscure some important sectors of London's population. This exclusion has been particularly unfortunate, given that these were people who had already been overlooked by more conventional social history. The female dining room proprietor, the German waiter, and the female Greek pastry cook have all featured far too rarely in both the social and cultural history of London in this period. Often difficult to fit within established categories of social demarcation, working in a precarious and highly transient trade, under-represented in the public face of organized labour, those employed in the restaurant have hopefully now been rescued from scholarly neglect. To turn from caterers to diners, this book has demonstrated the value of moving beyond the elite patrons of West End restaurants to restore the significance of (among others) the lower-middle-class clerk (male or female) taking lunch in the City, the workmen assembled in an unruly scrum at the counter of the cheap refreshment room, and the commercial traveller looking for a meal while on a visit to the capital. This study of the London restaurant therefore shows how we might be able to reach an understanding of Victorian and Edwardian society that is informed by the new cultural history, but that also incorporates a panoply of people—small-scale entrepreneurs, workers in the service sector, and non-elite consumers—who have all too rarely featured in histories of the metropol-itan experience. Such a recognition of those who have previously been left on the margins has important historiographical implications that range beyond the fields of the history of London and, indeed, modern British history.[18] By putting the restaurant at the centre of our understanding of London in the three-quarters of a century before 1914, we can raise the tantalizing possibility of bringing together the progressive ideals that inspired the emergence of both cultural history and social history in the first place.

[18] My argument here aligns itself with Geoff Eley's plea for 'a basic pluralism' in order to reconcile the cultural turn with a clearer sense of the large-scale concerns underpinning social history in its heyday. See his *A Crooked Line: From Cultural History to the History of Society* (Ann Arbor: University of Michigan Press, 2005).

Bibliography

UNPUBLISHED SOURCES (MANUSCRIPT, SCRAPBOOK, AND CUTTINGS)

Bishopsgate Institute
  London Press Cuttings
  Hotels, Cafes and Restaurants, Box D 91.15
  London Collection Pamphlets
British Library (BL)
  Evanion Collection
  Lord Chamberlain (Add. MSS)
  William Edmonds Collection
Brunel University Library
  Special Collections, Burnett Archive of Working Class Autobiographies
City of Westminster Archive Centre
  Collection of Menus
  Gallati Family Archive
  Misc. files related to London Hotels
London Guildhall Library (LGL)
  Norman Collection
  Noble Collection
London Metropolitan Archives (LMA)
  City of London Commissioners of Sewers (CLA)
  J. Lyons and Co., Ltd
  London County Council (LCC)
  Metropolitan Board of Works (MBW)
Museum of London (ML)
  Ephemera Collection
New York Public Library (NYPL)
  Rare Books Division—Buttolph Collection of Menus
Royal Borough of Kensington and Chelsea Library
  Edward Linley Sambourne Diaries
Savoy Hotel, London
  Cuttings Book, 1889–1890
The National Archives
  Records from the Home Office (HO), Registry of Friendly Societies (FR),
    Treasury Solicitor's Papers (TS), Court of Bankruptcy (B), Metropolitan
    Police (MEPO), Board of Trade (BT), pre-nationalization railway companies
    (RAIL), Companies' Jurisdiction and Bankruptcy (C), Copyright Office
    (COPY), Ministry of Labour (LAB), Privy Council (PC), Ministry of
    National Insurance (PIN), Prison Commission (PCOM)
Women's Library, London School of Economics
  Records of the National Union of Women's Suffrage Societies

PUBLISHED SOURCES

Parliamentary Papers
Bills, Public &c. 'Waitresses Bill'. 1898. Bill 244
Bills, Public &c. 'Employers and Workmen Law Amendment'. 1898, 1899, 1900. Bills 316, 131, 178
Hansard Parliamentary Debates
Report and Special Report from the Select Committee on the Shop Hours Bill (1892)
Report from the Select Committee of the House of Lords on Early Closing of Shops (1901)
Report from the Select Committee on the Shop Hours Regulation Bill (1886)
Reports to the Secretary of State for the Home Department on the Shops Acts (1912), as it applies to Refreshment Premises, v. 26 (1912/13)
Royal Commission on Labour: The Employment of Women (1893)
Royal Commission on Liquor Licensing Laws. 5th report (1899)

Newspapers and Periodicals
All the Year Round
Anti-Adulteration Review and Food Journal
British and Foreign Confectioner
British Journal of Catering
Caterer
Catering Trade Worker
Chambers's Edinburgh Journal
Chambers's Journal
Chef
City Waiters' Provident Society Journal
Coffee Tavern Gazette and Journal of Food Thrift
Daily Mail
Daily News
Echo
English Illustrated Magazine
Era
Evening News
Evesham Journal
Food and Sanitation
Fraser's Magazine
Good Words
Hotel
Hotel and Tavern Advertiser
Hotel News
Hotel Review and Catering & Food Trades' Gazette
International Travellers' Journal

Lady
Licensed Victuallers' Guardian
Mostly About People (M.A.P.)
Murray's Magazine
Nation
New Penny Magazine
Nineteenth Century
Organiser
Pall Mall Gazette
Penny Magazine
Punch
Quiver
Referee
Refreshment News
Refreshment World and Hotel Supplies Journal
Restaurant
Restaurant and Hotel Review
Restaurateur
Sharpe's London Magazine
Strand Magazine
Temperance Caterer
The Times (London)
Tit Bits
Tourist and Traveller, and Hotel Review
Travellers' Journal and Hotel Gazette
Vegetarian
Vegetarian Caterer
Waiters' Record
Week-End
Weekly Chronicle (London)
Weekly Star and Vegetarian Restaurant Gazette

Primary (Printed Books, Articles, and Ephemera)

Acton, Eliza, *Modern Cookery* (1845; London: Longmans, Green & Co., 1887).

Bedford, John Thomas, *Robert; or, Notes from the Diary of a City Waiter*, with illustrations by Charles Keene (London: Bradbury, Agnew and Co., 1885).

Beeton, Isabella, *Mrs Beeton's Book of Household Management* (1861); ed. Nicola Humble (Oxford: Oxford University Press, 2000).

Bon Viveur, *Where to Dine in London* (London: Geoffrey Bles, 1937).

Booth, Charles, *Life and Labour of the People in London* (3rd ser., vol. 4; London: Macmillan, 1902).

Bowman, Anne, *The New Cookery Book: A Complete Manual of English and Foreign Cookery on Sound Principles of Taste and Science* (1867; London: Routledge, 1890).

Brereton, Austin, *A Memory of Old London* (London: Spiers and Pond, 1903).

British Tea Table (1897) British Restaurants London Guide (London: British Tea Table Co., Ltd, 1908).

Brown, F. H., 'Indian Students in Great Britain', *Edinburgh Review*, 217 (1913), 150–1.

Chowdray, K., 'The Indian Students in England', *Student Movement*, 12 (1910), 86–8.

Companion to the British Almanac of the Society for the Diffusion of Useful Knowledge (London: Society for the Diffusion of Useful Knowledge, 1880).

Cook, Mrs E. T. [Emily Constance Baird Cook], *Highways and Byways in London* (London: Macmillan, 1887; repr. 1902).

Dodd, George, *The Food of London: A Sketch* (London: Longman, 1856).

Doss, N. L., *Reminiscences, English and Australasian; Being an Account of a Visit to England, Australia, &c* (Calcutta: M. C. Bhowmick, 1893).

Dubois, Urbain, *Cosmopolitan Cookery* (1870; London: Longmans, Green & Co., 1886).

Escoffier, Auguste, *Auguste Escoffier: Memories of my Life*, trans. Laurence Escoffier (New York: Van Nostrand Reinhold, 1997).

Francatelli, Charles Elmé, *A Plain Cookery Book for the Working Classes* (London: Routledge, Warne & Co., 1852).

Francatelli, Charles Elmé, *The Cook's Guide, and Housekeeper's and Butler's Assistant: A Practical Treatise on English and Foreign Cookery in all its Branches* (London: Richard Bentley, 1861).

Francatelli, Charles Elmé, *The Modern Cook* (London: Richard Bentley, 1846).

Francatelli, Charles Elmé, *The Royal English and Foreign Confectioner* (London: Chapman and Hall, 1862).

Gallati, Mario, *Mario of the Caprice: The Autobiography of a Restaurateur* (London: Hutchinson and Co., 1960).

Gissing, George, *The Private Papers of Henry Ryecroft* (London: Archibald Constable & Co., 1903).

Gissing, George, *The Town Traveller* (London: Methuen, 1898).

Goring, O. G., *Fifty Years of Service* (1960; repr. London: Goring Hotel, 1984).

Grossmith, George, and Weedon Grossmith, *The Diary of a Nobody* (Bristol, J. W. Arrowsmith, 1892).

Harper, Charles, *London: Yesterday, To-day and To-morrow* (London: Cecil Palmer, 1925).

Hawthorne, Nathaniel, *The English Notebooks, 1853–1856*, ed. Thomas Woodson and Bill Ellis (Columbus: Ohio State University Press, 1997).

Huntley, Tom, 'Waiter, Waiter!' (London: London Music Publishing, 1895).

Imeson, W. E., 'The Girl at the A.B.C.' (song, composed by W. G. Eaton) (London: Francis, Day and Hunter, 1898).

Johnson, Grace, *Anglo-Indian and Oriental Cookery* (London: W. H. Allen & Co., 1893).

Kelly's Post Office Trades' and Professional Directory (London: Kelly's Directories, Ltd, 1890, 1900, 1910).

Kenney-Herbert, Arthur Robert, *Wyvern's Indian Cookery Book* (1878; London and Madras: Higginbotham & Co., 1904).

Langham Hotel Guide to London Prepared for the Use of Visitors (London: Langham Hotel Co., 1881).

Leal, Frederick, *Holborn Restaurant Illustrated* (London: Holborn Restaurant, 1894).

[Leal, Frederick], *The Restaurant Frascati*, with illustrations by Horace Morehen (London: Spottiswoode and Co., *c.*1894).

Leppington, C. H. d' E., 'Work and Wages in Hotels and Restaurants', *Good Words*, 33 (1892), 753–8.

Le Queux, William, *The Invasion of 1910* (London: Eveleigh Nash, 1906).

Malabari, Behramji M., *The Indian Eye on English Life; or, Rambles of a Pilgrim Reformer* (London: Archibald Constable and Co., 1893).

Markino, Yoshio, *A Japanese Artist in London* (London: Chatto and Windus, 1910).

Masson, David, *Memories of London in the 'Forties'* (London: Blackwood and Sons, 1908).

Mayhew, Henry, *London Labour and the London Poor* (4 vols. 1861–2; repr. New York, London, and Toronto: Dover, 1968).

Medley, K. I. M., and Ernest Lesser, *An Inquiry into the Waiter's Calling* (London: Apprenticeship and Skilled Employment Association, 1911).

Morris, Helen, *Portrait of a Chef: The Life of Alexis Soyer, Sometime Chef to the Reform Club* (Cambridge: Cambridge University Press, 1938).

Morton, R., 'The Waitress' Love Letter' (song, composition by W. G. Eaton) (London: Francis, Day and Hunter, 1894).

Narrow Waters: The First Volume of the Life and Thoughts of a Common Man (London: W. Hodge & Co., 1935).

Nevill, Ralph Henry, *London Clubs: Their History and Treasures* (London: Chatto & Windus, 1911).

Newman, Francis William, 'Vegetarianism', *Fraser's Magazine*, 11/62 (February 1875), 156–72.

Newnham-Davis, Nathaniel, *Dinners and Diners: Where and how to Dine in London* (London: Grant Richards, 1899).

Newnham-Davis, Nathaniel, *Gourmet's Guide to London* (London: Grant Richards, 1914).

One of the Old Brigade [Donald Shaw], *London in the Sixties* (London: Everett & Co., 1908).

Pascoe, Charles Eyre, *A London Directory for American Travellers* (Boston: Lee and Shepard and Dillingham, 1874).

Pascoe, Charles Eyre, *London of Today: An Illustrated Handbook for the Season* (London: Sampson Low & Co., 1885).

Perry, Albert, and Steve Leggett, 'A Waiter's Tale of Woe' (song, composed by Albert Perry) (London: Francis, Day & Hunter, 1897).

Post Office London Directory (London: W. Kelly and Co., 1840, 1850, 1860, 1870, 1880, 1890, 1900, 1902, 1910).

Roberts, Morley, 'Waiters and Restaurants', *Murray's Magazine*, 7 (1890), 534–46.

Russell, Thomas (ed.), *Advertising and Publicity* (London: Educational Book Co., 1911).

Sala, George Augustus, *Gaslight and Daylight* (London: Chapman and Hall, 1859).

Sala, George Augustus, *London up to Date* (London: Adam and Charles Black, 1894).

Sala, George Augustus, *Twice Round the Clock, or the Hours of the Day and Night in London* (1858); with an introduction by Phillip Collins (Leicester: Leicester University Press; New York: Humanities Press, 1971).

Salt, H. S., *A Plea for Vegetarianism and Other Essays* (Manchester: Vegetarian Society, 1886).

Salter, Joseph, *East in the West; or, Work among the Asiatics and Africans in London* (London: S. W. Partridge & Co., n.d. [1896]).

Scott, Clement, *How they Dined us in 1860 and how they Dine us now* (London, n.d. [*c.*1900]).

Scott, Clement, and Cecil Howard, *The Life and Reminiscences of E. L. Blanchard, with Notes from the Diary of William Blanchard* (2 vols; London: Hutchinson & Co., 1891).

Simond, Louis, *Journal of a Tour and Residence in Great Britain during the Years 1810 and 1811* (2 vols; Edinburgh: James Ballantyne & Co., 1817).

Sims, George R. (ed.), *Living London* (3 vols; London: Cassell and Co., 1901–3).

Sims, George R., *My Life: Sixty Years' Recollections of Bohemian London* (London: Eveleigh Nash, 1917).

Smith, Albert (ed.), *Gavarni in London: Sketches of Life and Character* (London: David Bogue, 1849).

Soyer, Alexis, *Memoirs of Alexis Soyer, with Unpublished Receipts and Odds and Ends of Gastronomy*, compiled and ed. F. Volant and J. R. Warren [his late secretaries] (London: Kent & Co., 1859).

Tempted London: Young Men (London: Hodder and Stoughton, 1888).

Thatcher, John Wells, *Two Hundred Years: Simpson's Restaurant [A Souvenir]* (London, n.d. [1923]).

The Florence Restaurant (London, *c.*1900).

The Hotel Cecil (London: Hotel Cecil, 1896).

The London Al-N's Taste, or Pretty Sally of the Chop-House (London, 1750).

Thomas, Albert, *Wait and See* (London: Michael Joseph, 1944).

Thompson, Henry, *Food and Feeding* (London: Frederick Warne & Co., 1901).

Tickletooth, Tabitha, pseud. [i.e. Charles Selby], *The Dinner Question, or how to Dine Well and Economically* (London: Routledge, 1860).

Tristram, W. Outram, 'A Storied Tavern', *English Illustrated Magazine*, 75 (December 1889), 219–26.

Wagner, Leopold, *A New Book about London* (London: George Allen & Unwin, 1921).

Wells, H. G., *Ann Veronica* (1909; London: J. M. Dent, 1993).

Wintle, W. J., 'Round the London Restaurants', *Windsor Magazine* (1896), 445–50.

Wodehouse, P. G., *Psmith in the City* (1910; repr. London: Adam and Charles Black, 1923).

Yates, Edmund, *Fifty Years of London Life: Memoirs of a Man of the World* (New York: Harper & Bros, 1885).

Secondary (Books and Articles)

Abelson, Elaine S., *When Ladies Go A-Thieving: Middle Class Shoplifters in the Victorian Department Store* (Oxford and New York: Oxford University Press, 1989).

Agathocleous, Tanya, and Jason R. Rudy, 'Victorian Cosmopolitanisms: Introduction', *Victorian Literature and Culture*, 38 (2010), 389–97.

Aguirre, Robert D., *Informal Empire: Mexico and Central America in Victorian Culture* (Minneapolis: University of Minnesota Press, 2005).

Alborn, Timothy L., *Conceiving Companies: Joint-Stock Politics in Victorian England* (London: Routledge, 1998).

Allen, Michelle, *Cleansing the City: Sanitary Geographies in Victorian London* (Athens, OH: Ohio University Press, 2008).

Anderson, Gregory, 'German Clerks in England, 1870–1914: Another Aspect of the Great Depression Debate', in Kenneth Lunn (ed.), *Hosts, Immigrants and Minorities: Historical Responses to Newcomers in British Society, 1870–1914* (Folkestone: Dawson, 1980).

Anderson, Gregory, 'The Social Economy of Late Victorian Clerks', in Geoffrey Crossick (ed.), *The Lower Middle Class in Britain, 1870–1914* (London: Croom Helm, 1977).

Assael, Brenda, 'Beyond Empire: Globalizing the Victorians', *Victorian Literature and Culture*, 43 (2015), 643–50.

Assael, Brenda, 'On *Dinners and Diners* and Restaurant Culture in Late Nineteenth Century London' (2012), in Dino Felluga (ed.), *BRANCH: Britain, Representation and Nineteenth-Century History*, extension of *Romanticism and Victorianism on the Net (RAVON)* <http://www.branchcollective.org/?ps_articles=brenda-assael-on-dinners-and-diners-and-restaurant-culture-in-late-nineteenth-century-london> (accessed 11 October 2017).

Assael, Brenda, *The Circus and Victorian Society* (Charlottesville: University of Virginia Press, 2005).

Aston, Jennifer, and Paolo Di Martino, 'Risk, Success, and Failure: Female Entrepreneurship in Late Victorian and Edwardian England', *Economic History Review*, 70/3 (2017), 837–58.

Auerbach, Nina, *Private Theatricals: The Lives of the Victorians* (Cambridge, MA: Harvard University Press, 1990).

Auerbach, Sascha, '"Beyond the Pale of Mercy": Victorian Penal Culture, Police Court Missionaries, and the Origins of Probation in England', *Law and History Review*, 33/3 (August 2015), 621–63.

Auerbach, Sascha, *Race, Law and 'the Chinese Puzzle' in Imperial Britain* (New York: Palgrave Macmillan, 2009).

Baics, Gergely, *Feeding Gotham: The Political Economy and Geography of Food in New York, 1790–1860* (Princeton: Princeton University Press, 2016).

Bailey, Peter, *Leisure and Class in Victorian England: Rational Recreation and the Contest for Control, 1830–1885* (London, Routledge, 1978).

Bailey, Peter (ed.), *Music Hall: The Business of Pleasure* (Milton Keynes: Open University Press, 1986).

Bailey, Peter, *Popular Culture and Performance in the Victorian City* (Cambridge: Cambridge University Press, 2003).

Bailey, Peter, 'White Collars, Gray Lives? The Lower Middle Class Revisited', *Journal of British Studies*, 38/3 (July 1999), 273–90.

Ball, Michael, and David Sunderland, *An Economic History of London, 1800–1914* (London: Routledge, 2001).

Barber, Peter, and Peter Jacomelli, *Continental Taste: Ticinese Emigrants and their Café-Restaurants in Britain, 1847–1987* (London: Camden Historical Society, 1997).

Bar-Yosef, Eitan, *The Holy Land in English Culture, 1799–1917: Palestine and the Question of Orientalism* (Oxford: Oxford University Press, 2005).

Beetham, Margaret, 'Good Taste and Sweet Ordering: Dining with Mrs Beeton', *Victorian Literature and Culture*, 36 (2008), 391–406.

Benson, John, *The Penny Capitalists: A Study of Nineteenth-Century Working-Class Entrepreneurs* (New Brunswick: Rutgers University Press, 1983).

Bird, Peter, *The First Food Empire: A History of J. Lyons & Co.* (Chichester: Phillimore & Co., Ltd, 2000).

Brandon, Ruth, *The People's Chef Alexis Soyer: A Life in Seven Courses* (Chichester: Wiley & Sons, 2004).

Breward, Christopher, 'Fashion and the Man: From Suburb to City Street. The Spaces of Masculine Consumption, 1870–1914', *New Formations*, 37 (1999), 47–70.

Breward, Christopher, *The Hidden Consumer: Masculinities, Fashion and City Life, 1860–1914* (Manchester: Manchester University Press, 1999).

Burnett, John, *England Eats out: A Social History of Eating out in England from 1830 to the Present* (Harlow: Pearson, 2004).

Burnett, John, *Plenty and Want: A Social History of Diet in England from 1815 to the Present Day* (London: Scolar Press, 1979).

Burns, Elizabeth, *Theatricality: A Study of Convention in the Theatre and in Social Life* (London: Longman, 1972).

Burton, Antoinette, *The Postcolonial Careers of Santha Rama Rau* (Durham, NC: Duke University Press, 2007).

Burton, Antoinette, 'Who Needs the Nation? Interrogating "British" History', *Journal of Historical Sociology*, 10 (1997), 227–48.

Cannadine, David, *The Decline and Fall of the British Aristocracy* (New Haven and London: Yale University Press, 1990).

Carney, Judith A., *Black Rice: The African Origins of Rice Cultivation in the Americas* (Cambridge, MA: Harvard University Press, 2001).

Cheah, Pheng, and Bruce Robbins (eds), *Cosmopolitics: Thinking and Feeling beyond the Nation* (Minneapolis: University of Minnesota Press, 1998).

Cocks, H. G., *Nameless Offences: Homosexual Desire in the Nineteenth Century* (London: I. B. Tauris, 2003).

Cohen, Margaret, and Carolyn Dever (eds), *The Literary Channel: The Inter-National Invention of the Novel* (Princeton: Princeton University Press, 2002).

Collingham, Lizzie, *Curry: A Biography* (London: Chatto and Windus, 2005).

Collingham, Lizzie, *The Hungry Empire: How Britain's Quest for Food Shaped the Modern World* (London: Bodley Head, 2017).

Conlin, Jonathan, *Tales of Two Cities: Paris, London and the Birth of the Modern City* (London: Atlantic Books, 2013).

Cordery, Simon, *British Friendly Societies, 1750–1914* (Basingstoke and New York: Palgrave Macmillan, 2003).

Cowan, Brian, *The Social Life of Coffee: The Emergence of the British Coffeehouse* (New Haven and London: Yale University Press, 2005).

Cowen, Ruth, *Relish: The Extraordinary Life of Alexis Soyer, Victorian Celebrity Chef* (London: Weidenfeld & Nicolson, 2006).

Crook, Tom, 'Sanitary Inspection and the Public Sphere in Late Victorian and Edwardian Britain: A Case Study in Liberal Governance', *Social History*, 32/4 (2007), 369–93.

Cunningham, Hugh, *Leisure in the Industrial Revolution, c.1780–1880* (London: Croom Helm, 1980).

Daunton, Martin J., '"Gentlemanly Capitalism" and British Industry, 1820–1914', *Past and Present*, 122 (February 1989), 119–58.

Daunton, Martin J., and Bernhard Rieger (eds), *Meanings of Modernity: Britain from the Late-Victorian Era to World War Two* (Oxford: Berg, 2001).

Davies, Philip, *Panoramas of Lost London: Work, Wealth, Poverty and Change, 1870–1945* (Croxley Green: Transatlantic Press, 2011).

Davis, John, 'London Government, 1850–1920: The Metropolitan Board of Works and the London County Council', *London Journal*, 26/1 (2001), 47–56.

Davis, John, *Reforming London: The London Government Problem, 1855–1900* (Oxford: Oxford University Press, 1988).

Davis, Tracy C., *Actresses as Working Women: Their Social Identity in Victorian Culture* (London: Routledge, 1991).

Delap, Lucy, *Knowing their Place: Domestic Service in Twentieth Century Britain* (Oxford: Oxford University Press, 2011).

Diner, Hasia R., *Hungering for America: Italian, Irish, and Jewish Foodways in the Age of Migration* (Cambridge, MA: Harvard University Press, 2001).

Driver, Felix, and David Gilbert (eds), *Imperial Cities: Landscape, Display and Identity* (Manchester: Manchester University Press, 1999).

Duman, Daniel, 'The Creation and Diffusion of a Professional Ideology in Nineteenth Century England', *Sociological Review*, 27 (1979), 113–38.

Durbach, Nadja, 'Roast Beef, the New Poor Law, and the British Nation, 1834–63', *Journal of British Studies*, 52/4 (2013), 963–89.

Edgerton, David, *Science, Technology, and the British Industrial 'Decline', 1870–1970* (Cambridge: Cambridge University Press, 1996).

Ehrman, Edwina, Hazel Forsyth, Lucy Peltz, and Cathy Ross, *London Eats Out: 500 Years of Capital Dining* (London: Philip Wilson, 1999).

Eley, Geoff, *A Crooked Line: From Cultural History to the History of Society* (Ann Arbor: University of Michigan Press, 2005).

Emsley, Clive, *Crime and Society in England, 1750–1900* (New York: Longman, 1987; repr. 1996).

'Fatbergs: 90% of London Restaurants are Contributing to Problem', *Guardian* (online version), 11 October 2017, <https://www.theguardian.com/environment/2017/oct/11/fatbergs-london-restaurants-oil-food-grease-traps> (accessed 11 October 2017).

Feinstein, C. H., 'What Really Happened to Real Wages? Trends in Wages, Prices, and Productivity in the United Kingdom, 1880–1913', *Economic History Review*, 43/3 (1990), 329–55.

Forman, Ross G., *China and the Victorian Imagination: Empires Entwined* (Cambridge: Cambridge University Press, 2013).

Francis, Martin, 'The Domestication of the Male? Recent Research on Nineteenth- and Twentieth-Century British Masculinity', *Historical Journal*, 45/3 (2002), 637–52.

Freedman, Paul, *Out of the East: Spices and the Medieval Imagination* (New Haven: Yale University Press, 2008).

French, Michael, and Jim Phillips, *Cheated not Poisoned? Food Regulation in the United Kingdom, 1875–1938* (Manchester: Manchester University Press, 2000).

Fritzsche, Peter, 'Spectres of History: On Nostalgia, Exile, and Modernity', *American Historical Review*, 106/5 (2001), 1587–1618.

Gabaccia, Donna, *We Are what we Eat: Ethnic Food and the Making of Americans* (Cambridge, MA: Harvard University Press, 1998; repr. 2000).

Gazeley, Ian, 'The Cost of Living for Urban Workers in Late-Victorian and Edwardian Britain', *Economic History Review*, 42/2 (1989), 207–21.

Gazeley, Ian, and Andrew Newell, 'Urban Working-Class Food Consumption and Nutrition in Britain in 1904', *Economic History Review*, 68/1 (2015), 101–22.

Gilroy, Paul, *The Black Atlantic: Modernity and Double Consciousness* (Cambridge, MA: Harvard University Press, 1993).

Godley, Andrew, 'Immigrant Entrepreneurs and the Emergence of London's East End as an Industrial District', *London Journal*, 21/1 (1996), 38–45.

Golby, J. M., and A. W. Purdue, *The Civilisation of the Crowd: Popular Culture in England, 1750–1900* (London: Batsford, 1984).

Goodlad, Lauren M. E., *Victorian Literature and the Victorian State: Character and Governance in a Liberal Society* (Baltimore: Johns Hopkins University Press, 2003).

Goodman, Jordan, *Tobacco in History: The Cultures of Dependence* (London and New York: Routledge, 1993).

Grant, Kevin, Phillipa Levine, and Frank Trentmann (eds), *Beyond Sovereignty: Britain, Empire and Transnationalism, c.1880–1950* (Basingstoke: Palgrave Macmillan, 2007).

Green, David R., *From Artisans to Paupers: Economic Change and Poverty in London, 1790–1870* (Aldershot: Scolar Press, 1995).

Green, Jeffrey, *Black Edwardians: Black People in Britain, 1901–1914* (London: Frank Cass, 1998).

Gregory, James, *Of Victorians and Vegetarians: The Vegetarian Movement in Nineteenth-Century Britain* (London: I. B. Tauris, 2007).

Grimes, William, *Appetite City: A Culinary History of New York* (New York: Farrar, Straus and Giroux, 2009).

Gundle, Stephen, *Glamour: A History* (Oxford: Oxford University Press, 2008).

Hamlin, Christopher, 'Nuisances and Community in Mid-Victorian England: The Attractions of Inspection', *Social History*, 38/3 (2013), 346–79.

Hamlin, Christopher, 'Public Sphere to Public Health: The Transformation of "Nuisance"', in Steve Sturdy (ed.), *Medicine, Health and the Public Sphere in Britain, 1600–2000* (London: Routledge, 2002).

Harris, Jose, *Private Lives, Public Spirit: A Social History of Britain, 1870–1914* (Oxford: Oxford University Press, 1993).

Hauck-Lawson, Annie, and Jonathan Deutsch (eds), *Gastropolis: Food and New York City* (New York: Columbia University Press, 2009).

Heller, Michael, 'Work, Income and Stability: The Late Victorian and Edwardian London Male Clerk Revisited', *Business History*, 50/3 (2008), 253–71.

Holmes, Colin, *John Bull's Island: Immigration and British Society, 1871–1971* (Basingstoke: Macmillan, 1988).

Horrall, Andrew, *Popular Culture in London, c.1890–1918: The Transformation of Entertainment* (Manchester: Manchester University Press, 2001).

Hughes, Kathryn, *The Short Life and Long Times of Mrs Beeton* (London: Fourth Estate, 2005).

Humphries, Jane, 'Women and Paid Work', in June Purvis (ed.), *Women's History: Britain 1850–1945* (London: University College London Press, 1995).

Jackson, Lee, *Dirty Old London: The Victorian Fight against Filth* (New Haven: Yale University Press, 2014).

Joyce, Patrick, *The Rule of Freedom: Liberalism and the Modern City* (London: Verso, 2003).

Kay, Alison C., 'A Little Enterprise of her Own: Lodging-House Keeping and the Accommodation Business in Nineteenth-Century London', *London Journal*, 28/2 (2003), 41–53.

Kinross, Felicity, *Coffee and Ices: The Story of Carlo Gatti in London* (Sudbury: Lavenham Press, 1991).

Kiple, Kenneth F., and Kriemhild Coneè Ornelas (eds), *The Cambridge World History of Food* (2 vols; Cambridge: Cambridge University Press, 2000).

Kohn, Marek, *Dope Girls: The Birth of the British Drug Underground* (London: Lawrence & Wishart, 1992).

Koven, Seth, *Slumming: Sexual and Social Politics in Victorian London* (Princeton: Princeton University Press, 2004).

Kriegel, Lara, *Grand Designs: Labor, Empire, and the Museum in Victorian Culture* (Durham, NC: Duke University Press, 2007).

Kynaston, David, *The City of London*, ii. *The Golden Years, 1890–1914* (London: Chatto and Windus, 1995).

Lahiri, Shompa, *Indians in Britain: Anglo-Indian Encounters, Race and Identity, 1880–1930* (London: Frank Cass, 2000).

Lester, V. Markham, *Victorian Insolvency: Bankruptcy, Imprisonment for Debt, and Company Winding-up in Nineteenth-Century England* (Oxford: Oxford University Press, 1995).

Lewis, Jane E., 'Women Clerical Workers in the late Nineteenth and Early Twentieth Centuries', in Gregory Anderson (ed.), *The White Blouse Revolution: Female Office Workers since 1870* (Manchester: Manchester University Press, 1988).

Liggins, Emma, ' "The Life of a Bachelor Girl in the Big City": Selling the Single Lifestyle to Readers of *Woman* and the *Young Woman* in the 1890s', *Victorian Periodicals Review*, 40/3 (2007), 216–38.

Light, Alison, *Forever England: Femininity, Literature and Conservatism between the Wars* (London and New York: Routledge, 1991).

Lobel, Cindy R., *Urban Appetites: Food and Culture in Nineteenth-Century New York* (Chicago: University of Chicago Press, 2014).

Lockwood, David, *The Blackcoated Worker: A Study in Class Consciousness* (London: Allen & Unwin, 1958).

Loeb, Lori, *Consuming Angels: Advertising and Victorian Women* (Oxford: Oxford University Press, 1994).

Luckin, Bill, *Death and Survival in Urban Britain: Disease, Pollution and Environment, 1850–1950* (London: I. B. Tauris, 2015).

McCloskey, Donald N., 'Did Victorian Britain Fail?', *Economic History Review*, 23/3 (December 1970), 446–59.

McNeill, J. R., 'Observations on the Nature and Culture of Environmental History', *History and Theory*, 42/4 (2003), 5–43.

Mandler, Peter, 'Against "Englishness": English Culture and the Limits to Rural Nostalgia, 1850–1940', *Transactions of the Royal Historical Society*, 7 (1997), 155–75.

Mandler, Peter (ed.), *Liberty and Authority in Victorian Britain* (Oxford: Oxford University Press, 2006).

Mandler, Peter, *The English National Character: The History of an Idea from Edmund Burke to Tony Blair* (New Haven and London: Yale University Press, 2006).

Marsh, Peter T., 'Joseph Chamberlain', in *Oxford Dictionary of National Biography*, ed. Lawrence Goldman (Oxford: Oxford University Press, 2009) <http://www.oxforddnb.com/view/article/32350?docPos=2> (accessed 22 February 2014).

Marshall, David, *The Figure of Theater: Shaftesbury, Defoe, Adam Smith, and George Eliot* (New York: Columbia University Press, 1986).

Marshall, Nancy Rose, *City of Gold and Mud: Painting Victorian London* (New Haven and London: Yale University Press, 2012).

Mason, Michael, *The Making of Victorian Sexuality* (Oxford: Oxford University Press, 1994).

Metcalfe, Robyn S., *Meat, Commerce and the City: The London Food Market, 1800–1855* (London: Pickering and Chatto, 2012).

Michie, Ranald C., *Guilty Money: The City of London in Victorian and Edwardian Culture, 1815–1914* (London: Pickering and Chatto, 2009).

Milne-Smith, Amy, 'A Flight to Domesticity? Making a Home in the Gentlemen's Clubs of London, 1880–1914', *Journal of British Studies*, 45/4 (2006), 796–818.

Morgan, Simon, 'Celebrity: Academic "Pseudo Event" or a Useful Concept for Historians?', *Cultural and Social History*, 8/1 (2011), 95–114.

Morton, Sandra, 'A Little of what you Fancy Does you…Harm!!', in Judith Rowbotham and Kim Stevenson (eds), *Criminal Conversations: Victorian Crimes, Social Panic, and Moral Outrage* (Columbus: Ohio State University Press, 2005).

Nava, Mica, *Visceral Cosmopolitanism: Gender, Culture and the Normalization of Difference* (Oxford and New York: Berg, 2007).

Nava, Mica, and Alan O'Shea (eds), *Modern Times: Reflections on a Century of English Modernity* (London: Routledge, 1996).

Nead, Lynda, *Victorian Babylon: People, Streets and Images in Nineteenth-Century London* (New Haven and London: Yale University Press, 2000).

Nord, Deborah Epstein, *Walking the Victorian Streets: Women, Representation, and the City* (Ithaca, NY: Cornell University Press, 1995).

Norton, Marcy, *Sacred Gifts, Profane Pleasures: A History of Tobacco and Chocolate in the Atlantic World* (Ithaca, NY, and London: Cornell University Press, 2010).

Norton, Marcy, 'Tasting Empire: Chocolate and the European Internalization of Mesoamerican Aesthetics', *American Historical Review*, 111/3 (June 2006), 660–91.

O'Brien, Patricia, 'The Kleptomania Diagnosis: Bourgeois Women and Theft in Late Nineteenth Century France', *Journal of Social History*, 17/1 (1983), 65–77.

Oddy, Derek J., 'Food Quality in London and the Rise of the Public Analyst, 1870–1939', in Peter J. Atkins, Peter Lummel, and Derek J. Oddy (eds), *Food and the City in Europe since 1800* (Aldershot: Ashgate, 2007).

Otter, Chris, 'Making Liberalism Durable: Vision and Civility in the Late Victorian City', *Social History*, 27/1 (2002), 1–15.

Otter, Chris, *The Victorian Eye: A Political History of Light and Vision in Britain, 1800–1910* (Chicago: University of Chicago Press, 2008).

Palmer, Robin, 'The Italians: Patterns of Migration to London', in James L. Watson (ed.), *Between Two Cultures: Migrants and Minorities in Britain* (Oxford: Blackwell, 1977).

Panayi, Panikos, *Fish and Chips: A History* (London: Reaktion, 2014).

Panayi, Panikos, *German Immigrants in Britain during the Nineteenth Century, 1815–1914* (Oxford: Berg, 1995).

Panayi, Panikos, *Spicing up Britain: The Multicultural History of British Food* (London: Reaktion, 2008).

'Pay Staff their Tips, Business Secretary Tells Restaurant Chains', *Guardian* (online version), 21 August 2015 <https://www.theguardian.com/lifeand-style/2015/aug/21/business-secretary-giraffe-restaurant-tips-directly-to-staff> (accessed 15 November 2016).

Pennybacker, Susan D., *A Vision for London, 1889–1914: Labour, Everyday Life and the LCC Experiment* (London: Routledge, 1995).

Pennybacker, Susan D., *From Scottsboro to Munich: Race and Political Culture in 1930s Britain* (Princeton and Oxford: Princeton University Press, 2009).

Perkin, Harold, *The Rise of Professional Society: England since 1880* (London: Routledge, 1989).

Phillips, Jim, and Michael French, 'Adulteration and Food Law, 1899–1939', *Twentieth Century British History*, 9/3 (1998), 350–69.

Pilcher, Jeffrey M., 'The Embodied Imagination in Recent Writings on Food History', *American Historical Review*, 121/3 (June 2016), 861–87.

Plotz, John, *Portable Property: Victorian Culture on the Move* (Princeton: Princeton University Press, 2008).

Ponce de Leon, Charles L., *Self-Exposure: Human-Interest: Journalism and the Emergence of Celebrity Culture in America, 1890–1940* (Chapel Hill, NC: University of North Carolina Press, 2002).

Pottle, Frederick A. (ed.), *Boswell's London Journal, 1762–1763* (New Haven: Yale University Press, 1950; repr. 2004).

Rappaport, Erika D., *Shopping for Pleasure: Women in the Making of London's West End* (Princeton: Princeton University Press, 2000).

Rappaport, Erika, *A Thirst for Empire: How Tea Shaped the Modern World* (Princeton: Princeton University Press, 2017).

Reid, Alastair J., *United We Stand: A History of Britain's Trade Unions* (London: Allen Lane, 2004).

'Restaurants Fear Brexit Will Turn Boom to Bust', *Guardian* (online version), 11 November 2017, <https://www.theguardian.com/business/2017/nov/11/restaurants-brexit-boom-to-bust-uk-hospitality-industry> (accessed 11 November 2017).

Rich, Rachel, *Bourgeois Consumption: Food, Space and Identity in London and Paris, 1850–1914* (Manchester: Manchester University Press, 2011).

Richards, Thomas, *The Commodity Culture of Victorian England: Advertising and Spectacle, 1851–1914* (Stanford: Stanford University Press, 1990).

Roberts, J. A. G., *China to Chinatown: Chinese Food in the West* (London: Reaktion, 2002).

Roediger, David R., *The Wages of Whiteness: Race and the Making of the American Working Class* (New York: Verso, 2007).

Rubinstein, William D., *Capitalism, Culture and Decline in Britain, 1750–1990* (London: Routledge, 1994).

Rubinstein, William D., 'The Wealth Structure of Britain in 1809–39, 1860–1, and 1906', in David R. Green, Alastair Owens, Josephine Maltby and Janette Rutterford (eds), *Men, Women, and Money: Perspectives on Gender, Wealth, and Investment, 1850–1939* (Oxford: Oxford University Press, 2011).

Samuel, Raphael (ed.), *East End Underworld: Chapters in the Life of Arthur Harding* (London: Routledge and Kegan Paul, 1981).

Schmiechen, James A., *Sweated Industries and Sweated Labor: The London Clothing Trades, 1860–1914* (London: Croom Helm, 1984).

Schneer, Jonathan, *London 1900: The Imperial Metropolis* (New Haven and London: Yale University Press, 1999).

Schwarz, L. D., *London in the Age of Industrialisation: Entrepreneurs, Labour Force and Living Conditions, 1700–1850* (Cambridge: Cambridge University Press, 1992).

Schweitzer, Marlis, *When Broadway Was the Runway: Theater, Fashion, and American Culture* (Philadelphia: University of Pennsylvania Press, 2009).

Sinha, Mrinalini, *Specters of Mother India: The Global Restructuring of an Empire* (Durham, NC: Duke University Press, 2006).

Spang, Rebecca L., *The Invention of the Restaurant: Paris and Modern Gastronomic Culture* (Cambridge, MA: Harvard University Press, 2000).

Sponza, Lucio, *Italian Immigrants in Nineteenth Century Britain: Realities and Images* (Leicester: Leicester University Press, 1988).

Stearn, Roger T., 'William Tufnell Le Queux', in Lawrence Goldman (ed.), *Oxford Dictionary of National Biography* (Oxford: Oxford University Press, 2009) <http://www.oxforddnb.com/view/article/37666> (accessed 4 April 2014).

Stoler, Ann Laura, and Karen Strassler, 'Castings for the Colonial: Memory Work in "New Order" Java', *Comparative Studies in Society and History*, 42/1 (2000), 4–48.

Swift, Roger, and Sheridan Gilley (eds), *The Irish in the Victorian City* (London: Croom Helm, 1985).

Swislocki, Mark, *Culinary Nostalgia: Regional Food Culture and the Urban Experience in Shanghai* (Stanford: Stanford University Press, 2009).

Taylor, Miles, and Michael Wolff (eds), *The Victorians since 1901: Histories, Representations and Revisions* (Manchester: Manchester University Press, 2004).

Tosh, John, *A Man's Place: Masculinity and the Middle Class Home in Victorian England* (New Haven: Yale University Press, 1999).

Tosh, John, 'Home and Away: The Flight from Domesticity in Late-Nineteenth Century England Re-Visited', *Gender & History*, 27/3 (2015), 561–75.

Tosh, John, 'Masculinities in an Industrializing Society: Britain, 1800–1914', *Journal of British Studies*, 44/2 (April 2005), 330–42.

Trentmann, Frank, *Free Trade Nation: Commerce, Consumption, and Civil Society in Modern Britain* (Oxford: Oxford University Press, 2008).

Van den Eeckhout, Patricia, 'Cooks and Waiters on the Move: The World and International Exhibition in Ghent, 1913, as a Destination for Hospitality Workers', *Food and History*, 11/2 (2013), 287–316.

Van den Eeckhout, Patricia, 'Waiters, Waitresses, and their Tips in Western Europe before World War One', *International Review of Social History*, 60/3 (2015), 349–78.

Waddington, Keir, '"We Don't Want Any German Sausages Here!" Food, Fear, and the German Nation in Victorian and Edwardian Britain', *Journal of British Studies*, 52/4 (2013), 1017–42.

Walker, Lynne, 'Vistas or Pleasure: Women Consumers of Urban Space in the West End of London, 1850–1900', in Clarissa Campbell Orr (ed.), *Women in the Victorian Art World* (Manchester: Manchester University Press, 1995).

Walkowitz, Judith R., *City of Dreadful Delight: Narratives of Sexual Danger in Late-Victorian London* (Chicago: University of Chicago Press, 1992).

Walkowitz, Judith R., *Nights Out: Life in Cosmopolitan London* (New Haven: Yale University Press, 2012).

Walkowitz, Judith R., 'The "Vision of Salome": Cosmopolitanism and Erotic Dancing in Central London, 1908–1918', *American Historical Review*, 108/2 (2003), 337–76.

Walton, John, *Fish and Chips, and the British Working Class, 1870–1940* (Leicester: Leicester University Press, 1992).

White, Jerry, *London in the Nineteenth Century* (London: Vintage, 2008).

Whitlock, Tammy, 'Gender, Medicine and Consumer Culture in Victorian England: Creating the Kleptomaniac', *Albion*, 31/3 (1999), 413–37.

Wiener, Martin J., *English Culture and the Decline of the Industrial Spirit, 1850–1980* (Cambridge: Cambridge University Press, 1981; 2nd edn, 2004).

Winstanley, Michael J., *The Shopkeeper's World, 1830–1914* (Manchester: Manchester University Press, 1983).

Winter, Emma L., 'German Fresco Painting and the New Houses of Parliament at Westminster, 1834–1851', *Historical Journal*, 47/2 (2004), 291–329.

Unpublished

Burnett, John, 'The History of Food Adulteration in Great Britain in the Nineteenth Century, with Special Reference to Bread, Tea and Beer', Ph.D. thesis, University of London, 1958.

Mandler, Peter, 'The Creative Destruction of the Victorian City', unpublished MS.

Index

smoking 31, 146, 149, 188
songs 86, 93, 113–14
Soyer, Alexis 63
Spang, Rebecca 7
Spiers, Felix William, *see* Spiers and Pond
Spiers and Pond 20, 31–5, 54, 58, 69, 88, 127–8, 136, 202–3
Spread Eagle Bread Company 31, 146
Squire, Fred and Sons 133
Stockham, William 133
stomach ailments 123–4, 137–8
Stone's 24
strikes 83, 119–20
suicide 88, 93
suppliers 55, 69–70; *see also* food provisioning
Suzanne, M. 64, 125–6
swearing 42, 75

table d'hôte 42, 72, 73, 207–8, 209
taverns 17, 23–4, 41, 43, 61, 76 n.113, 103, 131, 135, 156, 197, 200–1, 211; *see also* chophouses
tea 49, 147, 194, 200
tea (meal) 180, 194
tea rooms 28–32, 35–6
telegraphs 32, 181
telephones 71, 181
temperance 27–8, 29, 30–1, 43–4, 47, 58–9, 145–8, 182–3
Tenchio, Mr 55
theatres 32, 36, 37, 50, 71, 113, 124, 181, 192 n.66, 196, 198–9, 200–7, 209–10
theft 91, 94, 104
Thomas, Albert 104
Thompson, Henry 180
Tickletooth, Tabitha, *see* Charles Selby
Tinelli, A. 92–3
tips and tipping 82, 83, 84–5, 87, 90, 100–6, 119, 215 n.17
Tivoli 72, 78, 203
toilets (and washing facilities) 43–4, 73, 118–19, 133, 139–40, 143
transnationalism 6, 8, 40–1, 74, 110–11, 154–5, 158, 163–4, 168–78
Trocadero Restaurant 36, 75, 140, 193
tronc system 104; *see also* tips and tipping

Ude, Louis Eustache 63
unions 77, 83–4, 98–101, 119–20, 162–3; *see also* friendly societies

Veeraswamy and Co. 167, 168, 168 n.69
vegetarianism 34, 47–9, 60, 124–5, 145, 147–52, 182, 192 n.62, 195–6
ventilation 31, 87, 125–6, 132–4, 143, 150
Verrey's 38
Vienna Café 110, 170
violence 75, 91–3, 195
Vogel, Paul 91, 99–100, 162

wages 86–91, 98–101, 119–20, 186 n.30
Wagner, Leopold 212
waiters 16, 24, 70, 81–112, 115, 121, 139–40, 194–5, 201, 204
foreign 26, 91–2, 96–9, 106–12, 121, 159–64, 174, 178
ill health 87–8, 97, 140
see also nativism
Waiters and Waitresses and Licensed Victuallers' Employees Union 99–100
waitresses 30, 35–6, 60, 73, 89 n.24, 112–20, 188
Lyons 35, 114–17, 119–20
waste disposal 125, 131–2, 133–4, 143
Webster's 78, 79
Welcome (the) 47
Wenzel's 159
Whitehall Restaurant and Dining Rooms 143
Wiener Bier Halle und Restaurant 74
windows 23, 39, 41, 42, 50, 59, 72, 73–4, 78, 126, 150
Woollan, J.C. 1–2, 3, 4, 15
Woolpack (the) 190
women's only dining rooms 46–7, 60, 196
Women's Trade Union League 120
Wells, H.G. 194–5
Wodehouse, P.G. 189–90
Wyvern, *see* Arthur Robert Kenney-Herbert

Yates, Edmund 201, 212–13
Young Men's Christian Association (YMCA) 47